THE HEART OF

INTIMATE ABUSE

New Interventions in Child Welfare,
Criminal Justice, and Health Settings

Linda G. Mills, PhD, LCSW, JD

Springer Publishing Company, Inc.
536 Broadway
New York, NY 10012-3955

Cover design by: Janet Joachim
Acquisitions Editor: Bill Tucker
Production Editor: Kathleen Kelly

98 99 00 01 02 / 5 4 3 2 1

Library of Congress Cataloging-in-Publication Data

Mills, Linda G.
    The heart of intimate abuse : new interventions in child wel-
fare, criminal justice, and health settings / by Linda G. Mills.
        p.   cm.
    Includes bibliographical references and index.
    ISBN 0-8261-1216-1
    1. Victims of family violence—Services for—United States.
I. Title
HV6626.2.M56   1998
362.82'928'0973—dc21   98-25575
                                                              CIP

Printed in the United States of America

For Ronnie

Contents

Part III: Empowerment Strategies and Affective Advocacy

Part IV: Future Interventions

List of Boxes and Figures

Boxes

Figures

Foreword

I am writing this Foreword in my role as the founding editor of the new Springer Series on Family Violence and editor of Volume I in the series entitled *Battered Women and Their Families: Intervention Strategies and Treatment Programs*, 2nd edition (1998).

The Heart of Intimate Abuse: New Interventions in Child Welfare, Criminal Justice, and Health Settings, Volume III in this new series, provides a unique, compelling, and critical analysis of traditional domestic violence intervention strategies and policies. It also offers the reader a visionary, empowering paradigm that considers the multidisciplinary context in which the battered woman seeks intervention. This original practice paradigm, called The Heart of Intimate Abuse, takes into account the specific emotional, cultural, religious, and safety needs of the individual battered woman and her children. It centers her in the relationship, helps break down denial, and helps clinicians, child welfare workers, and advocates find effective ways to engage the battered woman toward healing and recovery. This book offers the first alternative to Lenore Walker's Cycle of Violence and Ellen Pence and Michael Paymar's Power and Control Wheel. This is the first book to understand that we must help the survivor build on her inner strength, and to become aware that her intense connection to the batterer can be understood in new terms.

Dr. Mills is the first social worker and attorney in the United States to write a single-authored book on policies and practices that address battered women in the contexts of their lives. There are only a few people who are trained in both social work and law who have expertise in domestic violence. Dr. Mills brings new meaning and strength to empowerment strategies, legislative and policy analysis, community advocacy, and client advocacy in both the domestic violence and child welfare arenas.

The Heart of Intimate Abuse makes a significant contribution to knowledge building in the domestic violence field. This volume is groundbreaking, insightful, and futuristic. With the substantial number of child and spouse abuse fatalities, this book is vitally needed.

I predict that numerous child protective services workers, domestic violence advocates, training specialists, professors, graduate students, and social work administrators will read this book. The book should be required reading in graduate schools of social work, law, public health, and medicine. Most important, I am convinced that this outstanding work will stimulate controversy, spirited discussions, and intense debate on how best to intervene with abused mothers and their children.

Albert R. Roberts, Ph.D., Series Editor
Professor of Social Work and Criminal Justice
Administration of Justice Department
Rutgers University
Piscataway, N.J.

Preface

Creativity flourishes in the womb. This book was first inspired by Ronnie's birth in August, 1996, when by then, we had trained over 400 child protective services workers on the meaning of domestic violence in their practice. Before he came, I wondered how a feminist could love children. The rest is history.

This book was written because it had to be. I felt that no one had adequately explored the space that separates feminists from empiricists, the battered women's movement from child protection, the abuser from the abused. This book covers that space—an intellectual, political, and practical space—where I am woman and mother, femme forte and child advocate, feminist and scientist, abuser and the abused.

Three projects for which I received funding with my colleague, Colleen Friend, inspired this book. We first received a Department of Health and Human Services grant in 1995 to train child protective services workers in Southern California. As of this writing, we have trained over 1,400 workers.

The second grant was to prepare a curriculum for social work faculty, funded by CalSWEC, and designed to prepare future child protective services workers in the basics of the intersecting problems of intimate and child abuse.

We have just received another large Department of Health and Human Services grant to do more of this work. This is exciting because it will continue to nourish my new-found commitment to families, and it will also give me further opportunity to cherish my worktime with Colleen Friend.

I am thrilled and proud to be part of Springer's new Family Violence Series for which Dr. Albert Roberts is the Editor. His encouragement was one of the most important driving forces behind this book. His belief in my ability helped me to believe in myself, and his intellectual enthusiasm was the basis of the spirit within it.

Bill Tucker at Springer Publishing made doing this book a joy. Kathleen Kelly, the production editor, did the herculean task of making sense of my scribble and gave me invaluable editorial and design assistance. I enjoyed our lengthy phone editing sessions. Skip Wright, the compositor, went well beyond the call of duty and was meticulously perfectionistic. Louise Farkas, the production manager at Springer, was also wonderfully supportive when I needed her. Pat Brownell, a Springer reviewer and expert in the field of domestic violence, made valuable suggestions that recognized what I was trying to do. Spring Davis-Charles at One-of-a-Kind Designs made the graphics come to life.

So many colleagues have influenced my intellectual and emotional development. Martha Minow is always there in the pockets of my inspiration. I cherish my relationship with Joel Handler and Zeke Hasenfeld with whom I have grown professionally and personally. Duncan Lindsey, also a colleague at UCLA, encourages me to speak my mind. David Lewis, the spirit of peace, teaches me to appreciate the intersecting roots of violence. Peter Margulies, and more recently David Wexler, have contributed in innumerable ways to my interest in a therapeutic justice. The ever insightful Joe Nunn reminds me of the significance of the personal. Dana McPhall helped me refine my approach, especially in relation to working with African American women. Mieko Yoshihama keeps me critical. Kwame Anku's genius is in his bluntness. Carole Goldberg and Christine Littleton are there in the soul of the institution and in my heart. Frances Olsen has been consistently supportive. Laura and Alejandro Gomez always make me smile.

Colleen Friend is more than just a colleague, more than just a friend. She is truly a soulmate of the mind. The fact that I could find someone as neurotic and perfectionistic as I am, always astounds me. However, it is her generous spirit that moves me most. I called Colleen all hours of the day and night and she always stopped for me, and for this book. The ideas, many of them starting with her, flow like springs. She is simply brilliant.

It is through Colleen that I have cultivated enduring friendships with people on the front lines. Carol Arnett, Eleanore Baidoo, Sandie Einbinder, Suja Joseph Lowenthal, Judge Peter Meeka, Gail Pincus, Bruce Rubenstein, Tom Sirkel, Rex White, and Donna Wills are invaluable to the movement's success. Bernice Abram is a star that shines within it and Scott Gordon is a driving force.

Without students where would I be? They run, they chat, they suffer. They are my sounding board and they are still feeling. Emily Maxwell was the first of many; she dug the roads, she laid the tracks. Marie Mendoza helped in the summer with the dirty work; she was great. Tamara Nestle, wonderful Tamara, ran for cites everywhere on the UCLA campus, and even went beyond. Her analysis and feedback were always astute. Phuong Hoang was a staple, forever solid and unaffected, and always there. She made everything difficult easy. Kimberly Yang held my life together with silk threads. I never even noticed how out of control everything was. Kimberly was sent from heaven.

Dear friends contribute something totally different. Our ability to work out the practical details of the world's most vexing problems makes it seem simpler than it is, and for that I am grateful. Sue Greenwald, who is on the front lines every day, corrects my inaccuracies and does so with pure love. It is our disagreements that I cherish most. Linda Durston reminds me of the traumas of legal education and the importance of good mothering. Lynne Praver holds our history and Anton and Chantal Schütz are always song to my ears. Christina Turcic and Ed Cohen keep me honest. Carol Jones foresees my future.

We learn all our best and worst habits from family. They are our soul, our blood; they are our worries. My father sat with me when I was 10 and taught me to write; my mother delivered me hot lunches when I was too tense to eat anything less appealing. They paid for everything, including my bad moods, and they served me, and now Ronnie. They are amazing.

My sister Adele, my niece Marissa, and more recently my brother-in-law Paul, help my life glimmer. We carry the secrets and we know the truth. That cannot be replaced by anyone.

Claudia Rodriguez, who cares for Ronnie for more hours of the day than we do, is nothing short of a saint. Her unconditional love shows him the way; her patience is his guide. Thanks, too, to Judy and Sophie Thomason, who share in our daily child care rituals.

Brenda Aris, and the women I met briefly at Frontera Prison touch the veins. They are the blood of my commitment, the store of my stubbornness. They are the spirit.

A book of this type embodies the love and hate we all feel and express in the intimacy of true partnership. Peter Goodrich has been my teacher and my guide; we have navigated tough waters and we have found our way in the madness. Without that work I could never have talked across or within these spaces; they are our spaces. And as for Ronnie, he taught me how to hold it all—the heart, the mind, and the soul—at once.

LINDA MILLS
Los Angeles, California

Part I

The Heart of Intimate Abuse

Introduction

I first met Brenda Aris on December 23, 1996, when I visited Frontera Prison, California Institution for Women. Brenda was one of two incarcerated women for whom Governor Pete Wilson had shown his sympathy. In 1993, Governor Wilson commuted Brenda's 15 years to life sentence to 12 years to life. Brenda's parole eligibility date changed to July 1994. She was released 3 years later. All told, she had served 11 years.

Brenda Denise Aris had killed her sleeping husband. Only moments before, he had beaten her. Her face was so bruised that she needed ice to stop the swelling. She saw the gun. She shot him. She ran outside in fear for her life, certain he would come after her. She called the police from a neighbor's house. Rick Aris was dead. Brenda was convicted; her children were parentless.

We should have been there. We should have been there in a way that would have helped Brenda gather her strength—not for shooting—but for leaving for good. No doubt she had tried. She had tried so many times that all doors had closed. No one wanted to hear Brenda Aris' story again.

Most feminists would argue that Brenda's problem was that her husband was not in prison. For the last 20 years, battered women's groups have legislated, sued, and lobbied to get law enforcement to take Brenda Aris seriously. But the story is more complex than just what the criminal justice system, especially in its current form, can offer. No amount of influence would have

3

locked Rick Aris, and others like him, up for life. We need a larger strategy. We need Brenda.

This book argues that the criminal justice, child protective, and health care systems have to find ways of embracing battered women, of hearing their painful stories, of accepting that they might go back. It argues that, as a general rule, we should reject interventions by these systems that force battered women to choose. Instead, we should design strategies that tap into the strength that keeps her wed to the violence, methods that help her learn to value her own safety, and approaches that accept her while helping her move toward peace. While many of the strategies I propose are derived from good social work practice, my premise is that these principles have all but been ignored by domestic violence practitioners. This is what makes the book new and exciting.

These strategies, methods, and practices I collectively refer to as "empowerment." Empowerment for battered women is part of a growing literature which recognizes that personal transformation, especially when linked to trauma, can be realized when the survivor is the architect of her own recovery and that the helping professions at best offer support, advice, and the tools that can prompt change (Herman, 1997). The principle of empowerment in the domestic violence context rests on the assumption that the state is not the "perfect protector." An empowerment approach begins with the assumption that it is the battered woman's responsibility to embrace methods of self-protection and to learn to distinguish between healthy and unhealthy modes of intimate interaction.

This book develops interdisciplinary techniques for working with battered women like Brenda, strategies that are derived from social work, psychoanalytic, postmodern and critical legal theories. This, however, is not a theoretical book. It is an application or practice derived from the theory. This book involves the development of strategies that bear the imprint of these theories, in forms that enable scholars and practitioners to rethink how they connect, engage, and empower battered women.

Extricating oneself from a violent relationship is a process. The book respects that process, sees the risk, and balances it against the needs of advocates impatient to protect. From my perspective, the system can only help insofar as Brenda, and other battered women like her, want it to be different. Ultimately, without her, such policies as mandatory arrest of batterers by law enforcement or mandatory reporting by health care professionals won't work. This book exposes the limitations of these state interventions and teaches us strategies for engaging the battered woman in the process.

The book begins with the premise that we have all experienced, at one point or another, violence, both as perpetrators and survivors, as aggressors and victims. If you have not been a survivor of a violent relationship in your adult life, chances are you have struck, bit, or otherwise tortured a brother or sister. Or, your parents manipulated you, hit you with a belt, or forced you to bed without supper. From this vantage point, this book challenges us all to reconsider the assumptions and myths we hold about domestic violence and its perpetrators and victims and to rethink these often unexamined beliefs. Such myths as battered women care more about themselves than their children or that they are too weak to leave an abusive relationship are examined in the context of the realities that battered women face in their lives. Realities you too faced when confronted with whatever level of violence you endured.

At the heart of intimate abuse are the complex reasons we abuse and are abused. Its strength is embedded in our love for the abuser and for our children; for our religion, culture, and race; for the fear and financial dependence; and for the use of abuse we both tolerate and foster. These factors all contribute to our propensity to look the other way, make excuses, and forgive the perpetrator of the violence we tolerate. These too are probably the excuses we use when perpetrating acts of violence against the people we love. It is these repressed and so often ignored influences for which this book should be recognized.

Chapter 1 is an overview, an exploration of the intersections of domestic violence and child welfare practice; I define and examine the nature of these two very prevalent problems and how and where they traverse. In addition, I present the tensions between the two practices, focusing both on their expression as they apply to batterers and on their conflicting ideologies. I also examine the points of connection between practitioners committed to battered women and those who represent the interests of children.

In chapter 2, I explore what I consider to be the heart of intimate abuse: the dynamics of domestic violence and, more particularly, the roles that love, religion, culture, race, fear, and financial dependence play in the battered woman's life and how these factors similarly influence the batterer. In this chapter, I distinguish prevailing models of abuse, such as the Cycle of Violence and the Power and Control Wheel, from a new model which I call the Heart of Intimate Abuse. The Heart of Intimate Abuse captures both the pressures on the battered woman to endure the abusive situation and the dynamics of abuse imposed by the abuser on the woman being abused.

In chapters 3, 4, and 5, I explore the systems to which battered women are subjected and their inadequate, and even violent, response to the survivor's complex needs. More specifically, in chapter 3, I explore the effectiveness and ineffectiveness of criminal justice interventions that ignore the battered woman's preferences and critique the laws that govern this all too often abusive legal response. In chapter 4, I criticize the child welfare systems response to domestic violence and challenge agencies to find solutions that move beyond either blame or indifference. In chapter 5, I examine the health care system and the ambivalence of health care practitioners who are facing increased regulation through mandatory reporting statutes.

In chapters 6 and 7, I present a model of empowerment for working with battered women. This approach rejects prevailing assumptions that a feminist stance on violence against women in the family should focus exclusively on helping survivors become economically independent of their abusers so as to ensure a permanent escape from their abusive relationships. Instead, I present a strategy for first engaging with the battered woman (chapter 6) and second taking the necessary steps to intervene in a way that empowers her toward action (chapter 7). In chapter 6, I present a method that I call Affective Advocacy that encourages practitioners to reflect on the violence in their own lives in the service of understanding how unconscious assumptions about battered women may cause practitioners to judge them in stereotypical ways. Countertransference and a corresponding understanding of where a practitioner falls on the Continuum of

Intervention become key to responding to battered women in ways that help empower them, based on their individual strengths. In chapter 7, I present a method for working with the criminal justice, public child welfare, and health care systems that relies on several new conceptual tools for facilitating dialogue with the battered woman, including the Violence Tree, the Heart of Intimate Abuse introduced in chapter 2, and the Survivor's and Batterer's Actions and Vulnerabilities Continuums.

In chapters 8, 9, and 10, I present case studies in the context of the criminal justice, child protection, and health care systems. These case studies apply the strategies presented in chapters 6 and 7 in the contexts in which Children's Social Workers (CSWs), advocates, and clinicians are likely to be exposed to them. Each case study is presented using a different format. For example, in chapter 8, I present two case studies. The first is an example of a "typical" interaction between a victim advocate or prosecutor and a battered woman. The second is my proposal for how such interactions *should* unfold using the Affective Advocacy method. In the "model" interaction, I use emotional subtext as a way of revealing what the advocate is thinking. I summarize and critique the methods used at the end of each interaction.

In chapter 9, I present three interactions between a child protective services worker and a family (child, mother, and husband). Here I use the CSW's reflections to reveal what the worker is thinking. In addition, I develop the interview, particularly with the battered woman, in stages, presenting a systematic strategy for connecting and working with a survivor.

In chapter 10, I present two interactions between health care personnel and their patients. The first interaction uncovers the tensions created by mandatory reporting and the second involves a physician and her nurse who confront a survivor and later her batterer. None of the health care interactions have emotional subtext; instead, what these practitioners "feel" is revealed in the interaction itself. I then summarize the experience of the health care workers at the end of each interaction. I have deliberately varied the styles of interaction and descriptions of them in order to help the reader resonate with one or another style.

In the final chapter, chapter 11, I synthesize the issues presented and build an alternative model for intervention. In this chapter, I propose programmatic and policy changes and suggest directions for future research that fit with my theory that empowering the survivor is the only viable method for alleviating the vicissitudes of the violence she and her children endure.

This book is about battered women. Although I am not apologetic about its focus, I also acknowledge that it fails to capture the unique experiences of all victims of intimate abuse, including survivors of gay or lesbian violence or elder abuse. In the conceptual models, the Heart of Intimate Abuse (chapters 2 and 6), the Violence Tree (chapter 6), and the Continuums (chapter 6), I neutralize the language so that they may be used by all survivors. In general, I use the words victim, survivor, and battered women interchangeably. None of these references are meant to disempower.

My "audience" is the intimate abuse scholar and the seasoned practitioner—the CSW or Public Child Welfare Worker or supervisor; the legal, social work or other advocate; and the clinician (nurse, therapist, or physician). For the scholar, I offer the book as an opportunity to think critically about domestic violence practice; to decenter and challenge the complacency that affects some aspects of intimate abuse research and scholarship. This book endeavors to reassert the primacy of the battered woman's voice, of her self-determination, in the face of an emerging consensus that she has neither the wisdom nor the capacity to decide. For practitioners, I offer concrete methods for analysis and action. The book is also designed to be accessible to those who know little or nothing about domestic violence.

The book reflects my dialectical agenda. It demonstrates my interest in the moment and heartfelt concern for the future. The book is meant to reveal the voices of Brenda and Rick Aris, and of the children they left behind, and to transform, in some small way, how criminal justice, child protection, and the health care delivery system judge them. For Brenda and Rick Aris, and for their children, it was a matter of life and death. For the rest of us, it is the heart of an abuse we know intimately.

CHAPTER 1

Intersections and Tensions in Domestic Violence and Child Welfare Practice

OVERVIEW AND DEFINITIONS

> Shades of violence and dimensions of abuse penetrate every shared space. An uninvited interruption, a slammed door, a disregarding glance—a spit, a slap, a sock. One afternoon's folly can be next week's destruction. To be pushed may be play, a wrestling match, or abuse. When is rape, rape? Is it the night of the incident, or 2 years later when the denial lifts and you recall that he forced himself on you despite your pleas to stop?
>
> (Mills, 1996b, p. 1225)

Abuse permeates, in one form or another, all of our histories. Whether as children or adults, whether between siblings or friends, we have all been abusive and abused. This chapter challenges us to think about our own histories of violence in the context of prevailing definitions of abuse (see Box 1.1). In addition, this chapter explores the impact of that violence on battered women and their children. It also reveals the tensions between practitioners working with battered women and their children.

BOX 1.1 DEFINITIONS OF INTIMATE ABUSE

For the most part, the terms intimate *abuse, battering,* and *domestic violence* can be used interchangeably to describe an individual's involvement with a partner, married or unmarried, heterosexual or same sex, who hurts the partner physically and/or emotionally. Domestic violence is a pattern of assaultive and coercive behaviors. Generally, *battering* means punching, hitting, striking, or kicking—it is the actual physical act of one person beating another.

Abuse may include physical assault, but the term also covers a wide range of other hurtful behavior, such as sexual coercion, economic coercion, destruction of property, threats, and/or insulting talk. Not all verbal attacks or insults are acts of domestic violence, however. Usually, it refers to a pattern in which the perpetrator is using, or *threatening* to use, physical force.

In general, *batterers* are referred to as men, and *survivors* as women. The term survivor appropriately reflects most battered women's response to the domestic violence she endures, as most women show signs of strength and resistance.

Domestic violence or intimate abuse, like child abuse, spans the spectrum of severity. Domestic violence describes a pattern of battering or abusive acts in the context of an intimate relationship. In 95% of the cases, men abuse women, although in some cases women are the primary aggressors (U.S. Department of Justice [DOJ], 1994a). In many cases, violence occurs in the context of asymmetrical power relations between men and women in the family and is reflected in inequality evident in society at large. In other instances, violence has been learned—experienced or witnessed in childhood—and becomes a method for resolving conflicts or for asserting power and control over an intimate. Domestic violence occurs at about the same rate in heterosexual and homosexual relationships and is evident in all populations, including immigrants, elders, and women with disabilities. It takes many forms, including destructive acts and hurtful words or actions. Physical, emotional, and sexual abuse are all forms of domestic violence.

Physical abuse can take many forms, including a shove, occasional slap, pulling hair, twisting an arm, or putting a hand over someone's mouth to get his or her attention. Physical abuse may also include cornering someone and not allowing her to move or chasing a partner around the house and pinning her down until she says or does what is wanted. These actions may seem playful but often can progress to more serious acts, such as a punch in the face, a kick in the stomach, or a cut with a knife. Common manifestations of physical abuse are cuts, abrasions, sprained backs, punctured eardrums, black eyes, broken bones, and dislocated jaws. Women who are physically abused by their partners may suffer crippling, blindness, miscarriage, loss of consciousness, and death.

Emotional abuse can be as damaging as physical abuse. Also, when emotional abuse is present, there is often the threat of physical assault. Many battered women suffer more from the emotional wounds than from the physical scars. Whereas the bruises heal, it is difficult for a battered woman to forget the nasty comments he made about how she looks or how she cares for the children. Feelings produced by emotional abuse include depression, anxiety, shame, and powerlessness. A woman who is being emotionally abused may feel unattractive, worthless, and unable to survive on her own, and she may think that she brings misery onto herself.

Sexual abuse is a situation that can be very difficult and embarrassing to discuss. Attitudes about marriage or general views about sexuality are formed at a very early age and are influenced dramatically by their families of origin. A battered woman may believe it is her duty to perform any sexual act her partner desires, even if she doesn't find it pleasurable. Sexual activity that results in feeling demeaned, disrespected, or violated can be abuse, especially if these feelings affect other aspects of one's life, such as functioning at work or taking care of children. Sexual abuse occurs when a woman submits to sexual acts she doesn't like.

Destructive acts are also a form of abuse. Some men display their violent behavior by destroying objects or hurting or killing their lover's pets. These destructive acts may be their only demonstration of abusive behavior or other forms of abuse may also be present. When an intimate partner intentionally damages his mate's car or house or harms or kills her pet, he is abusive. Often these acts are accompanied by threats of violence aimed directly at her.

Economic coercion occurs when one party feels that he or she is completely dependent on another party's resources and therefore must comply with whatever is requested. This can be abusive if the individual controlling the resources forces his partner to do things she otherwise would not want to do.

STATISTICS AND IMPACT

In the United States it has been estimated that between 4 and 8.7 million women of all races and classes are battered by an intimate partner (Roberts & Burman, 1998; Straus & Gelles, 1986). Some scholars predict that 50% of women will be victims of domestic violence at some point in their lives (Littleton, 1989; Mahoney, 1991; Walker, 1979).

Violence against women by their intimate partners is a leading cause of injury and death to women. In a national sample, 28% of married couples report at least one episode of physical violence over the course of their relationship (Straus & Gelles, 1986). Indeed, in 1992, the U.S. Surgeon General ranked domestic violence as the most common cause of physical injury to women between the ages of 15 and 44 (Novello, Rosenberg, Saltzman, & Shosky, 1992).

Ten to 14% of all married women have been raped by their husbands, and from 33 to 50% of battered wives are raped by their husbands (Finkelhor & Yllö, 1987; Pagelow, 1988; Russell, 1983). Of all female homicides, one third are killed by their husband or boyfriend (U.S. DOJ, 1992). Among intimate homicides, 69% were committed by men against women (U.S. DOJ, 1992).

Although startling, these statistics may underestimate the occurrence of domestic violence. Precise quantification is difficult because victims often hesitate to report incidents of domestic violence out of love for the man or their children, religious or cultural commitment or pressure, fear, or financial dependence, or a combination of these. Indeed, Straus and Gelles (1986) estimate that less than 15% of victims report domestic violence inci-

> **BOX 1.2   CHILD WELFARE AND THE IMPACT OF DOMESTIC VIOLENCE**
>
> - One study found that when spouse abuse was severe, 77% of the children in the homes had also been abused (Straus, Gelles, & Steinmetz, 1980).
> - 50% of the men who frequently assaulted their wives also frequently physically abused their children (Straus & Gelles, 1986).
> - 3.3 million to 10 million children witness domestic violence every year (AHA, 1994).
> - Male children who witness domestic violence have a greater likelihood of becoming batterers in their adult relationships (Hotaling & Sugarman, 1986).

dents. More recently, the National Crime Survey Report (U.S. DOJ, 1994b) revealed that 48% of the estimated 4 million battered women in the U.S. did not report incidents of intimate abuse. Unreported cases are unlikely to be recorded elsewhere because medical personnel often fail to question patients concerning sexual, emotional, or physical aggression by partners (Nurius, Hilfrink, & Rifino, 1996). Similarly, children's social workers (CSWs), advocates, and clinicians who are concerned about domestic violence and the related issue of child safety lack adequate assessments to uncover domestic violence as well as methods to validate the mother's experiences.

THE INTERRELATIONSHIP BETWEEN DOMESTIC VIOLENCE AND CHILD ABUSE

Dear Step Father:
    When you beat mom, me and the rest of the kids, I hated you. My hate lasted a long time. I wasn't sad or upset when you died. I think I still have hate locked up inside of me, all caused by you. Why can't you just love us like we all wanted to love you?
Anonymous
(Jaffe, Wolfe, & Wilson, 1990, p. 25)

There is a direct link between domestic violence and child abuse (see Box 1.2). Batterers do not always limit abuse to adult partners but sometimes abuse their children as well. A survey of studies revealed that 45 to 70% of battered women in shelters reported that their batterers have also committed some form of child abuse (American Humane Association [AHA], 1994). Based on a sample of 184 ethnically diverse children, O'Keefe (1995) found that in 47% of families in which a batterer abused his adult partner, the batterer also abused his children. Some studies (Bowker, Arbitell, & McFerron, 1988; Hart, 1992) place the rate as high as 70 to 80%. Hart (1992) reports that daughters are more than six times more likely to be sexually abused in a household where intimate abuse occurs. Conservative estimates suggest that child abuse is 15 times more likely to occur in households where domestic violence is present than in those without adult violence (AHA, 1994). The United States Advisory Board on Child Abuse and Neglect (U.S. ABCAN) (1995) found that domestic violence is the single major precursor to child death in the United States. It has been estimated that in 70% of the cases in which an abused child dies, there has been ongoing violence against the mother (Messinger & Eldridge, 1993). Thus, children in a household with domestic violence are at an increased risk of experiencing abuse or even death.

Domestic violence provides a context in which child abuse readily develops (Stark & Flitcraft, 1988). Children may be hurt accidentally if they are in the "line of fire" and experience violence meant to harm the adult partner. In addition, children may be hurt when intervening to protect a battered parent. One study of battered mothers and their children found that 35.7% of the children surveyed attempted to intervene during the abuse to attempt to protect their mother (Hazen, Miller, & Landsverk, 1995). A batterer may also use child abuse to terrorize his adult partner (Zorza, 1995a). The batterer's intent to hurt his adult partner can lead to child abuse.

Danger of a batterer escalating violent incidents against both the mother and the child increases when parents separate. The victimization rate of women separated from their husbands was nearly two times higher than that of divorced women and six times higher than that of married women (U.S. DOJ, 1997). According to Hart (1988), battered women who attempt to leave their abuser are most at risk of death, or what has been referred to as femicide.

Separated battered women report abuse 14 times as often as those still living with their partner (Harlow, 1991). When parents separate, children are also at risk for abuse, especially during contact visits. Hester and Radford (1992) and Hester and Pearson (1993) reported varying types of abuse during contact with a separated parent, including the witnessing of physical or verbal abuse at the meeting point, abduction and use of the child to secure the partner's return to the marriage, and "grilling" the child for information on the mother, thereby exacerbating the child's feelings of divided loyalty.

Victims of domestic violence may also abuse their children. In 1984, Walker found mothers are eight times more likely to hurt a child when battered than when safe. More recent statistics reveal that women who have experienced abuse at the hands of their spouses are two times as likely as other women to abuse their child (AHA, 1994). Battered women may abuse their children to keep from escalating a situation, that is, to prevent the child from creating an excuse for the batterer to batter. The victim may be attempting to keep the children "in line," to prevent the batterer from abusing them. The victim may also abuse her children as an attempt to release her frustration from being abused. Understanding reasons for the abuse may help determine whether the battered mother would continue abusing her child if she were no longer subjected to the abuse of her partner or husband.

Another form of child abuse may be when they witness violence between their parents or the adult partners responsible for them (Echlin & Marshall, 1995; Hilton, 1992). The effect of witnessing domestic violence can be devastating. Children who witness or are exposed to domestic violence show symptoms similar to those of children who have directly experienced physical, sexual, or emotional abuse (Davidson, 1994; Echlin & Marshall, 1995; Hershorn & Rosenbaum, 1985; Jaffe, Wolfe, Wilson, & Zak, 1986; Westra & Martin, 1981). Children exposed to domestic violence are at risk for internalized and externalized behavior problems. Internalized behaviors include withdrawal, anxiety, and somatic complaints. Externalized behaviors include aggressive actions, delinquency, and noncompliance with parental and school requests. Some children are either asymptomatic or "nonclinical" and may be either resilient or having a delayed reaction (Carlson, 1996). Children who are both witnesses of domestic violence and victims of physical abuse are at even higher risk for behavioral problems, especially externalizing behaviors (see Box 1.3).

THE INTERGENERATIONAL TRANSMISSION OF DOMESTIC VIOLENCE

Dear Dad:
   I love and respect you very much. When I was young you wanted me to be tough. Well I am and I'm also a wife abuser. I wanted to be just like you and be the man of the house. I found as well as you [that] times have changed. Women want to be treated equal and I can't blame them. I'm not abusive to my kids as you were to me but I put them through hell. Well Dad, I forgive you for anything you might have done in my childhood. You did what you thought was right. Dad, this is my last chance for a family life. I screwed up lots before. Wish me well.

Anonymous
(Jaffe et al., 1990, pp. 24–25)

The intergenerational transmission of domestic abuse is alarming. Children exposed to domestic violence and children who are

---

Box 1.3 How Are Children Hurt in the Presence of Domestic Violence?

Children may be hurt when they are used as spies or reporters or are forced to choose sides.

Children may be hurt when they observe verbal and physical abuse at the meeting point during monitored visitations.

Children may be hurt accidentally when they are in the "line of fire" and are injured by blows or weapons meant to harm the adult partner.

Children may be hurt when intervening to protect a battered parent.

Children are also vulnerable to the effects of domestic violence even prior to birth. The unborn child may be injured during pregnancy.

physically abused are more likely to use violence in relationships with intimates. Boys who witness family violence are more likely, as adults, to batter female partners (Hotaling & Sugarman, 1986). Straus and Gelles (1986) found that in a comparison of violent men with a control group of nonviolent men, the sons of violent parents have a rate of wife beating 900 times greater than that of sons of nonviolent parents. These examples suggest that exposure to violence can have enormous long-term effects on a child.

Not all children who witness abuse or experience abuse adopt a pattern of abuse. There are mixed data concerning whether girls who grow up in homes with domestic violence experience violence in their adult relationships (Fantuzzo & Lindquist, 1989). Fantuzzo and Lindquist (1989) reviewed 29 published papers on children observing violence with a total sample of 1069 children. They found that externalized behaviors such as aggression appeared linked with exposure to violence in almost all studies but not consistently across all ages and genders.

In a 1986 study of attitudes conducted by Canadian researchers Jaffe et al., children exposed to violence condoned it to resolve relationship conflicts more readily than did control groups. Their findings also revealed that older children who had experienced extreme violence and other negative life events showed some tendency to hold themselves responsible. According to Wolfe, Jaffe, Wilson, and Zak (1985), 26% of the children remained well adjusted, despite living with abuse.

Because domestic violence creates a setting in which child abuse may develop, understanding their interrelationship is crucial. Understanding the interrelationship can improve the practitioners' ability to recognize the risks and to develop viable mother and child safety plans. Before partnerships between the domestic violence and child welfare communities can be forged, however, it would be helpful to understand the tensions that are likely to emerge between these practitioners.

BATTERED WOMEN'S ADVOCATES AND CHILD WELFARE WORKERS: THE TENSIONS

As the issues of domestic violence and child abuse have evolved in policy and practice arenas, tensions have developed between practitioners who advocate and work with battered women and those working in child welfare. These tensions can be attributed to a number of factors, including high caseloads, different philosophies, different terminologies, different mandates, and competition for funding (Schechter & Edleson, 1994). Indeed, battered women and child advocates do not have a history of working together.

Different perceptions of the role of the batterer might be one key tension between the two groups. For example, child welfare workers often place the burden of protecting the children on the mother, even when she has not in any way contributed to the child's abuse. Indeed, social workers whose primary concern is the child's safety often concentrate blame for child abuse on the mother rather than on the batterer (Schechter & Edleson, 1994). On the other hand, battered women's advocates, in general, believe that protecting the mother will help ensure protection of the children (Schechter & Edleson, 1994).

More significantly, however, are their differing philosophies. Battered women's advocates are ideologically committed to working on behalf of women and, specifically, on behalf of women's rights. Domestic violence has been one policy arena in which feminists have successfully penetrated. In comparison to such issues as equality of wages or welfare benefits for women, feminists have been relatively successful in lobbying on behalf of survivors of domestic violence. The feminist analysis of domestic violence is that men beat their wives because they *can*; it is the ultimate expression of patriarchy. To make the feminist analysis cogent and consistent with their underlying ideology on such issues as abortion, feminist advocates have vehemently argued on behalf of the adult woman: the battered woman has rights separate and distinct from her husband and from her children as well. As Peled (1996) has so astutely observed, "[t]his important and just cause seems to have led the movement to an ambivalent and, at times, detached treatment of children's issues" (p. 138).

The child welfare community, on the other hand, is concerned with the best interests of the child. All too often, however, practitioners concerned with the welfare of children are similarly unidimensional in ideology. They are unwilling to see abuse as attributable to one or another of the parents; instead, they unreflectively blame both (Enos, 1996). Partly, this can be explained by their philosophy that the mother *and* father are responsible for ensuring the child's safety, and partly this attitude is attributable to the overwhelming caseloads of CSWs and other practitioners who are responsible for intervening on behalf of children.

Although the foci of battered women's and children's advocates differ, these foci are not exclusive. Although the child welfare community focuses primarily on the child and the battered women's community focuses primarily on the woman, both groups are concerned with ensuring a safe environment for the mother-child unit. Child welfare practitioners focus this attention on the parents when agonizing over what is in the best interest of the child. Similarly, battered women's advocates struggle to ensure that battered women are safe and, hence, can keep their children safe as well.

Even with different mandates, child welfare practitioners and battered women's advocates have many goals in common. Both are concerned that a cycle of intergenerational abuse will haunt future victims. Both attempt to break the pattern of intergenerational transmission of violence by intervening in the abusive crisis. Recognizing these commonalities may help the two groups work together toward the safety of both the battered woman and the child. Pivotal to a constructive relationship between battered women's and children's advocates is an understanding of the dynamics of domestic violence and the structural causes of violence between intimates. These issues are addressed in the next chapter.

QUESTIONS

❐ How has domestic violence affected your life?
❐ What relationships in your own life were *explicitly* violent?
❐ What relationships in your own life were *implicitly* violent?
❐ What did you do about the violence you detected?
❐ What new facts about domestic violence did you learn?

❏ What statistic surprised you most?

❏ Do you believe that when a child witnesses domestic violence, that this is child abuse?

❏ How has the intergenerational transmission of violence affected you or your clients' lives?

❏ Are you inclined to or do you work on behalf of battered women or children?

❏ What tensions are you likely to encounter?

❏ How might you consider resolving them?

CHAPTER 2

The Heart of Intimate Abuse and the Dynamics of Domestic Violence

At the heart of intimate abuse are the dynamics of domestic violence and the role love, dependence, and fear play in battered women's decision making. Examining the heart of intimate abuse also requires an analysis of culture and race and the ways both form our views on relationship and commitment. This chapter explores why battered women stay in abusive relationships and the impossible decisions they face when contemplating a course of action for themselves and their children.

A commonly asked question is why would a battered woman stay in an abusive relationship. Addressing this issue directly helps illuminate why a battered woman might endure violence, even when she has children to protect. This question also reflects several judgments. First, the question assumes that battered women generally do stay in abusive relationships and that they don't take steps to protect themselves or to leave. It also assumes that women should always leave an abusive relationship. In addition, by asking why does she stay, the onus of leaving the relationship is placed on the woman. Using this analysis, the battered woman is all too often blamed for allowing the abuse to continue. Women are viewed as weak because they remain in a relationship and endure the violence that threatens their lives and the lives of their children.

Other critical questions that need to be addressed are: Why doesn't the abusive partner leave? Why are there no residential treatment centers for men who batter? Why do men hold onto relationships that are so destructive?

Despite these concerns, the reasons women stay in abusive relationships merit attention in order to help practitioners understand the competing pressures on them to maintain the status quo (Box 2.1). First, women stay in abusive situations because they are emotionally attached to the relationship (Ellard, Herbert, & Thompson, 1991). They often feel sympathetic to a batterer's family history of abuse and empathize with its expression in

---

Box 2.1 Reasons Why Battered Women Stay in Abusive Relationships

- Love gives rise to the hope that "he will change."

  Women often define themselves relationally; they stand by their commitments.

  They love their children and want them to have a father.

- Financial reasons

  Women may be unable to train for work.

  Women may be unable to afford housing.

  They may lack education.

  There is inequality of wages for women.

- Fear of retaliation

  Women perceive that their physical safety is threatened.

  Women may lack real options to be safe with their children; indeed, efforts to leave in the past have not been supported.

  Risk of violence increases with efforts to leave.

- Religious beliefs

  For many women, leaving may violate religious law.

  Religious leaders may have advised them to stay.

- Cultural and racial influences

  The community may encourage women to put up with the violence in the name of keeping the culture cohesive.

  Exposing the violence may put the abuser in the hands of the police, who are feared.

adulthood. In addition, battered women may feel that a family should stay together "no matter what" and that they should tolerate abuse to protect the nuclear family (Frisch & MacKenzie, 1991). Similarly, they may stay because their children, who have a good relationship with their father, express either directly or indirectly that they want the mother to stay (Zambrano, 1985). Women may worry that leaving will disrupt their children's lives by forcing them to change schools and friends.

Second, structural constraints limit the choices available to women. The current structure of society includes inequality in wages for men and women and more lucrative job opportunities for men (Faludi, 1991). This structure forces some women into dependence on their male partners. In addition, women may lack the education necessary to pursue employment. Finally, institutions change at a slow pace and the acceptance of violence against women has strong roots in our society. Indeed, family values emphasize the importance of a two-parent nucleus at *any* cost.

Also for structural reasons, a woman may lack the financial resources to leave a relationship (Aguirre, 1985). Women may not be able to afford housing, child care, or basic life necessities (Sullivan, 1991). Women may worry that their children will lack financial security if they leave. Indeed, many batterers use their more lucrative financial position to control the women they abuse. Batterers commonly withhold or control finances in order to ensure their position of financial strength in the relationship (Davis & Hagen, 1992).

Third, battered women may be too afraid to leave (Painter & Dutton, 1985). Often batterers threaten survivors who threaten to leave (Barnett & LaViolette, 1993). Indeed, women who leave are more at risk for death or femicide (Hart, 1988). As previously discussed, risk of abuse increases for both the mother and the child when parents separate.

Another reason why a battered woman stays in an abusive relationship is due to low self-esteem; she thinks that life can be no better (Gold, 1986; Mills, 1985). In addition, she has become isolated, feeling she has no one in whom she may confide (Barnett & LaViolette, 1993). Moreover, she fears being lonely (Turner & Shapiro, 1986) or that the batterer will commit suicide (Campbell, 1992). Finally, she stays because she thinks the criminal justice system will fail her (Hart, 1996; Jones, 1994).

One of the most compelling reasons battered women stay in abusive relationships is for cultural or religious reasons (Barnett & LaViolette, 1993). Orthodox Jewish women (Horsburgh, 1995) or Muslim women (Mama, 1996), for example, may feel trapped because Jewish or Muslim law forbids a woman from filing for divorce without her husband's permission. Some African American women (White, 1994) and Latinas (Rivera, 1994) fear that if they leave a relationship they will be ostracized for contributing to racial stereotypes. African American women may also resist intervention by a hostile police force (Crenshaw, 1991).

Women living in cultures that value community over individuality, as well as those that hold women fundamentally responsible for the preservation of community face enormous barriers when confronting domestic violence. Women may fear breaking up their families (Lee & Au, 1998; Zambrano, 1985). Nilda Rimonte (1991) explains that a woman abused by her husband in some Asian Pacific cultures, will "hesitate . . . a very long time before attempting to do anything about the violence at all" (p. 139). Rimonte continues, "To some, her inaction and silence suggest collusion. In fact, it is an indication of the desperation induced by the limited vocabulary of self-definition permitted by her culture, and the terrible price she must pay to preserve her identity within her culture" (p. 139).

RACIAL AND CULTURAL CONCERNS IN DOMESTIC VIOLENCE AND CHILD WELFARE PRACTICE

Brother
I don't want to hear about how my real enemy is the system
i'm no genius, but i do know that system you hit me with is called a fist

Pat Parker
(White, 1986, p. 25)

In order to respond to the individual needs of victims of domestic violence and to better appreciate the racial and cultural influences on their decision-making processes, it is helpful to explore the attitudes and experiences of particular groups as they relate to intimate abuse. In this next section, some of the cultural factors that might affect how an African American, Latina, Asian Pacific, or Native American woman responds to the violence in her life are examined.

THE AFRICAN AMERICAN WOMAN

Battered African American women may be reluctant to involve outsiders, especially the police, who may be hostile to them and to their batterer. Negative and violent images of Black men prevent Black women from reporting domestic violence, which would substantiate racist images (White, 1994).

In addition, the African American woman might feel that if she rejects her violent partner, then she may not find another man (White, 1994). She may have internalized racist feelings and believe that a "good" Black man is hard to find. In addition, the African American woman might be influenced by her cultural and religious beliefs, that is, that she should not separate or divorce under any circumstances (White, 1994).

THE LATINA WOMAN

One study indicated that U.S.-born Mexican American men and women (30.9%) were more likely to use physical violence against their partners than were Mexican-born Mexican Americans (20.0%) or White (21.6%) men and women (Sorensen & Telles, 1991). Traditionally, Latino culture is patriarchal, in which men and elders are in charge. Women are told that they are morally and spiritually superior to males and as such are considered the mediators (Rivera, 1994). Because Latinas do not want to bring shame on the family they try to keep the violence a private, family matter. Because of the influential role of Christianity, especially of the Roman Catholic Church, victims may have spoken to their priest about the abuse and may have been encouraged to stay in the relationship (Ginorio & Reno, 1986). Recognition of the rich and unique histories of Spanish-speaking women will be key to understanding diversity and for finding points of connection between them.

THE ASIAN PACIFIC AND ASIAN PACIFIC AMERICAN WOMAN

This is a diverse group encompassing populations from all over the world at various levels of acculturation to the "dominant" culture. The Center for the Pacific Asian Family in Los Angeles receives about 1,500 calls each year and about 100 families are sheltered there annually (Yoshihama, 1994). The Asian Women's Center in New York receives about 2,500 calls each year (Yoshihama, 1994). The family is a hierarchical and patriarchal system in which the man is considered the head of the household. There is an emphasis on family harmony and pressure to save face and prevent family shame (Lee & Au, 1998). The family's welfare as a whole is valued more than an individual family member's well-being. Suffering without complaint is considered a value by Asian Pacific cultures (Lee & Au, 1998; Rimonte, 1991). The belief in fate may make women feel that they have no way to control the violence. And finally, it is important to recognize that those Asian Pacific women who come from war-torn countries may not perceive the violence they suffer as abuse (Yoshihama, 1994).

THE AMERICAN INDIAN WOMAN

A 1991 report by the Navajo Nation Department of Law Enforcement revealed that 0.6 to 1% of Navajos over age 18 are victims of domestic violence (Zion & Zion, 1993). These figures are believed to be gross underestimates (Zion & Zion, 1993). The stereotype that "Indians" are savages causes racism among non–American Indians, which, in turn, effects the self-esteem of American Indians; this could account for the domestic violence that has been detected in the American Indian community (Allen, 1986). The problem is that American Indians may not want to discuss domestic violence among themselves because it reinforces negative stereotypes (Allen, 1986). This may lead to underreporting of intimate abuse in the American Indian community.

In American Indian communities, native people have legal standing in what determination is made regarding the custody of children. An American Indian woman may fear tribal repercussions if she acknowledges the domestic violence that devastates her life (Allen, 1986).

OTHER CULTURAL ISSUES

Four other groups warrant special attention when considering the unique needs of individual survivors and their children. In this section, we explore briefly the dynamics present when working with immigrants, gay clients, elders, and clients with disabilities.

IMMIGRANTS

Recent immigrants often face multiple stressors, especially the pressure to assimilate. They are trying to find employment, learn the language, understand the culture, and meet family demands. When figures of authority come to investigate domestic violence, child abuse, or both, perpetrators, survivors, and their children are likely to deny any wrongdoing (Brownell & Congress, 1998; Orloff, Jang, & Klein, 1995). To admit to domestic violence would be to distinguish the family, set them apart, make them different.

Other pressures to assimilate may also exacerbate the intimate abuse (Lee & Au, 1998; Yoshihama, 1994). For example, the batterer may be accustomed to a traditional role for women, whereas the survivor, struggling to become a part of the dominant culture, may want to participate in activities, such as attending college, that are seen as threatening to traditional values.

Big cities such as Los Angeles and New York have strong cultural enclaves. Members of Chinatown, Little Italy, and Koreatown communities often reject assimilation into the "dominant" culture; the traditional culture and customs of their ethnicity prevail (Rimonte, 1991). In such situations, there are several pressures on immigrant battered women to stay in the abusive relationship. First, a survivor of domestic violence may be hesitant to reveal the violence because the culture and community are unsupportive or because they are threatened by the revealing of secrets. Second, the old customs of the dominant ethnicity may actually perpetuate domestic violence by tolerating or even approving of such behavior; the battered woman feels trapped by this tradition (Yung, 1997). Third, the survivor may feel dependent on the batterer for her immigration status and may fear that he will report her to the authorities (Roche & Sadoski, 1996). Practitioners working with battered immigrant women should be aware of these very pressing concerns, and should inquire about them directly.

GAY AND LESBIAN RELATIONSHIPS

Domestic violence in gay and lesbian relationships poses unique challenges to practitioners (Carlson & Maciol, 1997). It is estimated that 10.9 to 20.0% of gay male couples experience domestic violence (Lockhart, White, Causby, & Isaac, 1994) and between 17 and 26% of lesbian couples experience violence (Lie, Schlitt, Bush, Montague, & Reyes, 1991; Loulan, 1987). In one survey of 1,099 lesbians, 52% had been victims of violence by their female partners (Lie & Gentlewarrior, 1991). Reluctance to report domestic violence is often related to the batterer's threat that he or she will "out" the survivor; this can be especially challenging to a victim with children (Carlson & Maciol, 1997; Hammond, 1986). Similarly, a survivor's attachment to the relationship is often associated with their feelings that they won't find anyone else who will love them (Carlson & Maciol, 1997; Hammond, 1986; Herr, Grogan, Clark, & Carson, 1998). Finally, intervention in gay battering relationships often turns on the size of the batterer rather than on an investigation of who was primarily responsible for the violence. Fear by survivors that they will be stereotyped as "butch" and therefore be identified as the perpetrators may deter them from reporting the abuse they endure (Gelles, 1997). These issues should be addressed through specialized education and training for law enforcement and other domestic violence personnel and through the development of referral networks of practitioners who are sensitive to these concerns (Carlson & Maciol, 1997; Herr, Grogan, Clark, & Carson, 1998).

ELDERS

Special issues are evident in working with survivors of elder abuse, a form of domestic violence (Aitken & Griffin, 1996). Abusers in elder abuse cases might include home health care providers who steal checks or forge the survivor's signature or the children of the elder who may have control over the elder's finances or may be responsible for ensuring that they are cared for properly. Elders are often the targets of con artists and lawyers, neighbors, or other people who are in a position of trust with the elder (Los Angeles County Department [LACD] of Public Social Services [PSS], 1992).

There are a number of reasons why an elder would be reluctant to complain about the abuse or may be unwilling to terminate the relationship. For example, when the elder's child is the abuser, the elder may feel responsible for the child, even when the abuse is severe. The elder may not want to jeopardize this relationship with the child. Moreover, the elder might not want to report the abuse because he or she feels totally dependent on the abuser. They may be afraid that if the abuser leaves, they will be sent to a retirement home. Finally, the elder may not want to report any financial loss because they are afraid they will lose credibility. Indicators of these fears may include making excuses for the batterer; expressing fear of being abandoned or isolated; being passive or confused; denying that the abuse is occurring; and expressions of agitation, helplessness, and depression (LACD of PSS, 1992). If the elder looks to the caretaker for permission to speak or is cowering or cringing in his or her presence, this too might be a sign of domestic violence (LACD of PSS, 1992). Physical indicators might include odorous, matted hair; maintenance problems, such as unclean clothing or environment; and malnutrition and dehydration (LACD of PSS, 1992).

Several models of intervention have been suggested for elder abuse, including the Roberts' Seven-Stage Crisis Intervention Model (Roberts, 1996b) and the Elder Abuse Diagnosis and Intervention Model (Quinn & Tomita, 1997). Both models involve assessment and intervention, and both methods encourage practitioners to recognize the unique problems that elders face, such as financial and medical emergencies, and to mobilize services accordingly (Brownell & Abelman, 1998). It is also important to remember that when working with this vulnerable population that you should value both their dignity and right to self-determination (Brownell & Abelman, 1988).

WOMEN WITH DISABILITIES

As with the elderly, women with disabilities are seriously at risk for domestic violence. More specifically, individuals with developmental disabilities (ranging from physical limitations to developmental disabilities, etc.) are at high risk for both domestic violence and abuse from home care workers (Carlson, 1997; Murphy & Razza, 1998; Wisconsin Council on Development Disabilities, 1991). Women with disabilities may be reluctant to reveal their abusive experiences because they may not recognize them as abusive; they are also exceedingly dependent on their caretakers (LACD of PSS, 1992).

In one study of new Social Security Supplemental Security Income disability recipients, many of whom receive benefits for addictions or mental illnesses, or both, childhood and adult intimate violence was prevalent. Recipients of these benefits were both victims and perpetrators of domestic violence and child abuse (Mills, 1997a).

Recently, scholars have been particularly concerned with addressing the specific needs of battered women with mental retardation (Carlson, 1997; Murphy & Razza, 1998). Although no exact statistics have been gathered, it has been estimated by experts in the field that 90% of women who are mentally retarded will be sexually or physically victimized during their lifetime (Sgroi, 1989). Assessment and intervention of this vulnerable population poses specific challenges to practitioners, who must take into account the complex interplay of cognitive and psychological factors that may be operating when a person with a disability has been traumatized by abuse (Murphy & Razza, 1998). The assessment should include a clinical interview, observations of the client, an interview with the caregiver, and psychological testing (Nezu, Nezu, & Gill-Weiss, 1992). Therapeutic interventions with these clients should be intersectional. Carlson (1997) recommends co-led therapy groups; one leader should be experienced in developmental disabilities and another should have worked with survivors of domestic violence. Many of the assessment and intervention strategies designed for women with developmental disabilities are transferable to women with other disabilities as well.

THE CYCLE OF VIOLENCE AND THE POWER AND CONTROL WHEEL

> To voy a dar nua ojera
> Y como llegaste a mi
> Alejate, bándolera
> Si te tiro por la ventana
> Tu subes por la escalera.
>
> I am going to hit you
> I am going to give you a black eye
> And the same way you came to me
> Go away, thief
> If I throw you out the window
> You climb up the stairs.
>
> Hector Levoe, 1976
> Musician
> (Rivera, 1994, p. 231)

Traditionally, practitioners working in the field of domestic violence have relied primarily on two paradigms to explain the dynamics of intimate abuse: the Cycle of Violence and the Power and Control Wheel (Figures 2.1 and 2.2).

According to the Cycle of Violence, the intimate abuse begins with the tension-building phase, and is characterized by minor battering and/or emotional abuse. During the acute battering incident, the violence escalates to the point of "rampage, injury, brutality, and sometimes death" (Walker, 1989, p. 43). According to this model, the tranquil or honeymoon phase is characterized by the batterer apologizing with promises never to repeat the pattern again.

FIGURE 2.1   Cycle of violence.

Source: Walker, 1984. Adapted from Los Angeles Domestic Violence Council, 1996.

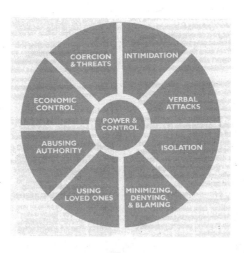

FIGURE 2.2   Power and control wheel.

Source: Pence & Paymar, 1993.
Adapted from Los Angeles Domestic Violence Council, 1996.

Of course, for many battered women this is not a cycle at all. Some battered women never enjoy a honeymoon phase and some never experience an acute battering incident. In a study done by Walker (1989), she found that the cycle was reported to occur in two thirds of the 1,600 incidents of violence recorded by battered women. For others, the buildup or tension-building phase is all they live with. Others may simply characterize the cycle as unpredictable.

Painter and Dutton (1985) describe a battered woman's response to these predictable and unpredictable patterns of violence as traumatic bonding. Traumatic bonding occurs when strong emotional ties link two people after incidents in which one person harasses, beats, threatens, abuses, or intimidates the other (Dutton, 1995). Traumatic bonding is particularly acute when the violence is intermittent and when the periods of nonviolence are characterized by calm and even pleasure. This dynamic is exacerbated by a power imbalance evident in many violent relationships, in which the victim internalizes the aggressor's negative appraisal, rendering her even more dependent and creating "a strong affective bond to the high power person" (Dutton, 1995, pp. 190–191). This dependency by the low-power person (in this case, the battered woman) masks the dependency of the high-power person that underpins this traumatic bond. It is the traumatic bonding, according to this theory, that keeps battered women enmeshed in violent relationships.

The Power and Control Wheel (see Figure 2.2) categorizes the abuse according to the means the batterer uses to control the battered woman; this model describes the dynamic as coercion and threats, intimidation, emotional abuse, and isolation. In addition, the wheel highlights the ways the batterer uses economic abuse, male privilege, and the children to exert control over his partner. According to the Power and Control Wheel the batterer minimizes and denies the abuse and blames the battered woman for his violence.

More specifically, the Power and Control Wheel highlights how the batterer makes or uses threats to hurt the victim; threatens to leave her, to commit suicide, to report her to welfare or to the immigration service; or makes her drop criminal charges against him by intimidating her. The wheel describes how he uses fear to control her, through stares and gestures or by threatening to smash things or destroy her property, or both. He might also display weapons. In addition, the wheel describes how he uses emotional abuse by putting her down, making her feel self-loathing, calling her names, making her think she is crazy or humiliating her. In addition, the batterer uses isolation, controlling what she does, who she sees and talks to, what she wears and reads, and where she goes. He also uses the children to relay messages or uses visitation to harass her, or he threatens to take the children away.

Economic abuse is another common form of power and control according to the wheel, preventing her from getting or keeping a job, making her ask for money, giving her an allowance, or counting her change. Also, economic abuse can take the form of not letting her know about or have access to the family income.

Using male privilege is another form of power and control the wheel describes. The batterer treats her like a servant, makes all the "big" decisions, and acts as "master of his castle." Finally he minimizes, denies, and blames (Dutton & Golant, 1995). He makes light of the abuse he inflicts and doesn't take her concerns about the violence seriously (Dutton & Golant, 1995). He even denies that the abuse occurs or shifts the responsibility for his abusive behavior onto her (Dutton & Golant, 1995).

Although all of these dynamics ring true of some or even most battering relationships, neither the Cycle of Violence nor the Power and Control Wheel fully take into account the survivor's conflicts and the influences which often keep her wed to the violent relationship. To help elucidate the roles that love, fear, dependence, race, culture, and religion play in the domestic violence dynamic, it is helpful to distinguish the Cycle of Violence and the Power and Control Wheel from a model that considers these factors from the victim's point of view. No explanatory tool introduced to date is adequate to help elucidate the conflicting experience of the battered woman, and to explore, from her perspective, how and why the violence re-occurs.

THE HEART OF INTIMATE ABUSE

The Heart of Intimate Abuse is a model designed to capture the dynamics that drive the violent relationship, taking into account the battered woman's experience as well as the batterer's perspective, from her point of view (see Figure 2.3). This paradigm is designed to go beyond the boundaries of the previous models such as the Power and Control Wheel and the Cycle of Violence to uncover the dynamic of intimate abuse from the battered woman's perspective. This conceptual model is critical for encouraging practitioners to stand in a battered woman's shoes by forcing the CSW, advocate, or clinician to discuss the abuse in a way that the survivor is likely to understand.

As the Heart of Intimate Abuse reveals, dynamics of domestic violence can be characterized by the pressures and influences on the survivor, which are likely to include love, religion, culture, race, fear, financial dependence, as well as the experience of the batterer to exert power and control through love for the survivor and her children; through religion, culture, and race; and through the use of abuse. The purpose of this paradigm is to understand a battered woman's conundrum and to help the practitioner better understand this particular battered woman's vulnerabilities. When the Heart of Intimate Abuse is shared in discussions with the victim, she herself can begin to understand the violence from her own vantage point, from the perspective of her love for the batterer; love for the children; religion, culture, and race; fear; and financial dependence, narratives which will resonate with her experience.

Similarly, a review of the dynamics of the batterer's violence, from her perspective, enables both the practitioner and the battered woman to share how she has come to understand his love for her and for her children; the role religion, culture, and race play in his mind (from her perspective); how power and control may be operating; and the many ways he uses abuse in their dynamic. The Heart of Intimate Abuse challenges practitioners to abandon, at least initially and assuming it is clinically appropriate, such paradigms as the Cycle of Violence and Power and Control Wheel, for a model that starts from the battered woman's perspective. This becomes especially important in chapters 6 and 7, when we start to explore a specific method for empowering the battered woman, and in chapters 8, 9, and 10, where we use the Heart of Intimate Abuse in dialogues with survivors through case studies.

Before proceeding to a fuller description of how empowering strategies might be used to interrupt the dynamics of intimate

The relationship is driven by...

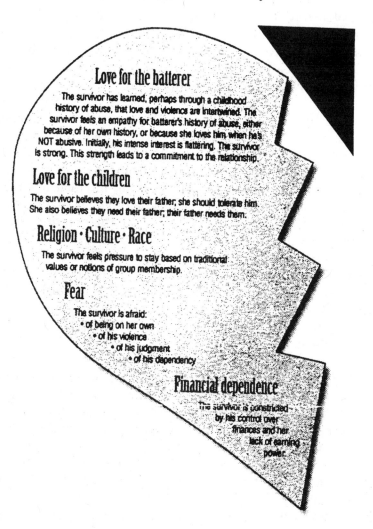

Love for the batterer

The survivor has learned, perhaps through a childhood history of abuse, that love and violence are intertwined. The survivor feels an empathy for batterer's history of abuse, either because of her own history, or because she loves him when he's NOT abusive. Initially, his intense interest is flattering. The survivor is strong. This strength leads to a commitment to the relationship.

Love for the children

The survivor believes they love their father; she should tolerate him. She also believes they need their father; their father needs them.

Religion · Culture · Race

The survivor feels pressure to stay based on traditional values or notions of group membership.

Fear

The survivor is afraid:
- of being on her own
- of his violence
- of his judgment
- of his dependency

Financial dependence

The survivor is constricted by his control over finances and her lack of earning power.

FIGURE 2.3 The heart of intimate abuse.

36

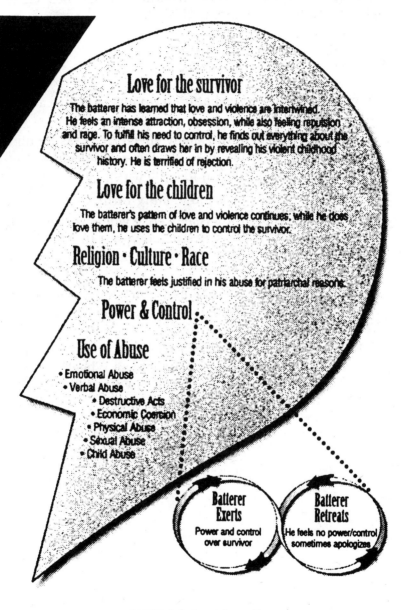

Love for the survivor

The batterer has learned that love and violence are intertwined. He feels an intense attraction, obsession, while also feeling repulsion and rage. To fulfill his need to control, he finds out everything about the survivor and often draws her in by revealing his violent childhood history. He is terrified of rejection.

Love for the children

The batterer's pattern of love and violence continues; while he does love them, he uses the children to control the survivor.

Religion · Culture · Race

The batterer feels justified in his abuse for patriarchal reasons.

Power & Control

Use of Abuse

- Emotional Abuse
  - Verbal Abuse
    - Destructive Acts
    - Economic Coercion
    - Physical Abuse
    - Sexual Abuse
    - Child Abuse

Batterer Exerts
Power and control over survivor

Batterer Retreats
He feels no power/control sometimes apologizes

FIGURE 2.3 *(continued)*

abuse, it is useful first to explore the systems that battered women confront and how they fare in those systems.

QUESTIONS

- ❏ What pressures force battered women to stay in abusive relationships?
- ❏ How do children in the family affect the pressure on a battered woman to stay in an abusive relationship?
- ❏ What pressures can you identify with?
- ❏ What pressures don't you identify with?
- ❏ What racial or cultural issues arise when working with battered women? What issues do you want to be sure to integrate into your practice? What issues are less legitimate in your mind?
- ❏ What myths or assumptions do most people make about battered women? What myths or assumptions do you make about battered women?
- ❏ How is the Heart of Intimate Abuse different from the Cycle of Violence or the Power and Control Wheel? What would you add or take away from this new paradigm for thinking about the dynamics of intimate abuse?

Part II

Systems' Responses to Domestic Violence

CHAPTER 3

The Criminal Justice System's Response to Domestic Violence

In January 1975, Frank Sorichetti attacked and punched his wife Josephine in the chest. That July, Frank attacked Josephine with a butcher knife and threatened to kill her and her children. In September, he destroyed the contents of their apartment.

Frank was well known to the officers at the 43rd Precinct in New York. On November 8, 1975, Frank picked up their daughter Dina during an authorized visitation and issued death threats to Dina and Josephine. Josephine immediately reported the threats to officers at the precinct and asked that Frank be arrested. She showed them her order of protection. The officers refused to arrest Frank.

The next day Frank was found passed out in his car. Dina had been attacked with a fork, a knife, and a screwdriver. Frank had also attempted to saw off her leg.

(Sorichetti v. City of New York, 1985)

Based on cases such as *Sorichetti*, many battered women's lawyers and advocates have come to believe that the most effective method for eradicating domestic violence is to arrest, prosecute, and jail perpetrators of intimate abuse, regardless of a battered woman's preference to avoid criminal intervention in her violent relationship (Frisch, 1992; Hanna, 1996). This chapter explores the prevailing criminal practices in domestic violence cases and examines those strategies critically in light of current research.

41

Some readers might wonder why an entire chapter is devoted to criminal justice responses. Critical to this analysis is the fact that the criminal justice system has become the predominant response to domestic violence in the United States and the lynchpin solution for those who believe we can eradicate intimate abuse. The issue of criminal interventions is particularly relevant when children are involved. Indeed, children who witness or become injured when violence erupts between intimates provide compelling support for aggressive interventions that disregard the battered mother's desire not to pursue criminal charges against her batterer.

As we have learned, and as the Heart of Intimate Abuse paradigm reveals, women stay in abusive relationships because they are too scared, poor, or unskilled to leave or because they love a man who is only occasionally violent (Hackler, 1991; Raphael, 1996). Economic factors that make it difficult for a woman to leave a dangerous family situation contribute to the potential violence (Hackler, 1991). In addition, women who are sympathetic to the traumas of their violent partners, especially those who are aware of a history of abuse in the batterer's family, may experience their lover's violence differently than those who are less tolerant or understanding.

Many women stay in abusive relationships because they are culturally pressured to endure violence. As Kimberle Crenshaw (1991) has argued, the specific "raced" and "gendered" experiences of women of color define and confine the interests of the entire group. For example, the Asian Pacific community's denial of violence against women—their beliefs about the family and the role of women within it—works to make violence against women acceptable, despite the diversity of Asian Pacific cultures. In so doing, these attitudes legitimize the victimization of women (Rimonte, 1991). An Orthodox Jewish woman who files for divorce could be accused of violating Jewish law, even if she wishes to divorce her husband because he abuses her (Horsburgh, 1995). Such consequences exemplify "the blatant and more subtle forms of intra-group oppression in the Jewish culture that foster the mistreatment of women" (Horsburgh, 1995, p. 203).

When experiencing abuse at the hands of men of color, African American women, Asian Pacific women, and Latinas must confront the layered identities of gender and culture in the context of a racist society prepared to label or blame. African American women and Latinas who complain that their partners are violent fear they will be ostracized for contributing to racial stereotypes (Crenshaw, 1991). Cultural pressures to identify with the larger Asian Pacific community may influence Asian Pacific women to fear rejection for revealing their secret (Rimonte, 1991).

These emotional, financial, and cultural factors become especially relevant when battered women must choose whether to rely on the criminal justice system for intervention in their abuse. Straus and Gelles (1986) found that less than 15% of battered women report severe incidents of violence, and the National Crime Survey Report (U.S. DOJ, 1994b) reveals that 48% of the estimated 4 million battered women in the United States failed to report incidents of intimate abuse. These statistics suggest women's ambivalence, or even outright hostility, toward involving the criminal justice system in their intimate lives.

Mandatory criminal interventions take two primary forms: mandatory arrest and mandatory prosecution. "Mandatory arrest" forces the police to detain a perpetrator of intimate abuse when there is evidence of violence such as bruises, cuts, or stab wounds (Box 3.1). The battered woman's claims no longer matter—the police arrest regardless. A "proarrest" or "presumptive arrest" policy encourages a law enforcement officer to arrest if she or he believes a domestic violence crime has been committed (Box 3.2).

"Mandatory prosecution," sometimes called a "no-drop" policy, requires a prosecutor to bring charges against the batterer regardless of the desire of the battered woman to pursue the prosecution; (Buzawa & Buzawa, 1996; Corsilles, 1994) (Box 3.3). Some variation among no-drop jurisdictions does exist. A "hard" no-drop policy never takes the victim's preference into consideration (Corsilles, 1994). A "soft" no-drop policy permits victims to drop the charges under certain limited circumstances, such as if the victim has left the batterer (Buzawa & Buzawa, 1996). In a hard no-drop jurisdiction, the battered woman's preference is irrelevant, except to the extent that she testifies, or does not testify, for the prosecutor. In these situations, prosecutions are pursued against the batterer by forcing the woman to testify (Buzawa & Buzawa, 1996), sometimes causing her to recant or lie on the stand. One study reports that 92% of prosecutorial agencies will use their subpoena power to require victim testimony (Rebovich, 1996).

BOX 3.1 MANDATORY ARREST POLICIES

Mandatory arrest eliminates officer discretion. The law enforcement officer, if she or he has probable cause to believe a misdemeanor or felony domestic violence crime has been committed, shall arrest regardless of the victims' wishes and regardless of whether the crime occurred in the presence of the officer (National Council of Juvenile & Family Court Judges [NCJFCJ], 1994).

If the officer receives complaints of domestic violence from two or more parties, the officer shall evaluate each complaint separately to determine who was the primary aggressor. Factors in determining the primary aggressor include:

• prior complaints of domestic violence;
• severity of injuries;
• likelihood of future injury; and
• whether someone acted in self-defense (NCJFCJ, 1994).

The arresting officer is discouraged from arresting both parties or from arresting no one insofar as they must submit a detailed report explaining their action (NCJFCJ, 1994).

This is exemplified in the Los Angeles County District Attorney's (1996) "Pledge to Victims" which presents the prosecutor's position in no uncertain terms: "We hope to convince you to cooperate with our efforts, but we will proceed with or without your cooperation. . . . "

Mandatory arrest and prosecution policies, which are emblematic of a "law and order approach," assume that the battered woman is weak and indecisive. Generally speaking, supporters of mandatory criminal interventions such as mandatory arrest and prosecution claim that their primary concern is for the battered woman's safety (arrest him and she will be safe) and argue that the battered woman is incapable of judging the dangerousness of the situation in which she is ensnared (Wills, 1997). Others have defended battered women's judgments arguing that although safety is on the minds of most victims, it is one of several concerns, such as: Where will I live? How will I support myself? How will I support my children? Will he kill us if we leave?

Box 3.2 Pro or Presumptive Arrest Policies

Pro arrest policies still allow for officer discretion. The law enforce-ment officer, if she or he has probable cause to believe a misde-meanor or felony domestic violence crime has been committed, shall presume that arrest is the appropriate response (NCJFCJ, 1994).

If the officer receives complaints of domestic violence from two or more parties, the officer shall evaluate each complaint sepa-rately to determine who was the primary aggressor. Factors in determining the primary aggressor include:

• prior complaints of domestic violence;
• severity of injuries;
• likelihood of future injury; and
• whether someone acted in self-defense (NCJFCJ, 1994).

The officer is discouraged from arresting both parties or from arresting no one insofar as they must submit a detailed report explaining their action (NCJFCJ, 1994).

I believe that the multifaceted nature of domestic violence de-mands that we adopt a more flexible approach than those embod-ied in mandatory policies. I begin with the assumption that many battered women deny the extent to which their intimate relation-ships are violent (Mahoney, 1991). For some women, a police response to a domestic violence call or prosecution forces them to realize that they have been abused and have legal recourse. For other women, however, such criminal intervention reinforces their denial, or the threat of their batterer, by sending them further underground (Hart, 1996). My concern is that battered women may not report the intimate abuse that plagues their lives for fear that they will be met with a response that takes the violence "out of their control."

A small but growing number of feminists are beginning to worry that universally applied strategies, such as mandatory arrest and prosecution, cannot take into account the reasons individual

---

Box 3.3 MANDATORY PROSECUTION POLICIES

If a "Hard" No-Drop Policy is adopted, the prosecutor's discretion is significantly curtailed. The prosecutor pursues a misdemeanor or felony domestic violence case regardless of the victim's supportive testimony. The victims' excited utterances (at the time of the crime), and pictures and other evidence gathered at arrest constitute evidence in the case (Corsilles, 1994).

If a "Soft" No-Drop Policy is adopted, the prosecutor's discretion depends on several factors. The prosecutor can drop the charges in limited circumstances, such as if the victim has decided to leave the batterer (Buzawa & Buzawa, 1996).

---

women stay in abusive relationships or the reasons for their denial (Bowman, 1992; Buzawa & Buzawa, 1993; Ferraro & Pope, 1993; Ford & Regoli, 1993; Littleton, 1993; Mills, 1996b). These feminists fear that the State's indifference to this contingent of battered women may be harmful, even violent (Mills, 1998b).

By violent, I refer to the institutional violence inflicted through the competitive dynamic that dominates the relationships between the State, the survivor, and the batterer. The State, in its obsession to punish the batterer, often uses the battered woman as a pawn for winning the competition. This destructive dynamic is, in itself, abusive to the woman. As one scholar described it, "once a survivor sets the remedial process in motion, there are partial constraints on her ability to restore the status quo" (Margulies, 1996, p. 184). Similarly, Cheryl Hanna (1996), a supporter of mandatory interventions, hesitantly admits: The battered woman's "fear and mistrust of the criminal justice system may be even greater than her fear of the batterer" (p. 1884).

MANDATORY ARREST: RESEARCH FINDINGS AND JUDICIAL INTERVENTIONS

> Twenty-seven states have laws that mandate arrest;
> 40 states have either mandatory or proarrest policies.
>
> (Zorza & Woods, 1994)

Ironically, results from studies on the efficacy of mandatory arrest are indeterminate. The first study to assess the effectiveness of arrest on recidivism, conducted in Minneapolis, revealed that arrest did, in fact, reduce future violence (Sherman & Berk, 1984b). It is important to remember that these studies are based on the percentage of women who *do* report violence to the police. The Minneapolis study was the first of six randomized field experiments on how police should respond to incidents of misdemeanor domestic violence. The randomized options in the Minneapolis study were (1) arrest; (2) remove the batterer from the premises for 24 hours; and (3) try to restore order (only).

Measurements used to determine recidivism rates included official records and victim follow-up interviews. Sherman and Berk's (1984b) study results found that arrest was the most effective means of reducing the likelihood of new violence. The arrest response, according to their findings, had a recidivism rate of 19%, whereas removing the batterer had a recidivism rate of 33%. The advise or try to restore order intervention had a recidivism rate of 37%. One interesting result is that in those cases in which arrest was the intervention, if the victim perceived that the police took time to listen when arresting the perpetrator, the rate of repeat violence was significantly lower. What they found was that arrest coupled with listening yielded a 9% rate of recidivism (Sherman & Berk, 1984a).

This study inspired a national response as mandatory arrest became the call of battered women's advocates across the country (Jaffe, 1986). More than one third of U.S. police departments surveyed said that their policy of presumptive or proarrest in misdemeanor domestic violence cases was the result of the Minneapolis study (Jaffe, 1986). A confluence of other compounding factors, such as court cases, also influenced police agencies to take domestic violence calls more seriously.

Two such influential court cases included *Sorichetti v. City of New York* (1985) and *Thurman v. City of Torrington* (1984). In *Sorichetti v. City of New York*, an appeals court upheld a $2 million award to the daughter of a batterer when this estranged husband and father attacked the child and nearly amputated one of her legs during a visitation with him (for further detail see p. 41). The police failed to investigate when the daughter did not return from the visit even though a family court order of protection had been issued. The Court of Appeals in New York held that issuance of a judicial "order to protect" (also known as a restraining order) indicated that a special duty to protect had been assumed by the authorities. The court noted that police are required to arrest violators of judicial orders of protection (Box 3.4).

In *Thurman v. City of Torrington* (1984), a federal court in Connecticut awarded Tracey Thurman $1.9 million in her lawsuit against the City of Torrington and 24 city police officers due to the city's policy and practice of nonintervention and nonarrest in domestic violence cases. The judge ruled that an ongoing pattern of deliberate indifference to victims of domestic assault violates the equal protection clause of the 14th Amendment. *Thurman* was the first civil rights case in which a battered woman was permitted to sue a police department for failure to protect.

Despite the Minneapolis study's initial finding of some deterrent effects of arrest and these influential law suits, none of the subsequent series of arrest studies confirmed the unequivocal result that arrest deters future incidents of violence (Berk, Campbell, Klap, & Western, 1992; Dunford, 1992; Hirschel & Hutchison, 1992; Pate & Hamilton, 1992; Sherman et al., 1992). Indeed, only one study, described later in the chapter, has replicated this result (Yegidis & Renzy, 1994).

Consider, for example, a study of the efficacy of arrest in Omaha, Nebraska (Dunford, 1992), which used official reports and victim interviews to examine three interventions in misdemeanor do-

---

BOX 3.4 ORDERS OF PROTECTION OR RESTRAINING ORDERS

A battered woman can obtain a "civil" order of protection to evict an abusive person from a common residence or to arrest a batterer should he violate the order by coming within a range from which he has been precluded, or both.

Orders may also relate to child custody and visitation, financial support, property allocation, payment of attorney fees, and counseling for the batterer.

mestic violence cases: (1) mediation, (2) separation, and (3) arrest. The overall finding was that arrest was no more effective than the other two interventions, with some minor caveats.

In a Milwaukee, Wisconsin, study Sherman et al. (1992) looked at three interventions: (1) full arrest, (2) short arrest, and (3) no arrest (with a warning if the police were called back). The research found a short-term deterrent effect for full or short arrest, with an overall finding that over a 7- to 9-month period violence increased with the arrest group. It also found that repeat violence increased with the arrest of groups who were unemployed, unmarried, high school drop-out, or African American. Similarly, they found a decrease in violence with the arrest of groups who were employed, married, and White. This study raised the disturbing question of the confluence of violence, recidivism, and the effect of arrest in the African American community, suggesting that mandatory arrest policies may have the uwitting effect of increasing abuse in African American women's lives.

In a Charlotte, North Carolina, study Hirschel and Hutchison (1992) also looked at three interventions: (1) advising and possible separation, (2) issuing a citation requiring the batterer to appear in court, and (3) arrest. The study found that arrest was no more of a deterrent than was citation or advise and separation. It also found that a prior criminal record and chronicity of the abuse suggested a likelihood that the perpetrator would reoffend.

In a Colorado Springs, Colorado, study Berk et al. (1992) looked at four interventions: (1) temporary arrest, (2) temporary crisis counseling, (3) emergency protective order (EPO) only, and (4) restoration of order without an EPO. The study found that arrest had a deterrent effect on good risk perpetrators, that is, perpetrators who had a lot to lose from the arrest. Similarly they found that arrest had no deterrent effect on bad risk perpetrators or perpetrators who had little or nothing to lose from their incarceration. Indeed, Berk et al. admitted that "an arrest can sometimes make things worse" (p. 198).

In yet another study conducted in Metro Dade County, Florida (Pate & Hamilton, 1992), it was found that arrest only marginally affected recidivism according to one official measure and victim data. This study examined the differential impact between arrests, which lasted on average 14.6 hours, as compared with an intervention by a special unit trained in handling abuse, the Safe Streets Unit. This study tested the effectiveness of ride-along support teams that have become popular in domestic violence police response efforts. The Safe Streets Unit had little or no impact on recidivism.

REASSESSING THE RESEARCH ON ARREST

> With the onslaught of mandatory arrest policies, there has been an increase in the arrest of women. In 1987, 340 women in Los Angeles and 4,540 men were arrested for domestic violence crimes; in 1995, 1,262 women were arrested and 7,513 men were arrested. In 1995, a record 14.3% of domestic violence arrests in Los Angeles were women.
>
> (Johnson, 1996)

The overall findings of these six studies reveal that arrest was effective in deterring "good risk perpetrators" who had ties to the community, especially those with key indicators such as marriage, military service, and employment status (Berk et al., 1992; Sherman, 1992). In addition, the studies documented that arrest actually increased violence to some women, particularly those whose batterers were unemployed or had previously been arrested (Berk et al., 1992; Sherman, 1992).

These studies revealed complex results. To better understand the trade-offs between policies for employed and unemployed batterers and arrest or warnings, researchers have performed a cost-benefit analysis. Assuming most batterers arrested were employed, a proarrest approach would contribute to lowering incidents of repeat violence. In Milwaukee, however, where most of the suspects were unemployed, mandatory arrest actually failed to produce the greatest good for the greatest number. Welch (1994), for example, does not advocate mandatory arrest for Chicago because of the high number of people who are unemployed.

Some obvious conclusions from these studies are that regional variations in unemployment or other factors should encourage regional solutions. It is noteworthy that no study, even those that included victim interviews, examined either victim preference and its impact on recidivism or the dampening effect of mandatory arrest on future reports (Mills, 1998c). The one study that did examine the role of victim preference in determining police response found that victims were generally satisfied with police intervention (85%) when the police followed the victims' preferences (Buzawa, Austin, Bannon, & Jackson, 1992). This study suggests that victim preference is linked to victim satisfaction but reports nothing regarding whether satisfaction correlates with recidivism. When considering all of the studies, Lawrence Sherman (1992), an influential researcher in the field, concludes that arrest does have a deterrent effect for a majority of perpetrators but not for all.

These obvious conclusions aside, a raging debate on the efficacy of mandatory arrest ensues (Bowman, 1992; Buzawa & Buzawa, 1993; Hanna, 1996; Lerman, 1992; Mills, 1996b; Mills, 1997b; Mitchell, 1992). The debate often turns on whether we should encourage domestic violence policies that disregard the battered woman's preference. The arguments forwarded in favor of mandatory arrest are that battered women need the State to act on their behalf because they are too afraid to assert what they really want, that is, the batterer arrested; that they are too confused or traumatized to know that arrest is in their best interest; or that they are unwilling, in the case of women of color, to betray racial or cultural norms. Other reasons advanced for mandatory arrest policies include the educational and political benefit of asserting, in no uncertain terms, a societal intolerance for intimate abuse.

Opponents of mandatory arrest policies claim that battered women are disempowered by interactions with police officers who disregard the complexities of their conundrums (Mills, 1998b). They argue that survivors will stop calling law enforcement if they feel dismissed in their interactions with them (Hart, 1996). These issues are addressed more directly, from a clinical and advocacy perspective, in chapter 8, where I explore, in a case study, how to work with battered women caught in this criminal justice web.

MANDATORY PROSECUTION AND
THE EFFICACY OF OTHER INTERVENTIONS

> Once I got the [restraining] order I thought, it's time
> to start all over . . . most abusers are bigger and
> stronger than you are, and the order gives you a little
> bit more of an edge . . . it makes you feel as if you ate
> a can of spinach, like Popeye.
>
> Anonymous
> (Fischer & Rose, 1995, p. 424)

The only randomized study of mandatory prosecution was conducted in 1986 by Ford and Regoli (1993). The Ford and Regoli
(1993) study involved 480 men charged with misdemeanor assault
of a conjugal partner in Indianapolis, Indiana. These men were
assigned to one of three tracks: (1) pretrial diversion to a counseling program, (2) prosecution to conviction with a recommendation of counseling, and (3) prosecution to conviction with
presumptive sentencing. The study found that the type of prosecution policy employed in a case (no drop versus drop permitted)
can affect batterer behavior. Ford and Regoli also found that
victims who were given the choice to drop the charges against
the batterer and chose not to prosecute, had the greatest risk of
reabuse, even greater than those who were placed in the no-drop
prosecution category. It also revealed that mandatory prosecution may be harmful to women in some cases. Indeed, the researchers found that a battered woman was most likely to ensure her
subsequent safety when she could drop the charges and yet chose
to pursue the prosecution on her own accord.

Ford and Regoli (1993) explained that when a battered woman
decidedly pursued the prosecution of her batterer, she could
express her power in the situation and that such expression
actually decreased the violence in her relationship. They hypothe-
sized that victims who chose not to drop the charges in a jurisdiction which granted them the option to drop were the most likely to
experience increased safety due to the victim's "personal power."
They suggest that this kind of power, which might also be characterized as empowerment, is derived from three sources: using
the prosecution as a bargaining chip with the batterer; providing

women with a means of allying with others, including the police, prosecutors, and judges; and providing women a voice in determining sanctions against the batterer.

Ford and Regoli's findings can be criticized on a number of grounds (Mills, 1998c). First, their study was limited, in that they looked only at "eligible" misdemeanor assault cases; they did not consider cases involving defendants with prior records of violence against the victim, with criminal histories of felony violence, or who posed a serious threat of imminent danger. Second, only some victims in the study were actually permitted to drop the charges. The victims who filed the complaint themselves were allowed to drop the charges if they wished, whereas those victims whose complaints were filed by the police, rather than by the victims themselves, were not allowed to drop the charges. Third, the study did not examine the effects of what happened in a case, only how the case was tracked (i.e., diversion, prosecution with a recommendation of counseling, and prosecution with presumptive sentencing). Finally, the small sample of 480 defendants as well as regional variations limits the generalizability of their results to other jurisdictions.

A more recent study of the combined effects of arrest and prosecution on recidivism found that subsequent incidents of violence decreased when the court process was pursued against a perpetrator (Yegidis & Renzy, 1994). The study revealed that perpetrators who were subjected to multiple stages in the criminal justice process (from arrest to prosecution to sentencing) were less likely to reoffend. Their most dramatic result, however, was that arrest did have a deterrent effect on batterers, an effect that lasted at least 18 months. This study was the first to reconfirm the Minneapolis results that arrest affected recidivism for all batterers. Yegidis and Renzy's (1994) study, however, was limited by its design: cases were not randomly assigned to an intervention but rather examined, after the fact, by reviewing police reports and court records.

Another relevant question is whether other methods designed to protect battered women are working. Orders of protection, orders that prevent the batterer from contacting or following the victim, have also been only marginally effective. In 1994, Keilitz reported that 60% of women who obtained a temporary restraining order (TRO) experienced physical or psychological abuse in the year following the issuance of the order. Chaudhuri and Daly (1992) also investigated TRO violations in a small sample of cases (30) in which the violation of the restraining order was arrestable. The authors concluded that the TRO did have some deterrent value, but 34% of the men still violated the TRO. Such factors as alcohol abuse, unemployment, and a prior criminal record contributed to those violations.

REASSESSING MANDATORY POLICIES

> He had threatened to smash my face in if I ever called the police . . . you know, for me to really go out and do it is real significant to me. To go out and really take the initiative to really do something for myself.
> Anonymous
> (Fischer & Rose, 1995, p. 418)

So why have we implemented unidimensional policies such as mandatory arrest and prosecution that actually increase the violence in some battered women's lives? Such policies are in effect largely due to the lobbying efforts of battered women's and feminist organizations who believe a strong public stance against intimate abuse is necessary to deter violence against women. They believe that a policy that has the State prosecute men for beating their neighbors but not for beating their wives is sexist and unjust.

Mandatory arrest and prosecution might initially appear to be a simple and preferable solution to domestic violence because it is easier to follow and forces law enforcement and prosecutors to take domestic violence seriously. History tells us that without mandatory arrest and prosecution, the police and prosecutors are reluctant to treat domestic violence crimes in the same way as other crimes. As recently as 30 years ago, injunctions were only available to "married" women, and no criminal penalties against a spouse ensued from violation of that injunction (Zorza, 1992).

The problem is that the policies may very well backfire. When we force arrest and prosecution on battered women, many victims may feel compelled to recant and lie. One prosecutor in Los Angeles estimated that most battered women are reluctant witnesses who are willing to perjure themselves when they are put on the stand against their will (personal communication, March 1997).

Don Rebovich (1996) has studied the problem of conflicts between prosecutor and victim in no-drop prosecution jurisdictions. He reports that many large prosecutors' offices have had considerable problems with "uncooperative" victims in domestic violence cases. Thirty-three percent of the prosecutors who responded to his survey claimed that more than 55% of their cases involved uncooperative victims. Sixteen percent of them believed that 41 to 55% of their victims were uncooperative, and 27% of the respondents believed that 26 to 40% of their victims were uncooperative. Only 27% of the prosecutors reported a 0 to 25% lack of cooperation by victims.

Given these perceptions by prosecutors, it is not surprising that they would become coercive with battered women in order to achieve their goals. As previously noted, 92% of prosecutors subpoena the battered woman to force her to testify (Rebovich, 1996). The least coercive methods for use on an "uncooperative" victim include victim advocate testimony and videotapes of initial victim interviews; however, only 10% and 6% of prosecutors used those two methods, respectively. Moreover, these methods may be criticized for leaving the battered woman out of the prosecution altogether, and robbing her of an important opportunity to partner with the State to ensure her safety (Mills, 1998b).

Statistics regarding the reluctance of victims to "cooperate" could mean one of two things: either the victim is too afraid to testify, or she isn't ready to prosecute. If she is too afraid, the prosecutor should help her negotiate a safe situation; if she is not yet ready, the prosecutor should respect her desire to choose, relying on the assumption that when she is ready, she will take the necessary steps not only to prosecute but also to change her life (Hart, 1996). This analysis assumes that victims are capable of acting on their own behalf, an assumption not held by many prosecutors or battered women's advocates who support mandatory interventions (Hanna, 1996; Jackson, 1990; Spagnoletti, 1998; Wills, 1997).

Buzawa and Buzawa (1996) summarized common arguments advocating for mandatory prosecution policies: (1) Domestic violence should be treated as an offense against the State, and not just the individual; (2) no-drop policies discourage unsympathetic court personnel from dismissing cases unless they can justify doing so; (3) no-drop policies limit the number of dropped cases; (4) no-drop policies deter intimidation or violence directed at the victim because the choice to prosecute is no longer hers; (5) more batterers will be deterred by the increased probability of conviction; and (6) society will benefit from the identification and conviction of batterers which will prevent them from reoffending by finding a new victim.

Buzawa and Buzawa (1996) also proffer arguments against such policies, pointing out that if victims are uncooperative or unconvincing, an increased conviction rate is unlikely. Furthermore, no-drop policies may deter victims from reporting violence because they may fear loss of control over the process. Feminists who typically eschew imposing a loss of control on women are ironically supporting the imposition of such loss of control on battered women. By advocating mandatory policies, feminists accede to the "infantilized" view of the battered woman. As noted above, Ford and Regoli (1993) found that a battered woman is safest when she has the choice to drop but elects not to do so. No-drop policies preclude battered women from having the option to make this empowering decision.

Perversely, in all too many cases, the effect of mandatory policies is to align the battered woman with her batterer, protecting him and further entrenching her in the abusive relationship (Mills, 1998b). The State, even with a policy of mandatory arrest and prosecution, cannot ensure that the batterer will be locked away forever, nor can it ensure that the battered woman will be free from his violence. Indeed, in one survey, only 1% of the batterers received jail time beyond time served at arrest (Barnett, Miller-Perrin, & Perrin, 1997). Therefore, it is critical that we teach the battered woman to yearn for her safety and to take whatever internal and external steps are necessary to achieve it.

Ironically, the opportunity to make decisive and empowering choices about criminal justice intervention may be the very action the battered woman needs to stop the violence in her life. The decision regarding whether to arrest and prosecute may be the first opportunity a battered woman has to take an affirmative step in a relationship in which she has previously felt powerless. A system is needed that encourages this expression of power and control. To offer it to her through state policy and practice is to encourage her to alter the abusive dynamic and to transgress the violence that devastates her life. To withhold it from her is to replicate the traumatic bond and to replace the abuse of the batterer with the violence of state intervention (Mills, 1998b).

SUMMARY AND REFLECTIONS

I suggest that inflexible policies such as mandatory arrest and mandatory prosecution be reformed to reflect the diversity of battered women's experiences and to expose the possibility that some battered women will need a legal response that does more than arrest and prosecute the batterer. Some battered women need a response that is intuitive to and insightful of their personal conundrum. I believe we should have a system that is flexible enough to respond to these varying needs when necessary. We should recognize the many hidden strengths and talents of battered women and acknowledge the need for legal interventions that help them find ways to reduce the violence in their lives. In chapter 8, I will explore how a practitioner's work with a battered woman can help her negotiate an empowering solution for her and her children when confronting the criminal justice system. I draw on principles from the Affective Advocacy and Systems Strategies methods, including The Heart of Intimate Abuse, developed more fully in chapters 6 and 7, to present an empowering model for helping survivors negotiate the complex and often hostile criminal justice system.

Before we explore how these empowering methods might be applied, it is useful first to learn more about the other systems battered women confront. In the next chapter I examine the public child welfare system and its approach to battered women and their children.

Questions

☐ How does a battered woman's cultural background affect her decision to pursue or not pursue arrest or prosecution of the batterer?

☐ Did you assume that a mandatory or proarrest policy was appropriate for every battered woman? If not, why not? If yes, which studies, if any, affected your opinion?

☐ In the criminal context, how is the system violent towards battered women?

CHAPTER 4

The Public Child Welfare System's Response to Domestic Violence

The twins, Helen and Heather A. were 3½ years old when they were first detained by Child Protective Services. At age 3, Helen and Heather accompanied their stepmother to the hospital after she had sustained a head injury. Heather had tried to prevent her father from hitting her stepmother by attempting to get her father off of her. Helen and Heather have witnessed three or four other incidents. On one occasion, one of the girls cut her finger and foot on glass that shattered when her father smashed a vase.

Their father denies hitting his wife. The injuries, he claims, were accidental.

In re Heather A., 1997

Public child welfare agencies have had, at best, an ambivalent and conflicted relationship toward battered mothers. They have either looked the other way and ignored the intimate abuse (if the child is not directly abused) or blamed the battered mother for the child's abuse or neglect. This chapter explores how these practices affect battered women and their children and examines ways of resolving these conflicting approaches.

To truly understand the conflicts, it is useful first to review how public child welfare agencies operate. Child Protective Services (CPS) cares about the safety of children. Indeed, what is in "the best interest of the child" is supposed to guide their interventions

59

in a family. Although the "best interest" standard sometimes conflicts with a policy commitment to "preserving" families (depending in part on the political current in any given community), public child welfare agencies are concerned, first and foremost, with the safety of the child (and not with keeping an abusive family intact).

If and when CPS intervenes, they have many options to pursue. The least intrusive intervention involves monitoring a case, keeping an eye on a family. This kind of supervision may take the form of parenting classes, surprise home visits, or interviews with the child at school. On the other end of the intervention spectrum is CPS' legal right to remove a child from an abusive family and to terminate parental rights through a court proceeding. All too often where a case falls on the spectrum depends on individual CSWs and their supervisors.

The number of child abuse complaints has risen dramatically in the last 10 years (Lindsey, 1994). The difficulty public child welfare agencies have in coping with the growing number of complaints is evident (Lindsey, 1994). Domestic violence presents a new challenge to an already overburdened system. Resistance to embracing domestic violence as child abuse is inevitable.

Yet the statistics that link domestic violence and child abuse are staggering. A survey of studies reveals that 45 to 70% of battered women in shelters report that their batterer had committed some form of child abuse (AHA, 1994). As was evident in chapter 1, domestic violence provides a context in which child abuse readily develops.

Several questions plague public child welfare practice in relation to domestic violence. How should intimate abuse be integrated into a practice that has essentially isolated the best interests of children from the interests of their parents? Should CPS intervene in families in which the child is only a "witness" to the domestic violence but not directly abused? When and if they do intervene in witnessing cases, what form should that intervention take? If domestic violence is suspected and it appears that the case demands intervention, what responsibility does the CPS agency have toward the battered mother? If the battered mother is aware that the abuse is occurring and has done nothing to stop it, should her parental rights be terminated?

This chapter begins by exploring the most extreme cases; instances in which CPS has terminated parental rights for domestic violence. These issues are discussed in relation to battered mothers and battering fathers. Next, I present the findings of a qualitative study of four programs that CPS agencies used to better integrate domestic violence into their public child welfare practice. I use these case examples to illustrate the resistance that even sympathetic CPS agencies feel in relation to this issue and to present the challenges that CPS agencies face if they are serious about integrating domestic violence into their practice in an empowering way. Third, I explore three policy questions that underlie the smooth integration of domestic violence into child abuse practice. Should the witnessing of domestic violence by a child be enough to open a CPS investigation? Should all domestic violence cases investigated by a CPS worker and confirmed be cross-reported to law enforcement? Should treatment be mandated for battered women when there is CPS involvement in a domestic violence case? Finally, I explore how legal and related systems reform can help alter the conflicts evident in public child welfare and domestic violence practice.

THE TERMINATION OF PARENTAL RIGHTS

California case law now recognizes that domestic violence constitutes a form of child abuse that can result in the termination of parental rights (*In re Heather A.*, 1997; *In re Jon N.*, 1986). Although the applicable legal standard is still evolving, the relevant cases begin to sketch out California law in this area. In child abuse cases, three elements are key when removing minors from their parent's custody: (1) neglectful conduct by the parent in one of the specified forms, such as a parent's failure to adequately supervise or protect a minor; (2) causation; and (3) serious physical harm or illness to the minor or a substantial risk of harm or illness (*In re Heather A.*, 1997, p. 194). The recent Court of Appeals decision *In re Heather A.* (1997) examines these elements in light of the intimate abuse that persisted between the father, Harold A., and the stepmother, Ramona. The court dramatically concludes that "domestic violence in the same household where children are living is neglect; it is failure to protect [the children] from the substantial risk of encountering the violence and suffering serious physical harm or illness from it. Such neglect *causes* the risk" (*In re Heather A.*, 1997, p. 194).

The Court of Appeals seemed influenced by a key feature of the *In re Heather A.* (1997) case. The court concluded that "secondary abuse," that is, the "effect on children of occurrences of abuse in their environment which are not directed specifically at them," (p. 186) was a form of child abuse. The court was particularly persuaded by the findings of a psychologist who evaluated the children and who reported that a form of secondary abuse is the "Battered-Women Syndrome," described as a "pattern of learned helplessness and dependency, *originating in childhood*, which, without intervention, is perpetuated throughout the victim's life that psychologically causes her to return again and again to relationships in which she is battered and abused" (p. 195). The court opined that if the children's "exposure to Father's domestic violence had not already sown the seeds in them for Battered Women's Syndrome, further exposure to Father could do so, thus resulting in substantial danger to their future physical health in that they would submit to being battered themselves" (pp. 195–196). No abuse directed toward the children was necessary for a finding of neglect in this case.

The most interesting, and in some respects chilling, aspect of the *Heather A.* decision is that parental rights can be terminated against the abusing father or the victimized mother. For battered women, the laws most often used to terminate their parental rights, and hence to deny them custody of their children, are "failure to protect" statutes. Under these laws, parents are found to have abused their children by "allowing" either physical or sexual abuse or "allowing" the conditions under which such abuse could occur (Miccio, 1995) (Box 4.1). These child protective statutes hold battered women accountable for the abuse of their husbands or partners, even though they were victims to it. Kristian Miccio (1995) documents the extent and nature of the problem of blaming the woman and suggests that protective laws should impose a legal standard that "speaks to the best interest of families, specifically those persons within the family who are its nonabusive members" (pp. 1106–1107).

It is interesting to note that men receive sole or joint custody in 70% of contested custody disputes (Zorza, 1995a). One factor that improves men's chances of custody are their financial resources (Harvard Law Review Association [HLRA], 1993). Indeed,

> **Box 4.1 Circumstances That Give Rise to Failure to Protect Cases Against Battered Women**
>
> - The mother was present and did nothing to prevent the abuse against the child (even if her own life is threatened).
> - The mother left the child alone with the batterer, knowing he had abused the child in the past (even if she is protecting herself).
> - The mother knew the child had been abused but failed to seek medical attention (or failed to reveal the abuse to the physician).
> - The mother would be unable to protect the child from the father's abuse in the future.

there is strong evidence that there are linkages between domestic violence and women's poverty and intimate abuse and the receipt of welfare benefits (Raphael & Tolman, 1997). In addition, the little income that battered women do have may be threatened by changes in welfare laws such as rigid requirements for employment and time limits for receipt of benefits (Brownell, 1998). Battered women have reason to worry that their poverty could be held against them in custody disputes. Joan Zorza (1995b) observes that "fathers win usually because the women are held to a far higher standard and are believed less often than are men because women's concerns are trivialized, as the many state court gender bias studies have concluded" (p. 2).

Court decisions are so erratic in this area that some judges have concluded that a father convicted of voluntary manslaughter for killing the mother of his children did not necessarily meet the standard for terminating parental rights (*Bartasavich v. Mitchell,* 1984). It is on these case and societal precedents that O.J. Simpson was able to secure custody of his children even though he had received a civil damage award based on the murder of the mother of his children. The courts' sympathy for men not only shed light on the favorable treatment they seem to receive before the law, but also reveal the lack of responsibility imposed on them for creating the abusive environment (Dohrn, 1995).

Judicial action aside, what gives rise in the Child Protective Services system to blaming the mother and excusing the father? To explore more fully what lies behind the actions of CSWs (the

CPS workers) who make many of the decisions on who should and should not have access to their children, I collected data on the experiences of four programs that received federal funding to help CPS agencies integrate domestic violence into their practice, mostly through training. In this study, I wanted to answer the following questions: How have Child Protective Services agencies integrated domestic violence into their child welfare practices? Do their methods blame the victim and excuse the perpetrator? What institutional barriers must still be overcome?

CPS RECEPTIVITY TO DOMESTIC VIOLENCE

> If the [battered] woman fears that she will be blamed
> for failure to protect her children from the abuser,
> she may be reluctant to cooperate, fearing the [CPS]
> agency will take her children away from her. If the
> agency's personnel is untrained in domestic violence,
> its personnel may indeed blame the mother for failure
> to leave her children's abuser.
>
> Judge Levin
> (*In re Farley*, 1991, p. 301)

Many battered women are deterred from reporting their abuse and their children's maltreatment because of their fear of losing custody (U.S. ABCAN, 1995). The U.S. ABCAN (1995) also found that many child abuse prevention programs direct their attention to mothers, failing to focus on the men who batter. The extent to which battered women actually lose custody of their children due to their status as battered women is unclear. The perception that reporting domestic violence could affect custody, however, may effectively close communication between the CPS worker and the battered woman (Felder & Victor, 1996).

Nationally, these issues have just begun to be addressed. In 1995, the Federal Register (U.S. Department of Health and Human Services [DHHS], March 9, 1995) announced that the National Center on Child Abuse and Neglect and the Children's Bureau Discretionary Funds Program were requesting applications to conduct child abuse research and training in innovative exemplary practice. The Request for Proposal wanted applicants to develop a training package to address "working with families contending with domestic and/or community violence" (p. 24715).

In the end, 200 groups and universities requested funds (M. Mannis, personal communication, October 1995), and five groups were awarded approximately $110,000 over a 2-year period. These five groups included Columbia University School of Social Work (New York, NY), Simmons School of Social Work (Boston, MA), Temple University's Center for Social Policy and Community Development (Philadelphia, PA), Tennessee State University (Nashville, TN), and UCLA's Center for Child and Policy Studies (Los Angeles, CA). To understand more about the general receptivity of CPS agencies to integrating domestic violence into their practice, data were collected from four of the five grantees, on the assumption that these groups had vied for federal funding during a competitive and peer-reviewed process and therefore were in an excellent position to assess the receptivity of their public child welfare communities to the issue of domestic violence. (The fifth group, Tennessee State University, never responded to numerous inquiries.) I begin with an overview of each of the projects and explore, in more depth, what the institutional climate was for integrating domestic violence into public child welfare practice.

Columbia University School of Social Work developed a 2-day training curriculum for CPS workers in New York City. They also developed a worldwide website for dissemination of information about the project. The first of a two day training focused on self-awareness of victimization and attitudes about domestic violence. Day two focused on batterers, assessment, and intervention.

Simmons College worked with Boston's CPS Agency, the Department of Social Services' (DSS) Domestic Violence Unit, a unique and important innovation in child welfare practice. In addition, they worked with the DSS training department to facilitate collaboration between units within DSS and to provide extensive on-site trainings in domestic violence to supervisors. A training manual on domestic violence was also prepared for DSS.

Temple University developed the "Training Project on Collaborative Responses to Community and Domestic Violence." They planned two sets of training sessions for violence prevention and intervention professionals and brought together a diverse group of violence prevention and intervention workers to foster understanding of the problems of family violence, to identify the roles and mandates of the different systems and to establish linkages between them, to recognize the interrelatedness of family violence, and to propose policy systems change.

UCLA's training program took a twofold approach. First, UCLA trained a large cohort of workers and supervisors on the intersections of domestic violence and child abuse and developed an assessment instrument that would make their interventions more effective when domestic violence was suspected. This training was a 1-day program. In addition, UCLA trained a smaller select group of CPS workers and supervisors over a 6-day training period as "fellows" or experts in domestic violence. These experts were scattered throughout Los Angeles County and were viewed as the domestic violence resource persons to the other workers and supervisors in those offices. Policy change was key to UCLA's interest in the training program; they wanted to ensure that their assessment instrument, or some instrument like it, became integral to a child abuse assessment in Los Angeles.

The specific successes of the four programs have been many and varied. The Columbia Program trained more than 400 CPS workers in New York City in a sophisticated method for intervening in cases involving both domestic violence and child abuse. In addition, they had 3,000 "hits" on their website, and they sent several hundred copies of their training manual to parties requesting it.

Simmons College was in the fortunate position of doing "second generation" domestic violence work in their public child welfare agency. Boston had already established a Domestic Violence Unit at DSS, a radical notion in a CPS agency, and saw their job as trying to infiltrate the other units at DSS. Simmons was not concerned with training large numbers (15 supervisors were trained); rather, they chose intensive involvement with one office to pilot their efforts, which included assessing needs, developing curriculum, and piloting training materials to be used systemwide.

Temple's project involved training more than child welfare workers. The diverse training group included domestic violence victims' advocates, public school educators, university faculty, police officers, drug and alcohol counselors, city government representatives, community-based organization representatives, hospital workers, and others. They provided two training sessions to 200 professionals total, the purpose of which was to bring together a diverse group of violence prevention and intervention workers, especially child welfare workers, to foster better understandings of the problems of family violence.

UCLA trained more than 900 CPS workers and supervisors in the Southern California region. Approximately 120 of those workers and supervisors participated in the 6-day training session over a 6-month period. Workers and supervisors came from every region in Los Angeles County and nearly all CPS workers in Orange County were trained. The assessment instrument was widely disseminated beyond trainees and was an integral part of a California Social Work Education Center (CalSWEC) curriculum developed as an offshoot of the federal grant (Mills & Friend, 1997). CalSWEC is responsible for training a Masters in Social Work cohort of California's child welfare workers.

A key feature of nearly all the programs was the development of a training curriculum involving multiple players from the child welfare and domestic violence communities that led to new and important alliances. Columbia gathered a diverse group of representatives from the child welfare and domestic violence communities and worked closely with one zone, or district, at CPS that was testing a special domestic violence assessment instrument.

Simmons worked with the Domestic Violence Unit as a starting point for facilitating collaboration between units within DSS. They also developed an interagency team that proved invaluable in their cross-training approach. This team continues to consult on DSS cases and helps to identify issues that arise among agencies represented.

Temple also found strength in their interagency Advisory Board, members of which represented many different systems involved in violence prevention and intervention. Because their trainees also came from diverse professional organizations and agencies, networking was facilitated between people and organizations that wouldn't otherwise have the time or inclination to communicate.

UCLA's interagency collaboration was also integral in its success: law enforcement, including prosecutors, judges, alcohol and drug treatment agencies; adult protective services; domestic violence advocates; and CPS supervisors were involved in the planning of the trainings and in the development of the curriculum.

The most striking feature of the four training programs was the similarities in the challenges they faced. Three issues, to one degree or another, challenged the success of each training program. First, each of the groups found the CPS "culture" resistant to large scale change. Second, each of the projects lacked the involvement of certain key players. Third, each group was challenged by differences in philosophical orientation between the domestic violence and child abuse communities that were represented or involved in developing the training.

All the projects felt that CPS culture was difficult to penetrate. Specifically, all the programs, even Simmons who had access to a specialized Domestic Violence Unit, found that there was no formal infrastructure to facilitate true collaboration between the training program and its genesis in a university or Center, and the public child welfare agency. This was despite the fact that each of the groups was operating in CPS environments that had integrated, to one degree or another, domestic violence into their child abuse interventions.

For example, all four programs were operating in communities where domestic violence had become a part of their assessment formats. This is *not* the norm. When the practices of the 58 counties of the State of California were examined, integration of domestic violence into child abuse assessment was rare (Mills, 1998a) (Box 4.2). Boston had the most elaborate domestic violence protocol, a method they found was rarely used. New York also had a special protocol that was developed and tested, at least by one particular zone. Philadelphia was using a form that had a reference to domestic violence, but found that few workers understood the nexus between intimate and child abuse. Los Angeles also had a reference to domestic violence in its assessment format, but had done little to help workers understand the implications of its application.

The indifference or resistance the four groups met seemed connected to the fact that certain key agency players were uninvolved or not involved enough in the projects. The lack of overall interest in the intersections between domestic violence and child abuse by high-level public child welfare administrators was a feature that impeded "buy-in" from other CPS agency personnel, including workers and supervisors. Even those groups that felt that top administrators had "bought-in" found that attendance at sessions

---

Box 4.2 CPS Risk Assessment in California: Is Domestic Violence Included?

To learn more about how CPS agencies assess child abuse cases for domestic violence, the risk assessment formats of all 58 counties in California were collected and reviewed (Mills, 1998a). In 47 counties in California, an actual form is used by CPS workers when assessing risk in a child abuse case. Eleven counties do not require their workers to use any special form or format when assessing risk in a child abuse case. As one might expect, those counties that use forms ask questions regarding the "the precipitating incident," "child characteristics," "caretaker characteristics," and "family factors." Some forms give further guidelines to workers, such as whether or not the case presents a "low," "moderate," or "high" risk (see Appendix I for details).

A further analysis of the forms reveals that only six counties, those using the "Los Angeles Risk Assessment Form," explicitly assess for "spousal abuse" or "marital conflict," or both. (One county uses this form with children under 5 when there is an allegation of physical abuse.) Twenty-four counties in California use the "Fresno Risk Assessment Form." In this form there is no explicit reference to spousal abuse, only a generic reference to "History of Abuse/ Neglect in Family" under the "Family Factors" section of the form. Sixteen counties in California use the "State Risk Assessment Form." Again, no explicit reference to spousal abuse is made. A "History of Abuse" appears under the "Family Factors" section of the form. The rest of the counties use no forms or use other forms of assessment with no explicit reference to spousal abuse.

Although the use of risk assessment forms is itself controversial (Nelson, 1994), a review of the forms used by nearly every county in California, except those six counties using the Los Angeles Risk Assessment Form, suggests that CPS workers have not yet begun to factor domestic violence into their assessment of child abuse. Without an explicit mandate to help facilitate these discussions, battered women will continue to be reluctant to divulge the intimate abuse that is plaguing their and their children's lives.

---

was sometimes low and that other agency demands impeded full participation. What seemed apparent is that no group was able to stop the CPS machinery long enough to heed the pressing call of domestic violence.

All groups found, to one degree or another, that differences in philosophy became one of their biggest challenges in making these multi-disciplinany programs a success. According to at least three of the groups, training sessions were often mired in CPS workers' stereotypical assumptions about battered women, especially in relation to their "staying" in abusive relationships, which sometimes prevented trainees from realizing that it was the batterer, not the battered woman, who was responsible for the abuse. Without overcoming that hurdle, workers would continue to judge the actions of battered women based on stereotypical assumptions such as "she should just leave." This tension seemed embedded in the larger philosophical conflict between domestic violence and child welfare, discussed in detail in chapter 1, and was often expressed by the program participants as a competition for mandates. As one group described it: "There was difficulty in trying to introduce a strengths or protective perspective into an agency culture focused on investigatory goals" (Fleck-Henderson & Krug, 1997).

All the groups expressed that much more work needed to be done. Each was convinced that training "was not enough" and that other structural changes were necessary. Some suggested that legal and legislative change would be necessary for final CPS agency "buy-in." Others believed that the collaborational efforts, if continued and institutionalized, would lead to lasting change. This experience is supported in the literature, which suggests that multiagency teams are critical for addressing public child welfare's ability to intervene in domestic violence cases (Aron & Olson, 1997a, 1997b; Peled, 1996).

In sum, three primary issues dominated the reflections of the training groups. First, CPS personnel come to the topic of domestic violence with stereotypical attitudes about battered women, especially in relation to judgments about their staying in the abusive relationship. Second, CPS agency personnel are, in varying degrees, resistant to adopting strategies that empower battered women to protect children. Third, CPS agencies are conflicted about whether the witnessing of domestic violence should be considered a form of child abuse and hence should be investigated by CSWs.

These same issues were identified in a recent Urban Institute Report (Aron & Olson, 1997a) that revealed that current approaches to child abuse, including investigation methods, risk assessment, and case planning, are inappropriate in cases involving domestic violence. Aron and Olson (1997a, 1997b) made site visits to five CPS agencies in California, Hawaii, Massachusetts, Michigan, and Oregon to determine what these innovative communities were doing to link child abuse to domestic violence. Community collaboration was a key feature of their study findings, and they found that this relatively low-cost form of intervention in domestic violence and child abuse cases was very effective. They concluded, based on the experience of these programs, that child abuse and domestic violence agencies should work together to address battered women's needs.

Despite these promising developments, the Urban Institute's findings suggest that if systemwide change is desirable, then more than just collaboration will be necessary. They recommend an investment of substantial resources, including the hiring of Domestic Violence Specialists at CPS agencies, a method that they believe will ensure that collaborative efforts become institutionalized in public child welfare culture.

As in the experience of the four programs, the Urban Institute Report (Aron & Olson, 1997a) reveals that cases involving domestic violence and child abuse may pose far greater challenges than cases that involve only violence against the child. They suggest that "staff awareness, understanding, and motivation, coupled with tools and resources, were all necessary ingredients for sustained system change" (Aron & Olson, 1997b, p. 13).

THE ISSUES

Assuming that the integration of domestic violence into child abuse practice is both desirable and inevitable, it is useful to examine three pressing questions that plague this evolving field. The answers to these questions could help agencies and other organizations struggling to merge domestic violence and child welfare to overcome the hurdles that prevent this integration.

1. Should the witnessing of domestic violence by a child be enough to open a CPS investigation?

2. Should all domestic violence cases investigated by a CPS worker, and confirmed, be cross-reported to law enforcement?
3. Should treatment be mandated for battered women when there is CPS involvement in a domestic violence case?

SHOULD THE WITNESSING OF DOMESTIC VIOLENCE BY A CHILD BE ENOUGH TO OPEN A CPS INVESTIGATION?

CPS involvement in a family means resources, support, and monitoring. Unfortunately, as the experience of programs working in this area reveals, CPS philosophy is all too often caught in political tides that affect the nature of the intervention delivered. Child deaths move CPS agencies to become more "authoritative" to ensure child protection (U.S. ABCAN, 1995). Authoritative intervention all too often lead to child removal from families rather than CPS monitoring. The worry, and reality, is that battered women will be punished for their perceived inaction in relation to the battering, and children will be removed without working with the battered woman, a victim herself, to strengthen her internal and external resources (Echlin & Marshall, 1995; Peled, 1996).

As CPS agencies begin to integrate domestic violence more fully into their assessment and intervention approaches, it would be advisable to develop methods for intervening in domestic violence cases where children are witnessing the abuse but not sustaining the blows directly. When both abuses are present, CPS involvement is inevitable and will merit a different response. The vexing question is what happens when the child is a "secondary victim"; an issue we explore in more depth in the case study in chapter 9.

From a policy perspective, I suggest that intervention is appropriate in witnessing cases if done sensitively and as free of judgment about the battered woman's conundrum as possible. Ideally, an agency outside CPS would take over the function of managing a case involving a child witness soon after CPS intervention. This could avoid direct CPS involvement and the ever-present tension presented by their investigatory and police functions. Under such a model, practitioners on contract with CPS could focus their energy on empowering the battered woman in relation to her child and could know intimately, the many challenges posed by domestic abuse cases where children are involved. The advantage of such an approach is that it can build on the strengths of both the child protection and domestic violence systems and can help work through the tensions between these two systems, which were explored more fully in chapter 1. Child protection can assess threat and recommend appropriate action; domestic violence advocates on contract with CPS agencies can begin the process of empowering the battered woman while being sensitive to the issues posed by children who are witnesses to intimate abuse.

Such an intervention would also be prevention. It would be a recognition that the intergenerational transmission of abuse must be interrupted and that reports of domestic violence to CPS agencies provide an opportunity to do that important work. It also allows the system to intervene to provide counseling and other treatment modalities to the child to ensure that an abuse sequela is prevented, if possible (Jaffe, Wolfe, & Wilson, 1990).

This kind of collaborative approach would also be a recognition that most battered women are reluctant to initiate police intervention (Straus & Gelles, 1986; U.S. DOJ, 1994b) and thereby provides an alternative service system that could respond to victims who might otherwise go underground. The worry is that even with the kinds of safeguards I am suggesting, battered women, especially women of color, might be discouraged "from seeking the help they need from social control agents" (Peled, 1993, p. 48).

SHOULD ALL DOMESTIC VIOLENCE CASES INVESTIGATED BY A CPS WORKER, AND CONFIRMED, BE CROSS-REPORTED TO LAW ENFORCEMENT?

Cross-reporting occurs when a CPS worker or supervisor calls the police to inform them that a crime has occurred when domestic violence is detected in their investigation. Cross-reporting is one method for increasing law enforcement involvement in domestic violence cases.

Given the mixed data on police intervention (chapter 3), I believe that cross-reporting should only be necessary in the most extreme cases in which the battered woman has made a firm decision to stay in the abusive relationship and when all assessments suggest that the abuser is likely to reabuse and that his abuse may be life threatening (Mills, 1998b). I believe that police involvement should be initiated by anyone other than the battered woman *only* when she is incapable of taking her own action and the threat is so great that she will be unable to protect herself or her children (Mills, 1998b). The methods presented in chapters 6 and 7 are designed to help workers ferret out these cases.

SHOULD TREATMENT BE MANDATED FOR BATTERED WOMEN WHEN THERE IS CPS INVOLVEMENT IN A DOMESTIC VIOLENCE CASE?

Many battered women's organizations complain that CPS, when it does intervene, focuses exclusively on the battered woman and does not account for the batterer's role in causing an abusive family dynamic (Bograd, 1984; Bowker, Arbitell, & McFerron, 1988; Dobash & Dobash, 1992). Treatment should be mandated for batterers, and visitation should depend on their compliance with that mandate (for a fuller discussion on issues of treatment for batterers, see chapter 9). This begs the question, however, as to whether CPS should mandate treatment for battered women when they are involved in a case. This decision should depend on how abusive the batterer is, whether the victim insists on staying in the relationship, whether the child has actually been abused by the batterer, and whether the battered woman has been abusive to the child. The danger in mandating treatment for all battered women is that they may perceive the violence "as their fault." It logically follows that if the abuse were not their fault, why would they be mandated to attend treatment?

I believe that CPS should make decisions about treatment on an ongoing basis. Using an empowerment model, the battered woman would be subjected to few mandates or requirements, assuming that she is willing to take some action to protect herself and her children. The tension arises when she is unwilling to take such action. My view is that mandated treatment is preferable, from an empowerment perspective, to calling the police without her consent (Box 4.3). If the CPS worker believes that mandating treatment might move the battered woman to the emotional edge she

---

Box 4.3   Evaluating Treatment Options for Battered Women

As a CSW, a clinician, or an advocate, you will be in a position to advise battered women on what kind of treatment program might be appropriate for them. Consider these questions in assessing a treatment program for battered women:

- Is there an individual assessment performed by program personnel to help determine a battered woman's suitability for this particular treatment?
- Does an individualized contextual perspective, taking into account culture and religion, guide intervention and treatment?
- Does the program have information concerning its effectiveness?
- Is it monitoring its short-term or long-term success?
- Does the program reflect the client's right to self-determination, or does it impose its own prejudicial assumptions on battered women?
- Are safety plans put in place immediately and periodically re-evaluated?
- Are there interventions designed to enhance her protective capacity for her children?
- Is the staff willing to provide you with periodic written progress reports if you have the battered woman's permission?
- What constitutes compliance, progress, and grounds for termination?

---

needs to realize that "enough is enough," then mandating treatment may in fact be an appropriate and even empowering intervention in this case (Horton & Johnson, 1993).

A SYNTHESIS OF RESEARCH AND PRACTICE

A synthesis of previous research on the current practices of child protective services agencies in relation to domestic violence and a review of the questions that still remain reveals that we have a long way to go before intimate abuse is identified as integral, or even related to child abuse. The experience of the four groups that received federal funding to do training on domestic violence teaches us that resistance about how, when, and where these issues should intersect remains, even among willing CPS agencies.

Since we have not yet fully integrated domestic violence into child protection, we still have time to consider the extent to which they should be partnered. I suggest that CPS involvement may be helpful in domestic violence cases to the extent that they can identify these dual abuses. Given the mixed data presented thus far and the apparent ambivalence by CPS agencies, I believe that organizations outside the CPS system such as contract agencies might be more appropriate for undertaking the empowerment work that needs to be done with battered women. The monitoring and police functions of CPS may make it impossible to meld empowerment with traditional notions of child protection.

Child witnessing and treatment for battered women in the context of intervention on behalf of children raise other important policy considerations that warrant theoretical and research attention. Whether or not child witnessing is "enough" to constitute child abuse is worthy of our consideration; what's most important, however, is that children who witness or are abused in the process of those observations are treated (Jaffe et al., 1990). Without that kind of attention to the issue, we will continue to reproduce violence in intimate relationships.

Treatment for battered women is important. Forced treatment is, in general, disempowering insofar as it is not victim-initiated. In appropriate cases, however, mandated treatment can provide the impetus necessary for change, a change you can imagine her imagining but that she has not yet imagined. These are delicate decisions and should be made with the understanding that one or two wrong steps can literally send a battered woman to her death.

On the other end of the intervention spectrum, it seems obvious that training is critical to changing the attitudes of CPS workers who intervene with myriad judgments about battered women. These assumptions are so pervasive that they lead CPS workers to file "failure to protect" petitions. The collective experience of the four programs that developed partnerships with some of the more enlightened CPS agencies is that training is probably not enough to fully overcome the essentializing attitudes of some public child welfare workers. Legislative change will probably be necessary.

The Model State Code developed by the Advisory Committee of the NCJFCJ (1994) is designed to help ensure that battered mothers are met with a sympathetic response when faced with termination or other custody proceedings.

MODEL STATE CODE FOR DOMESTIC VIOLENCE CASES

Child custody decisions in nearly all states require a determination of the fitness of both natural parents and a determination of a custody arrangement that is in the best interest of the child (Cahn, 1991). In practice, the fitness of both parents is presumed (Cahn, 1991).

Although variations in statutes do exist, according to Cahn (1991), states have started to link domestic violence and child custody. Family Violence: A Model State Code was developed for that purpose (NCJFCJ, 1994). A "model code" is just that, a model for states to follow in custody cases involving domestic violence. The Code is designed to protect the interests of battered women and their children when custody is at issue. Custody and the termination of parental rights are linked in that termination precludes custody. If adopted, these code sections could potentially prevent CSWs from filing a "failure to protect" allegation against a battered woman. The victim could rely on the Code to argue that her behavior, under the abusive circumstances, was predictable and that she should not be penalized for attempting to protect herself or her children.

Several provisions of the Model Code are designed to force judges to hold the batterer accountable for his violence by allowing the battered woman unrestricted custody of her children. For example, Section 401 provides that

> In every proceeding where there is at issue a dispute as to the custody of a child, a determination by the court that domestic or family violence has occurred raises a rebuttable presumption that it is detrimental to the child and not in the best interest of the child to be placed in sole custody, joint legal custody, or joint physical custody with the perpetrator of family violence (NCJFCJ, 1994, p. 33).

Section 401 is designed to address courts that are issuing orders for protection and adjudicating cases of divorce, delinquency, and child protection. The rebuttable presumption means that it will be assumed that placement with the abuser is inappropriate unless evidence to the contrary is presented.

Section 402 addresses the factors a court should consider in a proceeding in which the custody of a child or visitation by a parent is at issue when domestic violence is present:

a. The court shall consider as primary the safety and well-being of the child and of the parent who is the victim of domestic or family violence.

b. The court shall consider the perpetrator's history of causing physical harm, bodily injury, assault, or causing reasonable fear of physical harm, bodily injury, or assault, to another person (NCJFCJ, 1994, p. 33).

In addition, the Model Code provides that if a parent is absent or relocates because of an act of domestic violence by the other parent, the absence or relocation should not be held against the parent in determining custody or visitation. The purpose of these sections is twofold: first, to ensure that the well-being of the survivor and the child are linked and, second, to recognize that battered women may have to flee the abusive family home and should not be penalized or judged for leaving dependent children behind.

Section 403 of the Model Code provides that there is a presumption concerning the residence of the child. In this section the Code reads as follows:

In every proceeding where there is at issue a dispute as to the custody of a child, a determination by a court that domestic or family violence has occurred raises a rebuttable presumption that it is in the best interest of the child to reside with the parent who is not a perpetrator of domestic or family violence in the location of that parent's choice, within or outside the state (NCJFCJ, 1994, p. 34).

This provision of the Model Code is designed to give the nonperpetrating parent the option of living in another jurisdiction on the assumption that this will contribute to the survivor's safety and is in the best interest of the child. Each of these code provisions are designed to protect the survivor's right to custody of her child.

The Model Code is not the only legal recourse battered women can rely on, assuming it is adopted in their jurisdiction. Other states have changed the climate in which battered women seek custody of their children by changing the courts that hear their claims. Hawaii has attempted to address intimate and child abuse in a more comprehensive manner by developing a unified criminal and civil court that adjudicates woman and child abuse, divorce, and juvenile delinquency matters all in one forum (Mills, 1996a). This unified court has been hailed by some as a model for administering a more "therapeutic" justice. Yet, this approach has also been challenged for being unresponsive to the diverse needs of battered women. For instance, Barbara Hart, the Legal Director of Pennsylvania Coalition Against Domestic Violence, among others, has argued that revealing spousal abuse in one proceeding might affect a woman's credibility in another family matter (such as child custody) adjudicated by the same court (Unified Courts, 1993).

SUMMARY AND REFLECTIONS

The public child welfare system and the related child custody issues present vexing problems to CSWs, advocates, and clinicians concerned about the intersections of domestic violence and child abuse. On the one hand, to use the authoritative CPS system for intervention in woman abuse cases seems inappropriate if it is empowerment of the battered woman that is to be achieved. On the other hand, the CPS system is a point of entry for battered women who need the attention that the system might be reformed to give. Because of bias, both the legal system and the corresponding CPS system have failed battered women who need both a swift and a patient response and one that respects the shifting financial, emotional, and cultural uncertainty that the intimate abuse conundrum presents. Cases such as *In re Heather A.*, "failure to protect" allegations, and custody disputes should be scrutinized to ensure that battered women are not unjustly deprived of their children due to the abuse of their mates.

The collective experiences of the four programs who received DHHS funding suggest that CPS training is not enough to overcome the biases of CSWs. Legislative and legal changes, such as those suggested, offer hope in a system that is all too often ready to blame the battered woman. The Model Code and Hawaii's Unified Court attempt to recognize the complex problems of domestic violence and child abuse and to address them in an institutional setting of understanding and fairness. Both approaches provide hope for the battered woman who fears that whatever action she takes—staying or leaving—it will be misinterpreted and held against her in a custody or failure to protect proceeding.

In the next chapter we examine the health care system and the challenges posed by interventions performed by health care practitioners, including nurses, social workers, and physicians.

QUESTIONS

- ❑ What roles do CSWs play in blaming the battered mother for the batterer's violence?

- ❑ What resistance do CPS agencies pose to programs wanting to train CSWs on domestic violence and child abuse?

- ❑ What are the pros and cons of integrating domestic violence into child abuse assessment formats?

- ❑ What role do you think CPS should play in child "witness" cases involving domestic violence?

- ❑ Is cross-reporting an appropriate response by a CSW who detects domestic violence? What are its advantages and disadvantages?

- ❑ If you were a CSW, under what circumstances would you require a battered woman to undergo treatment?

- ❑ Does the Model Code address your concerns regarding the ways in which "failure to protect" statutes have been used against battered women? How does the Model Code protect fathers who are falsely accused of domestic violence crimes?

- ❑ Does Hawaii's Unified Court seem to offer a viable alternative to battered women?

CHAPTER 5

The Health Care System's Response to Domestic Violence

Danny Carter Jr. died on August 31, 1993. He was 2 years old. Danny's mother had brought him to the hospital claiming that he had been pushed down a flight of stairs by a sibling at their Springfield home. He was treated for a concussion. It was later revealed that Danny's father had picked him up by the throat, punched him in the chest, and thrown him to the ground. An autopsy discovered that Danny died of a bruised heart. Danny's mother told the truth about his injuries 1 month after his death, while her husband was dying from an overdose on Extra-Strength Tylenol®. She was charged in connection with Danny's death; she had provided false information to the physician who treated her son. Her defense was that she had been so severely battered by her husband over a period of years that she had been too terrified to tell the doctors what had really happened to Danny Jr.

(Davis, 1994)

PANDORA'S BOX

Medicine . . . often categorizes problems, fundamentally social in origin, as biological or personal deficits, and in doing so smothers the impulse for social change which could offer the only serious resolution.

Stark & Flitcraft, 1982, p. 32

81

Cases such as Danny Carter Jr.'s raise the specific problem of how the health care system should respond to child abuse and domestic violence and the reality that health care professionals have been reluctant to open this "Pandora's box." Although it is now well established that health care practitioners are mandated reporters in child abuse cases, extending these provisions to battered women has proved to be problematic. Should health care personnel perform diagnostic domestic violence interviews in every case or only in those cases in which the women have children? At what point should law enforcement or CPS, or both, be contacted in cases in which domestic violence is suspected? What legal mandates control these interactions? What liability may be imposed for health personnel inaction? What unintended consequences flow from a mandatory reporting policy in domestic violence cases? What are the pros and cons of these policies? These questions are addressed in this chapter. In addition, this chapter examines the underlying institutional limitations of our health care system, a system that focuses almost exclusively on treatment rather than on prevention, on crisis intervention rather than on family health.

WHEN BATTERED WOMEN HAVE CHILDREN

The domestic violence issues related to the health care system are exacerbated when they involve children. Indeed, the complex interplay of the two issues has led to a kind of analytical paralysis in this area. Child health advocates have been reluctant to fully embrace domestic violence as a health care issue for children, given competition from other, equally devastating problems, including and especially poverty. Similarly, feminist organizations have been reluctant to promote the issue of domestic violence and children's health for fear that battered mothers will be infantilized or essentialized, or both, as reproductive or protective agents (Solloway & Sonosky, 1996). Yet, there is little doubt that domestic violence is intimately connected to a child's health. Health risk behaviors such as a history of alcohol or other drug use, overeating, and a propensity toward violence are familial, insofar as they are genetically wired or learned by example (Schor, 1995). In the same way that it is difficult to distinguish where maternal and child health begins and ends, parental decisions about when, where, and how to seek medical attention for children's injuries, physical and psychic, are determined according to the parents' own values.

There is now little doubt that good parenting and hence good child health is fostered and profoundly influenced by good marital relationships. Studies reveal that mothers who feel supported seem to enjoy their children more and act or feel more competently in their relationships with them (Corse, Schmid, & Trickett, 1990; Goodyer, 1990; Seybold, Fritz, & MacPhee, 1991). We have learned that the opposite is also true. Mothers who have the least support and the highest levels of stress, including abuse, are less emotionally available to their children and may even abuse them (AHA, 1994; Billings & Moos, 1983; Walker, 1984). There is little question that children's needs must be met by their parents and that those needs span the corporeal and affective landscape; they are material, emotional, social, and educational. What is most interesting, however, is that parental income, education, employment, marital status, age, and sexual orientation are, on their own, not inherently predictive of successful development (Schor, 1995). Rather, such factors as family support and affection are most critical (Schor, 1995).

Analytically speaking, the issues of domestic violence and health care are plagued by the difficulty in pinpointing where the parent begins and the child ends. Definitions of "family health" have been fixed in traditional notions of adult or child illness and treatment or adult or child disease and intervention. We have been unwilling to fully embrace the parent and child as inextricably intertwined, and we have been ill equipped to see how their needs and interests converge and diverge. Indeed, we have been reluctant to see them both as one and as two.

These analytical limitations are evident in the agencies charged with the mandate to protect their interests. Maternal and Child Health (MCH) programs, situated in the U.S. Department of Health and Human Services, are committed, at least on paper, to recognizing the special vulnerability of women, infants, children, and adolescents. They provide pregnancy-related services to women as well as health care services for infants, children, and adolescents (Solloway & Sonosky, 1996). The primary focus of the MCH programs has been healthy birth outcomes for infants and the healthy development of children and adolescents. Until now, women's health care needs have only been included in MCH programs insofar as they are directly related to these goals. More recently, these programmatic limitations have been questioned. In light of evidence that there is a direct relationship between healthy mothers and healthy children, a debate has ensued regarding the extent to which MCH programs should address women's health needs more holistically. Although every expert who participated in a 1996 effort to reconsider how women's health should be integrated into MCH program goals was overwhelmingly supportive, "many also cautioned against MCH being too inclusive" (Solloway & Sonosky, 1996, p. 7).

The inclusion of women's health into MCH programs does not necessarily guarantee that domestic violence will be addressed. Indeed, discussions have just begun on whether MCH definitions of "family health" should include intimate abuse (anonymous communication, April 8, 1997). What is evident, both in the federal bureaucracy that addresses vulnerable children's health and in the attitudes of professionals who treat their mothers, is that there is much resistance to embracing intimate abuse as a health care problem.

As is often the case, sometimes treatment programs can stretch these analytic boundaries through practice. AWAKE (Advocacy for Women and Kids in Emergencies), a program at Boston Children's Hospital, works with abused children and their mothers as they are identified in the hospital setting. AWAKE is a program specifically designed to address the problem revealed in the Danny Carter, Jr. case and to constructively intervene to ensure mother and child safety and well-being. The program was started in response to a Boston City Hospital study that revealed that 59.4% of the mothers of abused children were themselves victims of domestic violence (Taylor, 1997). Working with CPS, AWAKE advocates try to keep mother and child together. They provide in-hospital counseling and support groups and continue working with families after they leave the hospital. Other social and financial support programs are also available to mothers and their children. Their results have been dramatic: Sixteen months after the children are released from the hospital, 85% of the battered women no longer live with their batterers. In addition, only 3 of the 500 children referred by various agencies have subsequently been placed in foster care (Taylor, 1997).

AWAKE's success demonstrates the possibility that innovative programs can overcome the analytical shortcomings of institutions that are otherwise slow to change. Because the health care system's mandate has been so narrowly focused on crisis intervention and treatment, it has been reluctant to embrace a broader agenda (Rosenberg, O'Carroll, & Powell, 1992). Although elements of the patriarchical state are probably in part responsible for the health care system's lack of attention—beginning, of course, in medical school education—other explanations are equally plausible. Western medicine is indifferent to prevention, and its disease model orientation all too often marginalizes the psychosocial and public health dynamics of injury or illness (Gordon, 1996). This has been particularly evident in its treatment of battered women, described in detail below.

TREATING BATTERED WOMEN

> Physicians will not ask questions if they do not know how to deal with them.
>
> Anonymous
> (Cohen, DeVos, & Newberger, 1997, p. S22)

At the U.S. Surgeon General's Workshop on Violence and Public Health, held in Leesburg, Virginia, on October 27 through 29, 1985, then Surgeon General C. Everett Koop began discussions on the limitations of the health care response to child abuse, domestic violence, and abuse of the elderly. The universal response to this issue has been legal reform. All but three states (South Carolina, Washington, and Wyoming) have some form of mandated reporting for health care professionals (Box 5.1).

Forty-one states, Puerto Rico, Virgin Islands, and Washington, D.C., have statutes that require health care practitioners to report injuries that appear to be caused either (depending on the statute) by a gun, knife, firearm, or other deadly weapon. These states are Alaska, Arizona, Arkansas, California, Colorado, Connecticut,

Box 5.1 Mandatory Reporting Laws

1. What is to be reported?
   Almost all states have laws mandating reports when the patient has an injury that appears to be caused by a gun, knife, or other deadly weapon. Other states require reports of injuries from crimes, acts of violence, or nonaccidental acts.
2. Who makes the report?
   Whoever is treating the injury in question (health care worker, institution, facility, or person in charge) makes the report. Some statutes require "any person" to report.
3. What level of knowledge or suspicion is required?
   Some statutes require "reasonable" cause, others only if in their opinion a criminal act was involved.
4. To whom do you report?
   In general, reports are made to a police agency. Generally, it is up to the police agency what to do with the report.
5. What are the penalties for failing to report?
   Fines range from $10 (e.g., Arkansas) to $1,000 (e.g., California) and may sometimes include a jail sentence.
6. Is immunity for reporting provided?
   Most states provide practitioners with immunity from civil/criminal liability when reports are made in good faith.
7. Is provider-patient confidentiality revoked?
   Some statutes have been interpreted to suggest that privileges do not apply to the information required to be reported.
8. When is provider liability at stake?
   A provider may be held liable for failure to diagnose a domestic violence-related injury and to file a report. In states where there is no reporting requirement, providers can be held liable for breaching confidentiality if they report.

Delaware, Florida, Hawaii, Idaho, Illinois, Indiana, Iowa, Kansas, Louisiana, Maine, Maryland, Massachusetts, Michigan, Minnesota, Mississippi, Missouri, Montana, Nevada, New Hampshire, New Jersey, New York, North Carolina, North Dakota, Ohio, Oregon, Pennsylvania, Rhode Island, South Dakota, Tennessee, Texas, Utah, Vermont, Virginia, West Virginia, and Wisconsin. Twenty states and Washington, D.C. require reports when the health care practitioner believes that the injuries are the result of a criminal or illegal act or otherwise related to the commission of a crime or offense of violence (depending on the statute). These states are Arizona, California, Colorado, Delaware, Hawaii, Idaho, Illinois, Iowa, Massachusetts, Minnesota, Nebraska, New Hampshire, North Carolina, North Dakota, Ohio, Oklahoma, Pennsylvania, Utah, West Virginia, and Wisconsin.

Eight states require reports of injuries that they believe are the result of an act of violence, which in some cases must be in connection with a criminal act (depending on the statute). These states are Arizona, Florida, Hawaii, Michigan, Nebraska, North Carolina, Ohio, and Tennessee. Six states specifically require reports under circumstances in which the injury appears to be inflicted intentionally or was otherwise not accidental. These states are Alaska, Arkansas, Colorado, Georgia, Nevada, and Oregon. In Alaska, Arizona, Hawaii, Indiana, Iowa, Kansas, New York, North Carolina, and Ohio, the seriousness or gravity of the injury is important to the health practitioner's decision to report. Five states have mandatory reporting laws that specifically require health professionals to call the police or other designated governmental agency when domestic violence or adult abuse, including spousal rape, is suspected. These states are Arkansas, California, Colorado, Kentucky, and Rhode Island.

These statutes were passed because battered women reported that they used the health care system and that they often had contact with emergency room doctors or family practitioners for their domestic violence-related injuries (Stark & Flitcraft, 1985; Yu, 1997). Since it was believed that only 15 to 48% of battered women report incidents of violence to law enforcement (Straus & Gelles, 1986; U.S. DOJ, 1994b), battered women's advocates began to put pressure on practitioners other than law enforcement to intervene. They hoped that these mandates would better ensure that batterers experienced consequences for their violence. Although the statistics are still unreliable on how many battered women use the health care system, there is little doubt that it is now viewed as a first point of system contact for some, if not most, battered women.

In a 1991 survey, the American Medical Association (AMA) (Yu, 1997) asked survivors of domestic violence to identify one person who could have had an impact in preventing their injuries. In total, 87% named their family physician. Yet, in a 1993 survey conducted by the Commonwealth Fund's Commission on Women's Health at Columbia University, 92% of women who were physically abused by their partners did not discuss these incidents with their physicians. In a study done by Stark and Flitcraft (1985), one in five battered women had seen a physician at least 11 times for trauma. Similarly, Stark and Flitcraft (1985) found that 23% of battered women had seen a physician 6 to 10 times for other reasons related to the abuse, including treatment for anxiety, depression, back and related pain, sleep disorders, hyperventilation, and other vague medical complaints.

In a 1992 study conducted by Sugg and Inui, the resistance of doctors in addressing domestic violence in their practices was examined. Thirty-eight physicians were interviewed in a large, urban, health maintenance organization (HMO) serving predominantly white, middle-class patients. The reasons they gave for their reluctance was lack of time and resources and their hesitation to interfere in private "family matters." One physician suggested that the reason he didn't ask about a patient's violence history is because he didn't want to "open Pandora's box" (p. 3158).

Studies of psychiatric patients have found that up to one third have a history of domestic violence (Carmen, Rieker, & Mills, 1984; Post et al., 1980). About 25% of women who attempt suicide are victims of domestic violence (American Medical Association [AMA], 1992). Straus and Smith (1990) found that depression and suicide attempts are four times more likely in female victims of severe assault compared with women who were not subjected to violence. Alcohol and drug dependency are also common in battered women because they search for ways to medicate the violence. A study by Barnett and Fagan (1993) revealed that the incidence of alcohol use by women during the abuse was 17.8%, and the male incidence was 30%. Following the abuse, 48.1% of women drank, compared with 24.2% of the batterers.

McFarlane and Parker (1994) report that abuse during pregnancy affects one in every six adult women and one in five teenagers. The Maricopa Medical Center, Department of Obstetrics and Gynecology surveyed all obstetrics and gynecology residencies in the United States and Puerto Rico (Chambliss, Bay, & Jones, 1995). Their study revealed that 75% of residents reported that they did not recognize any situations of battering.

Studies on emergency department visits have found that 22 to 35% of women presenting with any complaint are there because of symptoms related to ongoing abuse (Hasselt, Morrison, Bellack, & Hersen, 1988). In a study of 1994 emergency department visits, the DOJ (1997) found that 37% of injuries to women involved a spouse, ex-spouse, or boyfriend.

To address resistance to identifying and treating domestic violence cases by health care personnel, the Joint Commission on the Accreditation of Healthcare Organizations now requires all 200 hospitals to develop and follow protocols to help identify, evaluate, and treat adult domestic violence victims (Scott & Matricciani, 1994). The AMA (1992) has determined that its members have an ethical duty to diagnose and treat domestic violence, even though, in general, the AMA is opposed to laws which mandate reporting.

Given the incidence and prevalence of domestic violence and its obvious intersection with the health care system and given legislation to use the health care system as an avenue to criminal justice intervention, it is no surprise that a debate has ensued on the issue of mandatory reporting.

REASSESSING MANDATORY REPORTING

> I'm sorry, but if my doctor were to call the police and they went to my husband, my husband would have beat the shit out of me.
>
> Anonymous
> (Mooney & Rodriquez, 1996, p. 95)

The arguments in favor of and against mandatory reporting parallel some of the arguments in favor of and against mandatory arrest and prosecution. Health practitioners, like law enforcement and prosecutors, must acknowledge and accept their roles as participants in order for the policy to be effective. The inaction of health care personnel and law enforcement may also have similar negative results.

Those in favor of mandatory reporting rely on research that suggests that battered women are much more likely to visit their practitioner than call the police (Pierce & Deutsch, 1990). They argue, and statistics reveal, that battered women are often forced to go to the emergency department or to their primary care physicians seeking medical treatment. These women wouldn't otherwise talk about their domestic violence, and many of them wouldn't otherwise contact the police (Pierce & Deutsch, 1990). Advocates of mandatory reporting believe that it provides an otherwise missed opportunity to hold a batterer accountable for the violence they have inflicted (Hyman, Schilinger, & Lo, 1995; Jones, 1996).

Advocates of mandatory reporting policies are particularly concerned about the discrepancy between the percentage of emergency room visits and identification of the cause (Jones, 1996). In a 1987 study by Kurz, in 40% of cases in which the physician treated a battered woman in an emergency department setting, the staff did not discuss the abuse with the patients. Carole Warshaw (1989) reviewed emergency room charts at a large public hospital which were generated for women patients during a 2-week period in 1987 and found 52 cases involving women who were deliberately injured by another person (the most obvious cases). Warshaw's results (1989) revealed that even though these women gave strong clues about being at risk for abuse, they were only addressed directly in one case "and for the most part, were specifically avoided" (pp. 508–509). In a similar study by Goldberg and Tomlanovich (1984), only about 4 to 5% of cases of domestic violence were identified correctly by emergency department personnel.

Law enforcement officers who are interested in stopping domestic violence and in holding perpetrators accountable are in favor of mandatory reporting by health care professionals. According to Tim Williams of the Los Angeles Police Department, the mandatory reporting law "helps us get the victim out of harm's way. . . . If there was no Mandatory Reporting Law, we would never know about these things" (Roan, 1996, p. E1).

Many specific arguments are advanced in favor of mandatory reporting. First, advocates argue that it enhances patient safety by removing the threat to the woman and does so in a way that doesn't require her direct action (Hyman et al., 1995). Second, they claim that mandatory reporting improves the response of the health care system by requiring it to become involved in patients' lives and to learn the causes of their injuries (Hyman et al., 1995).

Third, advocates support a system of mandatory reporting because it holds the perpetrator accountable for his abusive action (Hyman et al., 1995). Finally, advocates argue that mandatory reporting improves data collection and documentation of domestic violence incidents, since more women are likely to access the health care system for assistance with their injuries than they are likely to access the criminal justice system (Hyman et al., 1995).

The problem, as in the case of mandatory arrest and prosecution, is that battered women's lives are too complex for a blanket policy *that* cannot tailor its response to a victim's unique circumstance. Mandatory reporting by health care personnel is inadequate without additional arrangements for a battered woman to go to a shelter, to seek other living arrangements, or at a minimum, to obtain a restraining order. All too often, she will return home from the doctor or hospital to a batterer who is angry that the police were called. Because of the short amount of time batterers actually spend in jail (Zorza, 1992), they can be arrested in the hospital emergency room and released before the battered woman returns from the hospital (Roan, 1996). Janet Nudelman of the Family Violence Prevention Fund in San Francisco (Roan, 1996) finds mandatory reporting to be the wrong approach "because it takes away doctors' ability to decide on a case-by-case basis what is best for that patient. It asks them to be cops. It asks them to assume a position that isn't appropriate for them" (p. 1).

Several specific arguments are advanced by opponents of mandatory reporting of domestic violence. The risk of retaliation is real. According to Hart (1992, 1993), batterers often escalate the violence when their partners either attempt separation or increase their contact with help-seeking organizations. Hart (1993) found that as many as half of the batterers in her study threatened retaliatory violence, and more than 30% may inflict further assaults if they are prosecuted. Although it may be argued that battered women benefit from mandatory reporting, insofar as they themselves do not have to take direct action against the batterer, they might still be blamed for having revealed the abuse in the first place.

As Hyman et al. (1995) have argued, reporting has been shown in other arenas, such as elder abuse, to be less effective than education (U.S. General Accounting Office [GAO], 1991). Moreover, it is unclear whether reporting actually improves the care of battered women. In some cases, especially when intervention by law enforcement has been slow in responding or short in consequences such as jail time, mandatory reporting can actually increase the battered woman's vulnerability to violence. Studies in San Francisco and New York City reveal that in 1991 only 25 to 30% of law enforcement officers prepared the required written reports related to domestic violence calls, and only 7 to 12% resulted in arrests (Hyman et al., 1995).

In other instances, the reporting can be done by a health practitioner who doesn't truly appreciate the complexity of the battered woman's life and therefore fails to use the intervention in a way that improves her safety (Jones, 1996). Indeed, an inadequate intervention can send battered women underground as opposed to increasing their access to helping organizations (Bryant & Panico, 1994).

In addition, some opponents have argued that it is unethical to risk women's lives by imposing mandatory reporting laws in order to collect more accurate data on domestic violence incidents. Some opponents have even argued that the data collected in the confusion of a crisis are inaccurate (Hyman et al., 1995).

Of particular concern in mandatory reporting cases are the discriminatory attitudes of the mandated reporter: Reporting in child abuse cases reveals that a greater percentage of African American and Latino families are identified as abusive than are white families. In one important study by Cohen, et al. (1997), nearly all the health professionals surveyed, most of whom were white, asserted that family violence was a problem associated with people in poverty. Using the example of child abuse reporting, these respondents believed that reporting was necessary only when cases involved the poor. Although some professionals did in fact recognize that child abuse was indicated in their middle class or wealthier private patients, they "did not deem it 'appropriate' to report these cases" (Cohen et al., 1997, p. 23). Interestingly, even though they believed that the cases involving poor patients should be reported, they often didn't report those incidents as well. Latino, African American, Native American, or Southeast Asian communities were found to have, according to these health professionals, the majority of family violence.

These biased attitudes on the part of health professionals were also detected in their criticism of battered women and were relayed by both male and female health care providers (Cohen et al., 1997). Battered women were criticized for not following the advice of health care providers. These attitudes were similarly detected in a 1992 study by Bokunewicz and Copel of emergency nurses' attitudes about domestic violence. The researchers found that stereotypes about battered women were common: beliefs such as that the battered woman could leave or was masochistic or that the violence was a one-time incident were prevalent. Despite the fact that Kurz (1987) found that 75% of battered women volunteered that they had been injured by a husband or boyfriend, emergency department staff still stereotyped battered women as "evasive" or as possessing "troublesome" traits, or both.

Doctors themselves are sometimes uncooperative because they fear that by reporting they will make the situation worse. Dr. Larry Bedard, President of the American College of Emergency Physicians, was quoted as saying "I feel a lot of trepidation when I am faced with a situation where a woman says, 'Please don't report, because if you do, my husband will kill me' " (Levy, 1996, p. D1).

The refusal of doctors "to get involved" in cases of domestic violence may have criminal or fiscal consequences. In some states, such as California, noncompliance with domestic violence reporting laws is a misdemeanor. In addition, battered women have started to hold doctors liable for their inaction, in much the same way they held police agencies liable (Jones, 1996). Tort law in this area is still evolving; for now, physicians can be held liable under civil law for failing to report abuse to the police. The issue is particularly thorny because it involves an adult, not a child, an elder, or a dependent or "incompetent" adult. In child, elder, or dependent adult abuse cases, liability is clearer when the cases involve people who aren't otherwise competent to protect themselves. The threat of money damages can be a powerful incentive for physicians to act, while also compensating the victim financially for her injuries (Jones, 1996).

Mandatory reporting, of course, relies on the interest of the health care professional. Health personnel have been extremely reluctant to ask how a victim sustained an injury, avoiding the problem of reporting by avoiding the relevant inquiry. In one study by Reid and Glasser (1997), it was found that physicians failed to identify the majority of domestic violence victims, even though they were often the first and only individuals to whom the victim presented. The study assessed a total of 143 primary care physicians in three midwestern counties to determine the physicians' knowledge of and attitudes toward domestic violence, the importance and prevalence in their practice of intimate abuse, and their attitudes toward responsibility. In addition, the study collected information on current practices and protocols, level of education on domestic violence received, and opinions on how best to distribute information concerning domestic violence. The response rate was 52 of 83; 53% of respondents were family physicians; 47% were general internists. Thirty-four percent of the respondents were women. Their results revealed that 100% of the physicians agreed that finding and treating domestic violence was important, yet less than half agreed that domestic violence was a significant problem in their patient populations. Almost 96% of the physicians surveyed believed that more should be done to educate physicians about domestic violence. Indeed, 94% agreed that domestic violence should be included in a doctor's professional medical training. Yet, nearly half of those surveyed reported that they would not participate in a domestic violence forum. Although 41% reported that they had received some formal education regarding domestic violence, 57% felt that their medical school education had not prepared them to deal with the issues related to domestic violence. Less than 25% reported that they had been trained to diagnose domestic violence. In total, family and female physicians were more comfortable addressing issues related to domestic violence, whereas older physicians were less comfortable and less likely to agree that education about domestic violence should be a part of medical training.

Another study (Tilden et al., 1994) that included dentists and dental hygienists revealed some very interesting and disturbing results. Compared with physicians, psychologists and social workers, dentists and dental hygienists received the least education in abuse and had the least frequent rate of suspecting abuse and the greatest proportion of respondents who felt they were not responsible for intervening in suspected abuse (Tilden et al., 1994). In total, 45.9% of the dental hygienists and 47.3% of the dentists did not agree with the statement: "Professionals in my discipline have as much responsibility to deal with problems of family violence as they do to deal with other clinical problems" (p. 630). This finding is particularly striking when one contemplates that so many domestic violence incidents involve the face (68%), the eyes (45%), and the neck (12%) (Meskin, 1994).

In another study, it was confirmed that health professionals were reluctant to ask the questions that would trigger a reporting situation. Allert, Chalkley, Whitney, and Librett (1997) reported the results of domestic violence training provided to health care professionals in Utah. Included in the training were Emergency Medical Technicians and paramedics, as well as emergency department personnel. The trainers and researchers found that, although providers felt confident asking questions about abuse, the providers were unwilling to question patients unless they suspected domestic violence was the cause of the injury. The reason, according to Allert et al. (1997), is that these providers did not believe domestic violence was a problem in their communities.

In one study of five communities (Cohen et al., 1997), the researchers examined how domestic violence had been integrated into the health care system. It was found that charismatic leaders were the people responsible for inspiring change in how a health care organization addressed domestic violence but that those leaders often found themselves marginalized in the health care setting and without resources for ensuring the program's ongoing success. When the charismatic leader left, the domestic violence program usually fell apart.

Occasionally, program advocates are successful in fully integrating a domestic violence agenda into a hospital setting. Woman-Kind (Taylor, 1997) is one of the oldest hospital-based programs and is located in two suburban hospitals and one urban hospital in the Minneapolis–St. Paul area. With an annual budget of $200,000, a director, four full-time program coordinators, and 75 volunteers, WomanKind trains hospital staff to identify and respond to domestic violence. Crisis intervention for victims and ongoing support during and after their hospital stay is available, as is access to other resources, including safe housing, legal aid, and welfare.

These findings suggest that despite the various forms of mandatory reporting laws, physicians' reluctance must be overcome if the goal is to involve the health care system in domestic violence intervention. This limitation aside, it is highly questionable whether mandatory reporting actually serves the complex and highly individualized interests of most battered women who need services.

BATTERED WOMEN DENIED INSURANCE

A related development to the implementation of mandatory reporting laws has been the loss of health and life insurance coverage to battered women whose violence histories are documented in their medical records (Wagner, 1996). In 1994, a study by the U.S. House Judiciary Committee concluded that 8 of the 16 largest insurance companies admitted to using domestic violence as a factor when making decisions about issuing insurance policies and setting premiums (Morrison, 1996). Since the survey, at least two of the insurers, State Farm and Nationwide Insurance Companies, have reported that they have changed their polices and claim that they no longer discriminate against domestic violence victims (Morrison, 1996). It is reasonable to assume that if half of the nation's largest insurance companies use or have used domestic violence as a criterion for denying health insurance, then many of the smaller insurance companies do too (Morrison, 1996).

The National Association of Insurance Commissioners (NAIC), which represents state insurance regulators, drafted model state legislation to outlaw this kind of discrimination (Morrison, 1996). The NAIC reports that 6 states—Connecticut, Massachusetts, Delaware, Florida, Iowa, and California—have passed antidiscrimination laws and that 14 other states are considering similar action. A 1997 law in Utah has been designed to encourage battered women to get help and not to fear the repercussions of reporting domestic violence. This law makes it illegal for insurance companies to discriminate against victims of domestic violence by either limiting or canceling their insurance policies.

The Utah law was inspired when State Farm denied coverage to a battered woman, whom they claimed "continued to put herself in danger" (Wagner, 1996). State Farm compared the battered woman to a person with diabetes who refused to take insulin. State

Farm did report that they would reinstate coverage if the battered woman left her battering husband of 2 years, which she eventually did. As noted, State Farm Insurance has now revised their policy of denying coverage to battered women.

When this same battered woman attempted to get coverage from another insurance company, she was refused. The insurance company was quoted as saying that they denied life insurance coverage to victims of domestic violence because it might "provide an incentive to murder" (Wagner, 1996).

Morrison (1996) argues that it is difficult to know why any given applicant is denied insurance and hence to learn more about the extent of discrimination in this area. He explains that insurers are not obliged to file public documents disclosing the reasons they use when making coverage decisions, nor are they required to expose their underwriting standards. Moreover, insurance companies are not required to disclose reasons for rejecting individual applicants.

The unintended consequence of denying insurance coverage to battered women, which flows from the use of the health care system in identifying domestic violence, presents a complex problem for policymakers. Doctors must now document domestic violence, given the various mandatory reporting laws, and document their screening in the records, often to protect themselves from future liability. The insurance company requests a release from the applicant of all medical records, and when they receive those records, evidence of domestic violence appears in the records requested. Other methods of sharing medical information include subscriber databases, such as Equifax and the Medical Information Bureau, both of which are industry-funded organizations that share computerized information about applicants with more than 600 insurance companies. The third method for learning more about insurance applicants comes from court documents and credit reports, which often contain information regarding orders of protection.

Advocates of legislation regulating what insurance companies can do with this information conclude that the denial of insurance coverage can deter a battered woman from reporting incidents of violence to her medical practitioner or to a police agency. It may even deter her from getting an order of protection. Indeed, it seems reasonable that legal advocates working with battered women who are applying for, or are about to lose, insurance should advise them not to disclose their abuse histories to medical personnel.

SUMMARY AND REFLECTIONS

> A national public health objective for the year 2000 is for at least 90% of hospital emergency departments to have protocols for routinely identifying, treating, and referring victims of sexual assault and spouse abuse.
>
> (Family Violence Prevention Fund, 1997)

The road to health care for domestic violence survivors, both mothers and their children, has been a bumpy one. Although it is too early to tell whether mandatory reporting is effective in reducing recidivism or, as some have claimed, in increasing violence against women, it is clear that policy reform has taken a legalistic and punitive approach. Physicians can be held criminally liable and can be sued for not reporting cases of domestic violence, even when victims plead with them not to report; victims can be denied health and life insurance if they are finally honest about the violence in their lives. Despite these threats, most health care practitioners are reluctant to inquire into a patient's domestic violence history or are oblivious to the consequences of documenting it. Many believe it is isolated by race and class and that it is only relevant in populations unlike themselves.

The reluctance of maternal and child health experts to fully embrace domestic violence as a mother and child issue contributes to the frenzy to mandate health care professionals to act through reporting laws. This preoccupation with reporting neglects the possibility of contemplating more global public health strategies that treat individual cases according to individual needs. Not unlike the criminal justice and child protection systems, the health care system relies on professionals who are ill-equipped to respond to the complex needs of domestic violence victims and their children or to intervene. The fear is that all too often the intervention can exacerbate the problems of the violent family and send women and their children further underground, moving them closer to the violence that threatens their lives.

Although studies in health care treatment are just beginning to address issues of paternalism in relation to victims of domestic violence (Hyman & Chez, 1995), concerns already embraced by critics of criminal justice policy, it is obvious that similar issues are clearly emerging. Taking the decision out of the battered woman's hands to report or not to report an incident of domestic violence robs her of an important opportunity to make decisions about her and her children's future and robs her of her wisdom to respond to the violence she knows best.

Programs such as AWAKE and WomanKind should be replicated, and the methods of empowerment described in the next two chapters should be used to ensure that interventions by health care personnel do not mimic the actions of the batterer by disempowering the battered woman. In chapter 10, case studies in health settings are presented that will help explore exactly how those interactions can turn violence into an opportunity to realize change.

QUESTIONS

☐ As a matter of policy, how should Maternal and Child Health programs address the complex intersections of abuse? Where would you draw the line on what services they should or should not provide?

☐ What are the pros and cons of mandatory reporting? If you are a health care professional, would you report, or live with, the consequences of defying the law?

☐ Should battered women be treated differently by insurance companies because they are at greater risk of harm? Are you willing to pay higher premiums for the risk to herself and her children?

Part III

Empowerment Strategies and Affective Advocacy

CHAPTER 6

Engaging the Battered Mother: Empowerment Strategies and Affective Advocacy

> If we had a keen vision and feeling of all ordinary human life, it would be like hearing the grass grow and the squirrel's heart beat, and we should die of that roar which lies on the other side of silence.
>
> George Eliot (1871/1992, pp. 177–178)

In general, systems responses to battered mothers, whether criminal justice, child protection, or health care, have one feature in common: The battered woman is almost never adequately engaged by the practitioners working within them. In the case of the criminal justice system, in many instances the battered woman is only important insofar as she will or will not cooperate in the arrest and prosecution of domestic violence crimes; even her own assessment of her safety is often ignored (Mills, 1998b). In the case of child welfare, the mother is blamed for her failure to protect or is otherwise seen as an unfit mother (Peled, 1996), or the domestic violence is disregarded altogether by agency policy (Mills, 1998a). In the case of health care, the cause of her injury may be deemed irrelevant, or her cries for individualized attention are punished by statutes which mandate reporting. In other instances, insurance companies hold a battered woman's abuse history against her.

I begin with the assumption that practitioners who address the needs of battered women and their children must refocus their attention on engaging and empowering the mother-child unit. It is not enough, however, to see the mother and child as one; we must begin to view them as the cradle of hope for interrupting the intergenerational transmission of abuse and for reversing the trend toward violence that plagues, in one form of another, all families.

A model of empowerment for battered mothers requires that we critically analyze our interactions with survivors. In this chapter I present an approach for connecting with a battered mother that will prove critical to the CSW, advocate, and clinician's efforts to reach her through the cloud of violence. What generic skills are necessary to embrace a battered mother honestly and without judgment? What specific techniques can an advocate use to help smooth the bumpy road to connection? In the next chapter, we examine in greater depth some specific methods for interacting with the battered mother beyond the critical techniques of connection presented here. Chapter 7 explores these systems methods more generally and in chapters 8, 9, and 10, these approaches are synthesized in case studies that demonstrate how these techniques can take expression in specific interactions.

BUILDING CONNECTION THROUGH EMPOWERMENT

AFFECTIVE ADVOCACY

How should clinicians or advocates concerned with the needs of battered mothers, and hence their children, interact and connect? What generic clinical or advocacy principles can help guide professionals and hence enhance their capacity to start where she begins? What mixture of clinical distance and connection will help ensure the trust necessary to make change?

My theory is that interventions should mirror the survivor's uncertainty (Mills, 1996a). Recognizing the dialectical complexity of a clinical and advocacy relationship with a battered woman acknowledges that the dynamic will involve a mixture of intervention and treatment, empathy and shared suffering. Such an approach suggests that should a battered woman be ready to leave her abusive relationship, a practitioner should simultaneously be ready and able to respond, with minimal prodding and significant support if necessary. If on the other hand, she is unprepared to leave, the practitioner should, without judgment and with respect, provide alternative remedies according to her needs and desires. Toward this end, practitioners should strive for an approach that respects the complexity of any given battered woman's experience and also recognizes that true empowerment for battered women will be achieved not through obedience to the expectations of CSWs, advocates, or clinicians but rather through self-paced and self-initiated change.

Although I address the issues related to women leaving their abusive relationships throughout the book, it is important to note here that leaving is not always the safest strategy. Hence, a practitioner's judgment of a battered woman's commitment to her and her children's safety should never turn on her willingness to leave the abusive relationship alone. Rather, it should be contingent on her willingness, with your help, to take reasonable steps to ensure her own safety and the safety of her children.

Some practitioners have argued that a feminist stance on violence against women in the family requires an unequivocally woman-centered approach, one that helps survivors become economically independent of their abusers to ensure permanent escape from the abusive relationship (Davis & Hagen, 1992). Indeed, one study revealed that the staunchest feminist advocates believed that a survivor who decided to remain married should be encouraged to change her decision (McKeel & Sporakowski, 1993). I believe that a battered woman should be seen in the constantly shifting context of her relationship. I believe that empowerment interventions recognize that a battered woman's uncertainty and emotional and cultural loyalties demand a safe and nonjudgmental space in which to explore issues of violence. Practitioners should take the lead in establishing interventions to domestic violence that are based on theories and practices that provide an environment in which to explore all the battered woman's options and that embody an institutional ethos for empowering her through self-paced and self-initiated change.

Domestic violence practice in the United States can occur in such diverse settings as hospital emergency rooms and criminal courtrooms. These places have the potential to be important institutional settings within which women who experience violence can come to face the abuse in their lives. My work with these agencies and the research described in chapters 3, 4, and 5 overwhelmingly affirm that these institutional approaches, rather than helping the majority of battered women to address the violence in their lives, unwittingly force some survivors to suppress it. Frontline workers must be trained to ensure that no battered woman feels prejudged or forced underground because of her unwillingness to pursue one course of action or her desire to pursue another. One way to reduce that likelihood is to ensure that advocates trained in Affective Advocacy methods are available for survivors of domestic violence who may not yet be ready to take any formal action against their batterer. First, I describe this affective approach more generally; then I incorporate it into a specific strategy for working with a battered mother.

Affective Advocacy involves a deliberate attempt to reach a client emotionally and to train clinicians and advocates to understand that every interaction contains an emotional subtext and that in that subtext lies the key to a deeper and more empowering relationship. The possibility of change occurs in the communication, in the shared language, and in the space in between.

Affective practices address the survivor in her own emotional space and respond to the specific relationship and subjectivities where she is to be found. Rather than adopt a normative approach, such clinical interventions respect the survivor's relational structure and provide the space, time, and fluidity necessary for self-guided resolution (Pozatek, 1994). Such a method recognizes, too, that true empowerment for battered women will be achieved not through obedience to the expectations of practitioners but rather through a model that acknowledges that she must reconsider and reevaluate the meaning of the trauma in a time frame and an environment that supports the fluctuating complexity of her particular circumstance. It would go a significant way toward establishing this affective client dynamic if practitioners who work with battered women were trained in three basic, interrelated clinical principles.

First, working on the principle that practitioners are ineffective when unaware of their own histories, it is the practitioners' responsibility to reflect on the violence, in all its various forms, that they have experienced or have tolerated in their own lives both personally and professionally, intimately and institutionally. To be truly effective, in other words, practitioners must make an ongoing, concerted effort to understand their own experience of violence in relationships before working with battered women. Only in this way do they have a chance of leaving their own histories, prejudices, and presuppositions in relation to intimate violence behind them. This in itself is no simple task; the potential of practitioners to internalize the other two basic principles depends on their success with this first.

Second, domestic violence practitioners must treat their clients as they themselves would want to be treated. Again, however, practitioners can accept the survivor for who she is and where she is in her emotional development only if they recognize from their own personal experience the multifaceted, insidious, paradoxical, complex, and confusing character of intimate abuse.

Finally, and most important, frontline practitioners must encourage battered women to take the incremental steps they feel they are prepared to take (Box 6.1). To be effective, then, practitioners must take the individually paced clinical journey with each of their clients. They must venture with the client just far enough to encourage the client's safety and to help her learn more about her

---

Box 6.1 Empowerment and Affective Strategies

Reflect on the Violence in One's Own Life

- With whom do you fight?
- Whom have you forgiven?

Accept the Battered Woman As She Is

- What weakness in this battered woman reflects your own?
- What strength can you tap into?

Baby Steps Only

- Offer information, insight, and options.
- Hope for but expect nothing.
- Process . . . process . . . process is progress!

conundrum. Practitioners, however, must not venture so far as to alienate their clients from professional resources available when and if they are ready to take the next step. I address each of these issues more specifically below.

Reflect on the Violence in One's Own Life

"We can't judge a battered woman's decision to stay in an abusive relationship until we explore the violence we deny or accept in our own lives," I warn my students in my domestic violence class. "How many people tolerate abuse from parents, lovers or friends?" I continued. A few raised their hands. "Consider the following possibilities: Did your brother ever hit you? Did you hit him back? When was the last time your mother, your father, your lover humiliated you? Interrupted you? What did you do about it? When was the last time you humiliated others dear to you? How did they respond?" Suggesting to my students that we all tolerate and perhaps even inflict or at least participate in intimate violence, I encouraged them to explore the abuse in their own lives before rendering judgment or offering advice to the battered women they would counsel. In journals kept specifically for this purpose, nearly all of the students who worked with battered women realized that their own history of violence was not entirely unlike the clients' they served and, further, given that similar or different forms of violence had gone so completely unnoticed or tolerated in their own lives, that there were no legitimate grounds on which to judge their clients for their decision to leave or stay.

Several theorists and practitioners have argued that instead of asking "Why doesn't she leave?" the appropriate question is "Why does he batter?" (Littleton, 1993; Mahoney, 1991; Schneider, 1992). Of course the problem is that it is nearly impossible to train people not to ask "Why doesn't she leave?" when so many of us are so busy denying or ignoring the violence in our own lives and hence seeing the battered woman's conundrum as more obvious than it actually is. I suggest that the means for getting to the "Why does he batter" question is to explore, in therapeutic settings, including individual treatment and group support, and under supervision, the ways we (particularly those of us who think they are among the so-called nonabused) tolerate violence in our own lives. My students who did this work found that working with battered women is as much about helping their clients take incremental steps toward self-discovery and insight as it is about taking concrete steps toward addressing the violence in their own lives. To do so, we all concluded, is to undertake a radical program of long-lasting change that is achievable only through personal decision making arrived at through a means and in a time frame with which we as individuals and as members of our particular cultures and communities are comfortable.

Accept the Battered Woman as She Is

Once practitioners begin their self-discovery and they recognize and start to grapple with the violence they tolerate, they are prepared, regardless of their professional training, to work with a battered woman, a woman who is probably no more equipped than the practitioner to address the violence in her own life, just less confident and in more danger. Toward this end, practitioners must be painstakingly sensitive to achieving a most delicate balance. On the one hand, the battered woman seeks from the practitioner insight, guidance, and expertise. On the other hand, the exigency of the battered woman's situation can only contribute to her overriding fear that the system will judge whatever action (or inaction) she has taken to date and diminish the little power she may have to act in the future. If she feels prejudged, implicitly or explicitly forced to act, or pressured to take steps she is not prepared to take, then she may become alienated from the practitioner and from the process and reject whatever help is offered (or pretend as if she is accepting it but later fail to follow through on appointments) (Fischer & Rose, 1995). This aspect of "meeting" the client is in some respects the most important because it involves drawing the client in, affirming her strengths, and sustaining her involvement long enough for her to identify with a vision of a better, freer life for herself and to develop a plan for achieving it that keeps her safe in the meantime. To lose her to prejudgment not only may encourage the woman's probably already well-developed sense of hopelessness and despair but also could have life-threatening consequences for the future.

Baby Steps Only

Gently, ever so gently, the task of the advocate, the practitioner, is to offer enough information, enough insight, and enough options to empower the client to think, imagine, and possibly act. Most importantly, then, the practitioner should hope for everything but expect nothing and be thrilled if and when, in the gentle nonjudgmental, interactional space, the battered woman decides to act. Recognition that movement comes incrementally, that denial is fierce, and that immediate action is rare are the only assumptions practitioners should make. Most important, though, the practitioner should realize that, in most cases, the point is not to eradicate violence as we know it by ending a relationship now but rather to enable a battered woman to realize that it is she alone who can understand the violence in her life and how she wants to respond to it.

A FEELING-DRIVEN APPROACH

Three emotive or affective theoretical principles, including shared suffering, transference/countertransference, and when and when not to share, underlie how I would suggest interacting with the battered woman using an empowerment approach (Box 6.2).

BOX 6.2   A FEELING-DRIVEN APPROACH

Shared Suffering
- Empathy through your own suffering.

Transference/Countertransference
- Vigilance in monitoring the transference and countertransference keeps the therapeutic relationship clean.

When & When Not to Share
- Reveal your own vulnerabilities.
- Expose your own weaknesses.
- Know when and when not to tell your story.

Shared Suffering

Empathy, derived from an openness to suffering, is most detectable in people whose early childhood experiences were characterized by some suffering, particularly as it relates to separation and attachment (Henderson, 1988). This initial suffering, according to Henderson (1988), determines one's ability to "empathize" later in life. Empathic responses may often be hindered when inhibited by external conditions. Traditional clinical training, for example, can cause one's empathy to be "foreclosed" or sent "underground" (Henderson, 1988). In its alienation, it can also rekindle a lost lifetime of suffering. Suffice it to say that empathy is relevant to an affective empowerment method insofar as it begins with suffering. Suffering, however, whether ours or our clients', is a unitary process until one suffering being meets another in the space in between them. This geography suggests that the practitioner meet the battered woman, not in the usual distance created by the CSW, advocate, or clinician, but rather through the deliberate (conscious or unconscious) expression of shared suffering revealed in the space created between the battered woman and the practitioner.

Transference and Countertransference

So how do we share our suffering? This is best explored in the context of two psychoanalytic principles: transference and countertransference. Transference refers to the experience of the patient in psychoanalysis. When the patient meets the therapist, she is encouraged to see the therapist as someone with whom she has emotional conflict or attachment (Borch-Jacobsen, 1991). I suggest that we be aware that transference will occur in our interactions with battered women. Clients naturally engage in transference with their therapists and search for and even create emotional spaces in which they transfer feelings for others onto the clinician. Relying on this reality, it becomes possible for any intimate meetings such as those between practitioner and battered woman to create the possibility of an affective base on which to connect.

Countertransference, on the other hand, exposes the fact that the therapist too is influenced by the patient (Jung, 1966). Hence, countertransference encourages us to realize that every interaction with a client could evoke a history that might, and probably would, directly affect how the practitioner reacts to the client's biography. Indeed, the principles of transference and countertransference provide the possibility that such an emotional connection can occur. The question is how.

Demeanor, body language, facial expressions, and conversational techniques all affect how we communicate with others. A softness, a comfort with yourself, a nonjudgmental pose contribute to creating a welcoming space, as does a recognition of the barriers when meeting someone different from yourself. None of these postures are possible without a desire and capacity to self-reflect, however. Knowing yourself well enough, what interactions "push your buttons," and the transference and countertransference issues likely to be evoked by your own biography are necessary components for creating a space for exploring the shared suffering. Self-reflection then is necessary to help understand and acknowledge the reality that transference and countertransference are operating and hence can be more fully explored.

When and When Not to Share

Although transference, countertransference, and self-reflection provide the spaciousness and the possibility for emotional meetings, they do not provide a blueprint for making those interactions a success. First and foremost, it is helpful to remember that emotional interactions, like almost all meetings, begin with one's assessment of one's apparent differences (including race, class, education, etc.). On initial contact, those differences are either reinforced or reified through judgment or rejection, or they are overcome through other means. Affirming a client's anger at the system or sharing a history of domestic violence or child abuse, all the while feeling together, helps transform these experiences into connection. Second, engagement can only be achieved if practitioners reveal their own vulnerabilities and expose their strength within them. They can do so with a glance or a story, a touch, or a word. For the client to feel, the practitioner must also feel. To feel, practitioners should know where, when, and how they hurt. Finally, once the practitioner's feelings are exposed, remember it is in order that dialogue can and should lead wherever. Never assume what the client is feeling. Navigate together and directly.

It is the silence that oppresses, the unspoken subtext that denies. Go the conversational distance to know for sure that you have met the wall that separates you and the battered woman, do not stop before.

EMPOWERMENT AND AFFECTIVE STRATEGIES FOR MEETINGS WITH BATTERED MOTHERS: MAKING THE CONNECTION

> I just thought that . . . in order to be a battered woman you had to be really battered. I mean OK, I had a couple of bad incidents, but mostly it was pretty minor . . . violence.
>
> Anonymous
> (Mahoney, 1991, pp. 16–17)

Translating an Affective Advocacy approach for use with a battered mother can be a challenging undertaking. Being aware of the transference and countertransference is difficult enough. Challenging CSWs, advocates, and clinicians to explore their own histories of violence can present complex considerations that need to be explored. First, however, it is useful to present a *strategy* for working with battered women using the Affective Advocacy approach. In exploring this strategy, it is helpful to reflect back on the critiques presented of the criminal justice, child welfare, and health care systems and to ask the following questions. Are these systems responsive to the needs of battered mothers? How might you encounter battered women differently so that interactions in these systems could be more empowering? This section synthesizes what we have learned so far about connection and presents a specific method for engaging the battered woman. This guide, together with the approaches and applications presented in chapters 8, 9, and 10, will help you assess whether prevailing interventions facilitate or impede empowering interventions.

WHAT'S GOING TO HAPPEN?

An affective method in working with battered mothers always begins by explaining what is going to happen and, in doing so, connecting with the battered woman. Who the practitioner is, what agency she represents, and what reporting requirements she has are all necessary components of an affective interview. It is critical that the battered woman not feel manipulated by the practitioner; being honest is necessary to ensure a model of relationship that can be distinguished from the dynamic that has evolved with the batterer. Should the battered woman have to choose between two "dishonest" people, chances are she will choose the one with which she is most familiar—the batterer.

Depending on the kind of practitioner doing the intervention, it is always important to let her know that her child has been or might be interviewed because the well-being of both the mother and the child is necessary when doing a comprehensive assessment. If you are representing CPS, it is useful for the practitioner to explain that their primary purpose is not to take her child away but that it is a possibility.

It is always helpful to convey that a specific strategy for working with (battered) women helps the practitioner better understand their relationship and that the structural, emotional, cultural, racial, and financial problems they face must be part of the solution. It is useful to avoid referring to the victim as a battered woman, because she might not identify with being abused. It is also helpful especially in the early stages of the interaction, to name the violence as she names it—a slap, a sock—so as to avoid alienating a woman who does not yet recognize these acts as violent.

BE HONEST AND LISTEN TO HER

It is critical that the practitioner listen to the battered woman's story and that she do so after creating a space of honesty that is facilitated through modeling. Tell the battered woman what the practitioner's institutional constraints are and that she is there to listen if the survivor wants to talk. The practitioner may be the first person who has ever asked her about the violence in her life, or the advocate may be the 30th. Each time, however, the battered woman is given the opportunity to hear herself tell her own story, to describe her experience. Each rendition gets her closer to breaking through the layers of denial and shame that keep her emotionally tied to the abusive relationship.

SHARE YOU WITH HER

In the beginning stages of the interview, I suggest that the practitioner find a way of enhancing a connection with the battered woman by sharing a bit of her own history (if appropriate) or by telling her why the practitioner does this work. This introduction should be brief so that the battered woman feels that she has the space to tell her story and that she isn't there to hear your story. Finding this place of connection marks the beginning point for the affective relationship and enables you to cross racial, cultural, class, or even gender barriers that might otherwise be resisted.

VALIDATE HER

It is always useful for the practitioner to clarify, close to the beginning of the interview, that she is not going to ask her to leave the abusive relationship permanently. The practitioner may also suggest that she hopes that together you will develop short- and long-term strategies to ensure that she and her children are safe and that this may involve leaving the batterer at least temporarily.

Especially in the beginning of an interview, it is important to give validating messages: "The cultural pressures must be hard" or "I know he is good to the children." Be specific to her own cultural and socioeconomic background. In addition, it is critically important that the practitioner use the batterer's first name when eliciting information. Ask about both the positive as well as the negative aspects of the relationship in order to enable her to feel that she can share all dimensions of her relationship. If the practitioner presents, in any way, that she is judgmental of him or against him, she is likely to feel she needs to defend him or her reasons for staying with him.

It is critical that the practitioner elicit from her what she has done to protect herself and her child. It is likely that she has taken a number of steps that will reveal just how empowered she is; it is always useful to mark these steps and to acknowledge them in her presence. Chances are she has not seen the action she has taken thus far as evidence of her strength.

Use Direct and Indirect Questions

Direct and indirect questions are useful techniques, depending on the battered woman the practitioner is interviewing. Using an indirect approach, you might ask "What happens when you fight?" Using a more direct approach, you might ask "Have you ever been physically, emotionally, or sexually injured by your partner?" In the most direct approach, the practitioner asks "Is there hitting, intimidation, and so on between you and your partner?" It is also helpful to make comments on her affect and on the injuries observed; don't collude with the batterer through silence.

Team Approach

It is always helpful to explain that you want to establish a team relationship with her, and that together you can develop a plan that will ensure her safety and the safety of her child. Reinforce that the system can *help* protect her and her children, especially if she can clearly communicate how and when intervention is necessary and appropriate.

Monitor Countertransference

Blaming the battered woman for the actions of the abuser can be so damaging that it can alienate the survivor from seeking any further assistance. This is where the practitioner's countertransference might be operating. There is some evidence that people working in the helping professions are more likely to have a history of victimization (Jackson & Nuttall, 1996). CSWs, advocates, and clinicians who have not examined their histories of abuse are likely to impose their own judgments on battered mothers. It is useful for the practitioner to ask herself: Am I connecting with this battered woman? Have I considered her strengths? Have I provided all possible resources to this woman to facilitate her strength?

One way to monitor countertransference is to consider where the practitioner falls on the Continuum of Intervention (Figure 6.1). What I have found in training CSWs, advocates, and clinicians is

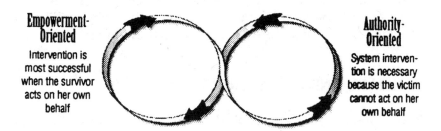

**Empowerment-
Oriented**

Intervention is
most successful
when the survivor
acts on her own
behalf

**Authority-
Oriented**

System interven-
tion is necessary
because the victim
cannot act on her
own behalf

FIGURE 6.1   Continuum of intervention.

that they bring their own assumptions about intervention to their domestic violence work. Some practitioners are comfortable allowing battered women to make their own decisions; in general, they trust them to act, over a period of time, in their own and their children's best interest. This may be called an "Empowerment-oriented" practitioner. This kind of practitioner realizes that a battered woman may need some time to build up strength and is comfortable giving it to her, even when this may pose some risk to the battered woman's physical safety. Empowerment-oriented practitioners believe that the only way to end violence, or ameliorate its effects, is to help the battered woman do her own internal work. An obvious influence on this process is whether the battered woman will ever be willing or ready to act, a topic that is discussed in more detail in chapter 7. If the battered woman will never be willing to act on her own behalf, it may affect the empowerment-oriented practitioner's inclination to let her move at her own pace.

"Authority-Oriented" practitioners, however, may be unwilling to let the battered woman take the time she needs to decide her own fate. This kind of practitioner would tend to see most battered women as weak, as incapable of acting on their own behalf, requiring a more paternalistic approach. Authority-oriented practitioners intervene earlier and feel that their decisive action is necessary to protect the battered woman.

Most practitioners fall somewhere along the continuum, often shifting their propensity toward authority or empowerment, depending on the battered mother and the practitioner's assessment of her ability to act. Knowing where they fall on the continuum helps practitioners understand more fully what they are likely to bring in terms of countertransference to these interactions.

SUMMARY AND REFLECTIONS

Practitioners working in criminal justice, public child welfare, and health care settings often maintain a policy of disconnection—they either ignore or overlook the battered woman's particular experience or they blame the battered woman for her conundrum (Callahan, 1993). Recognizing the battered woman's strengths and relying on an Affective Advocacy method that is committed to engaging with the survivor, CSWs, advocates, and clinicians can begin to forge a new relationship with a battered woman and her child, one that recognizes the unique and particular challenges each family faces.

In the next chapter, I present a practitioner's strategy for working in systems that moves beyond the connection described in this chapter. In chapters 8, 9, and 10, I merge the two complimentary methods and present case studies that illustrate how these principles can be applied.

QUESTIONS

- ❏ How is Affective Advocacy different from other advocacy and clinical approaches you use?
- ❏ In applying Affective Advocacy to battered women, what principles seem most critical to achieving the necessary connection with her?
- ❏ When you visualize working with a battered woman, what would be your first few words?
- ❏ How would you bridge the apparent divide between the two of you?

❐ How would you address, in a sensitive manner, her emotional or cultural commitment to the batterer? Or her commitment to her children in the face of the violence?

❐ In general, where do you fall on the Continuum of Intervention? What circumstances are likely to influence movement on the continuum in one direction or another?

CHAPTER 7

Systems Strategies for Working with Battered Mothers and Their Children

The strategies presented here build on the principles of engagement and connection set forth in the previous chapter. It cannot be emphasized enough that engaging a battered woman, as with any other client, is the CSWs, clinicians, or advocate's greatest and most critical challenge. Without connection, the interaction is all too often plagued with resistance, hesitation, or even dishonesty.

The specific strategy presented in this chapter is applicable to any systems-oriented interview with a battered mother, whether one is working as a child advocate investigating a protective services allegation, a nurse or physician in a hospital emergency room, a social worker in a shelter, or a law enforcement officer in the criminal justice system. These systems strategies, combined with the Affective Advocacy approach described in the previous chapter, will help ensure both an honest and forthright connection with the battered woman and a systematic technique for assessing the threat posed by any given situation.

Any method of assessment is rendered even more significant when children are involved. Under these circumstances, the battered woman is acting, or not acting, not only on her own behalf but also on behalf of her dependent children. Interactions under these circumstances become even more critical, more often than not evoking mandated child abuse reporting requirements as well as our internal desire to protect the "innocents." What is helpful to remember in interactions with battered mothers is that a practitioner's connection can be enhanced if they can share in the concern for a battered woman's children.

Once the practitioner has engaged the battered mother and relied on some of the specific techniques outlined in chapter 6 to connect with her, several important tasks must be accomplished. First, the practitioner must assess the history and pattern of violence. Were there physical injuries to the battered woman or to the children? What methods were used to inflict them? What kinds of violence, in general, does she endure? What threats does the batterer make? What means or weapons does he have?

Second, the practitioner must assess this battered woman, especially in light of stereotypes about victims of domestic violence: Will she take baby steps? How does she view why she stays in the abusive relationship? Where does she stand in relation to the violence he inflicts on her?

Finally, the practitioner must assess the threat the batterer poses to the battered woman and her children's safety. To what profile does he most closely conform? What does the future seem to hold?

The institutional context of this interview will affect what specific information the CSW, clinician, or advocate will disclose to the battered woman. If the practitioner is a CPS worker or working in a hospital or medical setting in a state that requires that she report suspected abuse, the practitioner's honesty about her mandated reporter status is crucial to ensure and maintain connection. If the practitioner is a victim advocate in a prosecutor's office, she should disclose that whatever the victim tells her will be revealed to the prosecutor assigned to her case. These issues are discussed in more detail in the chapters that follow, working through the case studies in criminal justice, child protection, and health.

ASSESS THE HISTORY AND PATTERN OF VIOLENCE

Sensitivity and honesty should underlie a practitioner's effort to find out what happened. Usually, some event precipitates her contact with a battered woman. How does the survivor view what happened? Listen and don't interrupt, empathize, share when appropriate. Stay attuned to the transference and countertransference issues. If the victim describes ways she remained strong or protected her children, give her positive feedback. Identify and highlight those strengths. Once the practitioner has the gist of what happened, it is necessary to determine the severity of the incident.

It is important that the practitioner and the battered woman work together to determine her overall level of danger. The Assessment of Threat described later will assist in this effort. In the meantime, however, it is useful to identify the kind of abuse the battered woman has experienced in this relationship. Is the abuse mostly verbal, verbal and physical, verbal and sexual? Locating the kinds of abuse she has tolerated on the Violence Tree (Figure 7.1) can help her understand the extent and seriousness of the abuse and can help the practitioner determine what kind of action might be necessary. It also allows the advocate to discuss violence in its larger context, such as how it is glamorized on television or in movies or tolerated in the community. Connecting the abuses through the use of the Violence Tree can highlight the interrelatedness, significance, and origins of the behaviors.

How the interview proceeds depends on the practitioner's assessment of the incident and of the entire history of abuse. For example, this particular precipitating incident may have involved only emotional abuse and wouldn't normally evoke any action by law enforcement or CPS. The history may reveal a pattern of other abuses, however, making the current incident of emotional abuse evidence of something more dangerous. If the practitioner is satisfied that the abuse is not life threatening in the eyes of the law, that is, that it would not warrant removing the children or making a report to law enforcement, the interview may end here. I would suggest, however, that no interview with a battered woman should end without the development of a Personal Safety Plan (Appendix II), which includes referrals to relevant agencies.

Interviewing the children and other parties to the violence complaint may help to elucidate what is actually occurring in the family. If the practitioner decides that the event warrants a longer conversation with the battered mother, the next step would be

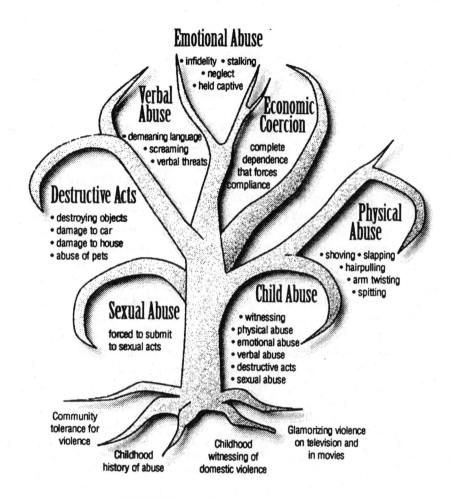

Emotional Abuse
• infidelity • stalking
• neglect
• held captive

Verbal Abuse
• demeaning language
• screaming
• verbal threats

Economic Coercion
complete
dependence
that forces
compliance

Destructive Acts
• destroying objects
• damage to car
• damage to house
• abuse of pets

Physical Abuse
• shoving • slapping
• hairpulling
• arm twisting
• spitting

Sexual Abuse
forced to submit
to sexual acts

Child Abuse
• witnessing
• physical abuse
• emotional abuse
• verbal abuse
• destructive acts
• sexual abuse

Community
tolerance for
violence

Childhood
history of abuse

Childhood
witnessing of
domestic violence

Glamorizing violence
on television and
in movies

FIGURE 7.1   The violence tree.

to assess the battered woman's vulnerabilities and her ability to act. Any assessment strategy relies on the practitioners capacity to evaluate an individual battered woman, independent of preconceived assumptions about the abuse and her reaction to it. A critical analysis of how battered women have been characterized will help illuminate how CSWs, clinicians, and advocates may stereotype and pre-judge them.

ASSESSING *THIS* BATTERED WOMAN

SOCIAL CONSTRUCTIONS OF BATTERED WOMEN

Feminist efforts to capture a battered woman's essential character have profoundly influenced our tendency to stereotype them. Lenore Walker's *The Battered Woman* (1979), and the corresponding development of a syndrome (Walker, 1984), has medicalized the experience of woman abuse and, hence further entrenched it in patriarchal roots while alienating it from its feminist tradition. Television footage of Hedda Nussbaum's badly beaten body and photos from Nicole Brown Simpson's murder trial, images embraced by feminists as indications of violence against women, haunt our psyches while functioning to repress the ways in which violence permeates our own lives.

A typical battered woman isn't us. They can't "fight back," they can't leave their abusive lover, and they can't resist his apologies. The typical battered woman is so entrenched in a cycle of violence that she experiences a "learned helplessness." The learned helplessness theory posits that after living with domestic violence, women do not view their behavior or actions as having any consequence. As a result of this perceived powerlessness to predict or control the violence, women become demoralized and paralyzed by fear. They are unable to take the steps necessary to improve their situation (Walker, 1984). Walker (1984) also notes the tendency of battered women to believe in the omnipotence, or strength, of their mates and thus to feel that any attempt to resist them is hopeless.

Walker (1984) draws on the work of Martin Seligman, who with his colleagues discovered that when dogs were repeatedly and noncontingently shocked, they became unable to escape even though a way to escape was possible and readily apparent to animals that had not undergone helplessness training. Seligman related their inability to escape to a kind of human depression.

Although at some level I don't question the assumption that leaving the abuse is more difficult when it is administered unpredictably (often a feature of violent relationships), what is troubling is our *assumption* that her staying is indicative of some underlying pathology unique to her. A reflection on the assumptions we have made about battered women, mapped in some detail below, would be incomplete without an exploration first of the reasons why feminists have been forced to essentialize women trapped in intimate abuse.

Some analysts suggest that as many as 50% of women will be battered at some time in their lives (Walker, 1984; Littleton, 1989). One in five females victimized by their spouse or ex-spouse reported that they had been a victim of a series of three or more assaults in the last 6 months (U.S. DOJ, 1994b). Verbal abuse, a feature of nearly all intimate relationships and considered by some to be more devastating than physical or even sexual abuse (Mahoney, 1991), is familiar to nearly all men and women who engage in the intimacy demanded of a partner.

The abuse doesn't stop there. In a 1985 national survey, Gelles and Straus (1987) reported that 10.7% of parents had been severely violent (including kicking, biting, hitting with fist, etc.) toward their children. Straus (1991) has reported based on the classic study of *Patterns of Child Rearing* (Sears, MacCoby, & Levin, 1957) that 99% of parents in the United States have, at some point in their children's lives, used physical punishment. Again, this does not account for the emotional abuse family members inflict on each other.

Not only are we quick to judge others on actions we ourselves inflict or endure, but we are also ready to repress the legal, religious, and cultural history that is responsible for fostering intimate abuse in the first place. A little more than a century ago, American men were legally permitted to beat their wives. It was not until 1891 that a British court in *Reg. v. Jackson* (1891) concluded that "the moral sense of the community revolts at the idea that the husband may inflict personal chastisement upon his wife, even for the most outrageous conduct." The transition from court decision to practice was very slow in coming. Thirty years ago, injunctions were only available to "married" women. Indeed, injunctions had no effect: No criminal penalties against a spouse ensued from violation of a restraining order (Zorza, 1992). Victims in some jurisdictions were required to pay prosecutors a fee to prosecute their batterer (Zorza & Woods, 1994).

In Christian texts, a hierarchical family structure was embraced and celebrated. The scriptures taught such principles as "wives be in subjection to your own husbands" (Holy Bible, I Peter, 3:1);

"the head of the woman is the man" (Holy Bible, I Corinthians, 11:3); "but I suffer not a woman to teach or to usurp authority of man, but to be in silence" (Holy Bible, I Timothy, 2:12); and "[women] are commanded to be under obedience" (Holy Bible, I Corinthians 14:34). Similarly, in chapter 2, we explored in some depth how race and culture might affect battered women's construction of the violence inflicted on them.

So who is the essentialized battered woman and how do these images contribute to how we assess her in professional interactions? The Battered-Woman Syndrome and the use of it as a defense for the charge of murder is one dominant construction of a battered woman. The Battered-Woman Syndrome defense provides, in a homicide case, a legal justification designed to exonerate a defendant (wife) who kills someone (her husband) when the defendant is confronted with an imminent threat of death or serious bodily harm. The law of self-defense requires that the defendant act reasonably, that is, that the defendant respond proportionally to the threat and that the threatened harm be imminent. Lethal force is permitted if and only if there is threat with force designed to produce death or serious bodily harm.

The problem with the efforts of feminists and battered women advocates to define a Battered-Woman Syndrome is that it is a medicalized or psychiatric definition, one that can only be supported by experts such as psychiatrists or psychologists and one that reveals a psychodynamic reason a battered woman stayed in the abusive relationship. For example, in 1989, Robin Elson was acquitted of murder using the defense based on the Battered-Woman Syndrome (Fiore, 1989). During their 6½-year marriage, Robin Elson's husband Jack told her what to wear, determined what list of chores she would do, restricted the nail polish she would wear, and decided what she would cook for dinner. He told her what groceries she could buy and checked the change against the receipt she was required to bring home. He beat her, at first sporadically and then more regularly. She would be beaten because the food wasn't cooked well or the toast was overdone. On December 17, 1988, Robin Elson murdered her husband with his 9-mm rifle while he was asleep in his chair.

"It's like the scientific experiment where they shocked dogs to the point that even when the gate was left open, the dogs never left" said her defense attorney Lynda Vitale. "The dogs saw the open gate not as a means of escape, but an invitation to more punishment" (Fiore, 1989). The prosecutor, on the other hand, is reported as saying: "She could have left the state, gone to a neighbor, called the police. He was asleep when the first shot was fired. He wasn't posing any threat. And when we start allowing citizens to take matters into their own hands, we are back to the law of the jungle" (Fiore, 1989).

All the press and the related legal maneuvering on behalf of women who have killed their batterers have had an effect on how we view battered women more generally. The only way to win these cases is to think of them unidimensionally, or in the extreme. Defenders of the Battered-Woman Syndrome must argue that the battered woman couldn't leave the abusive relationship, that she was stuck there, that she was emotionally and physically prevented from escaping. Defense attorneys portray the image of a battered woman as "helpless" or, like Zeligman's dogs, a trapped child. Similarly, she is seen as dependent, with low self-esteem, seeing murder as her only way out. Of course she is portrayed as "in denial," unable to cope with the violence until she had no choice but to kill. Prosecutors, on the other hand, portray her as weak (they should have or could have left if they really were of good character) or manipulative, or both. We begin to conjure up the image of a battered woman that is in agreement with our own denial—battered women should find the strength and will to leave.

The research on battered women suggests that they are not weak, that they are determined, and that they pursue strategies that will protect them from their abusers (Bowker, 1993; Gondolf, 1988a; Valle Ferrer, 1998). Three factors influence a battered woman's ability to demonstrate her strength: severe and prolonged abuse, her resources, and the belief that such efforts will be successful (Bowker, 1983). Consistent with these factors is the finding that when the violence first begins, women hope that they will be able to prevent it from happening without outside intervention (Reidy & Von Korff, 1991).

Other relevant factors that determine battered women's freedom are income, other than the abusive partner's, and other financial and child-related resources. When women have outside employment, education, or the possibility of housing, child care, transportation, and social support, they are more likely to seek help. Hofeller (1982) found that 58% of her sample stayed with their assailants because they felt they could not support themselves and their children. In addition, Okun (1986), who studied shelter residents, found that there was a direct correlation between the woman's income, in relation to her partner's, and the likelihood of her eventually terminating the relationship.

The research conducted reveals that battered women repeatedly look to the outside for help (Hamilton & Coates, 1993). The studies show that 80% of victims take actions of self-protection (40% take actions by protecting themselves verbally and 40% take actions by protecting themselves physically) (U.S. DOJ, 1994b). Indeed, battered women resist their batterers at two times the rate of other female victims, including demanding that he stop, seeking help and support, manipulating the environment to ensure their safety, and making attempts to leave (U.S. DOJ, 1994b). Assessing a battered woman in light of these strengths and tensions can help practitioners evaluate more realistically the survivor's capacity to act.

THE SURVIVOR'S ACTIONS AND VULNERABILITIES ASSESSMENT

The Survivor's Actions and Vulnerabilities Assessment helps practitioners determine first an individual battered woman's willingness to take action—action that might take the form of a protective order, testimony against the batterer in court, or going to a shelter—and second her particular vulnerabilities in relation to the Heart of Intimate Abuse (see Figure 2.3). Doing a Survivor's Actions and Vulnerabilities Assessment requires that the practitioner employ the Affective Advocacy Approach described in chapter 6 and that the CSW, advocate, or clinician be vigilant of her own countertransferences and preconceived assumptions that she may hold about battered women.

Some women, once abused or once they realize they are abused, are ready and willing to leave the abusive relationship. If they are ready to leave, whether or not they have children, a Personal Safety Plan is necessary given that her danger level increases once the battered woman takes this action (Mahoney, 1991). A Personal Safety Plan usually involves doing a Social Support Inventory and assessing and evaluating the strength of the battered woman's system of support.

One can never be absolutely sure that a battered woman will leave an abusive situation for good. The underlying assumption is that physically and legally terminating the relationship is the only guarantee that the violence will actually stop (Bowker, 1983; NiCarthy, 1987). Of course, it is critical to remember that the violence often escalates when separation, or a threatened separation, occurs (Mahoney, 1991). When the battered woman is ready to leave, she will express little doubt or reservation—you will know.

The figures vary on how many women return to their batterer. In a study by LaBell (1979), 74.2% of battered women staying in a shelter had separated at least one time, and some had separated more than 10 times. Johnson, Crowley, and Sigler (1992) found that about one third of battered women staying in shelters return to their partners. This finding was confirmed by Gondolf (1988a), who found that 24% of shelter women had planned on returning, with 7% undecided. Snyder and Scheer (1981) found a 33% return rate. The practitioner should tailor her questions and interventions to this battered woman's expression of certainty or doubt.

Locating a battered woman on the Action and Vulnerabilities Continuum (see Figure 7.2) helps the CSW, clinician, or advocate become clearer in their assessment of her willingness to respond to their suggestions. If she has decided to leave the abusive relationship and the practitioner feels she is settled in that decision, she would mark her as "Settled" on the Continuum. If the practitioner is unsure whether the survivor's expressions of resolve are genuine, she may want to postpone completing the Continuum and proceed to the second part of the Actions and Vulnerabilities Assessment, which locates what ties the survivor has to the relationship based on her review of the Heart of Intimate Abuse.

In this part of the assessment, the practitioner would determine which, if any, of the five factors presented on the left side of the Heart of Intimate Abuse are this battered woman's vulnerabilities. Displaying the Heart of Intimate Abuse to the survivor helps

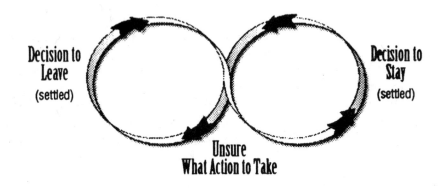

Decision to Leave (settled)

Decision to Stay (settled)

Unsure What Action to Take

FIGURE 7.2   Survivor's actions and vulnerabilities continuum.

facilitate this dialogue. What role does love play in her decision to act or not to act? Does she feel pressured to stay or leave because of the children? What racial, cultural, or religious pressure does she feel? Is she afraid to leave? Is she dependent on the batterer financially?

The answers to these questions provide the practitioner with important information. First, it can help the CSW, clinician, or advocate assess what vulnerabilities are likely to keep her tied to this relationship. If she is staying because her religion forbids divorce, this tells the practitioner first that she may be unwilling to take the "drastic" step of separation and second that it might be helpful to try and deconstruct the role religion plays in her life. If she is staying because she believes her children should have a father, the practitioner might want to focus their conversation on the dangers of witnessing domestic violence and the intergenerational transmission of abuse.

This part of the interview might focus on such questions as "Why do you think you have stayed with your husband (use his name) even though it has been so difficult at times?" Or, the practitioner may want to ask her what her breaking point is in relation to the religious or financial stronghold in her life? The practitioner may want to ask her if she would be less inclined to stay because of religious reasons if he threatened her with a weapon? If her priest or rabbi said it was okay to leave, would that help? Would it matter if her partner started hitting the children? If the battered woman seems clear about leaving but the practitioner senses some hesitation, she may want to "test" the survivor's resolve (for the battered woman's own benefit) by asking what event helped her decide that enough was enough. It is also helpful, when interviewing a battered woman and trying to understand her vulnerabilities and propensity toward action, to explore with her the nature of this batterer's violent dynamic.

For this kind of conversation, it is again useful to refer to the right side of the Heart of Intimate Abuse, which attempts to put into her words what factors influence the batterer's behavior. Some or all of these factors may be operating, including his "love" for the survivor; his love for the children; his religion, culture, or race; his power and control issues, including his feeling that he lacks both power and control; as well as his use of abuse to instill fear. To explore with a battered woman what factors seem to drive a batterer's violence can help illuminate for the practitioner both how the battered woman sees his behavior and what psychological and other techniques the batterer uses to keep her in his control.

Given that we know that leaving is often a process, the practitioner is probably working with a battered woman who will be placed at the "unsure what action to take" point on the Survivor's Actions and Vulnerabilities Continuum. It is critical to remember that battered women are taking steps all the time to protect themselves and their children, so her unwillingness to act more dramatically, that is, to leave either temporarily or permanently on this occasion, may not necessarily indicate her indifference or inaction.

Some women the practitioner will meet and work with will clearly have made the "decision to stay" on the Survivor's Actions and Vulnerabilities Continuum and are settled on that decision. They have resigned themselves to staying in the abusive relationship and there is little or nothing anyone can do about it. These women are far from "hopeless," because by working with them there is always the possibility that they might come to imagine a different kind of life. You should, at least, proceed knowing that whatever interventions you design must consider her propensity to stay. Respecting her statements about staying and not judging her for her decision will be the beginning point for the possibility of connection and therefore helping her to design strategies that help her address the violence she has endured and is likely to experience again.

ASSESSING *THIS* BATTERER AND HIS THREAT

SOCIAL CONSTRUCTIONS OF BATTERERS

Evidence reveals that not all batterers are the same. Edward Gondolf (1985), a leader in the field of domestic violence, advocated more than 10 years ago for a research agenda that distinguished batterer types. He was particularly interested in finding ways to differentiate the angry batterer from the oppressive batterer. He describes two conflicting approaches to understanding the men who batter women. The first approach, that of the empiricists, suggests that anger is the trigger of men's violence. The second approach, that of the feminists, asserts that men are predisposed to oppressing or dominating women, which they call "gender terrorism" (Gondolf, 1985, p. 313). Feminists criticize the empiricists for their "gender neutrality," Gondolf (1985) argues, a neutrality that implies that women are as much to blame for the violence aimed against them as the men who commit it.

The points of this debate are significant because they have implications for how interventions, services, and benefits are delivered to battered women and to batterers. If interventions implicitly rely on feminist principles, for example, police, prosecutors, and shelter workers will incorporate patriarchical notions into their response. Hence, the police using a feminist approach would mandate arrest, irrespective of a batterer's profile or type. If the police, on the other hand, take the empiricists' approach, they might be more interested in other factors associated with this batterer's behavior. Indeed, they may even consider whether arresting this batterer might make him more abusive toward his partner, given the findings of the arrest studies described in chapter 3 that suggest that violence can be exacerbated when the arrest involves a "bad risk" perpetrator.

Knowing the complex reasons why men batter helps us learn how to assess them and to intervene in the battering relationship. Indeed, the effective treatment of batterers often depends on characterizing them one way or another (for a discussion of treatment, see chapter 9). Anger psychologists argue, and have empirical evidence to support their contention, that the reason men batter is because they are angry. More specifically, psychological research supports the view that emotive or cognitive reasons explain the internal process of the man who batters. Berkowitz, for example (1983), using a frustration-aggression analysis, reports that violence is a means to release the emotion of anger or to remove the source of the anger. In other words, according to Berkowitz, anger causes some "unpleasantness" that the individual must remove. Here, the response is more impulsive.

Dutton (1995), on the other hand, supports the theory that the batterer perceives certain events to be threatening and the violence becomes a way of expressing his insecurity. Attachment, according to Dutton (1995), is key; abandonment of that intimacy evokes the greatest anger reaction. These views support the theory that battering can be controlled by helping men control their anger and by identifying situations that trigger their alienation.

Feminists, on the other hand, argue that it is the exploitation of women, and their accompanying oppression in intimate relationships, that is responsible for the abuse inflicted on them. The man does not beat his wife to release anger, or to relieve it, but rather to exert his power and control. Many studies support this contention (Goode, 1971; Dobash & Dobash, 1979; Straus, Gelles, Steinmetz, 1980; Yllö, 1983; Bowker, 1983; Finkelhor, 1983). Their argument is that abuse occurs more frequently in relationships between men and women in which there are differentials in power, education, or status. Using this theory, women may attempt to escape from the violence, or hope that it will stop, but no matter what they do, the violence will continue. As Gondolf (1985) so aptly summarizes, they become "trapped by society's lack of response" (p. 316).

Feminist literature argues that men are socialized to be in control, as much as they are taught to express anger and violence (Goldberg, 1984; Kurz, 1993; Pleck, 1981). Sattel (1976) has argued that the anger and violence are the means to that power and control. The "excessive masculinity" found in batterers, therefore, proves this theory (Barnett & Miller, 1984; Neidig, Collins, & Friedman, 1984). This excessive masculinity and even rigidity is directed against women in particular. Assuming that this feminist interpretation is embraced, which it largely has been, batterer intervention will not only attempt to control angry outbursts but also address the sexism that underlies the violence (For an analysis of feminist treatment approaches to battering, see chapter 9.)

A subsequent analysis of batterers by Gondolf (1988a), and other research on batterers suggests, as with battered women, that there is no stereotypical batterer (Hamberger & Hastings, 1986). In a study by Saunders (1992), attitudinal and behavior measures were employed in a preliminary clustering of 182 men entering treatment. Depression, anger toward a partner, and attitudes toward women were measured, along with generalized violence, severity of abuse against women, and alcohol use. Men were clustered into three categories. One cluster (N = 31) was characterized as "emotionally volatile," high on anger, having depression and jealousy scores, with moderate levels of violence and alcohol use. The batterers in the second cluster (N = 48), which he called "generally violent," were more likely to score low on the anger and depression measures and were the most likely to be violent outside the home. The third cluster (N = 86), or the "over-controlled" type, was composed largely of batterers who suppressed their feelings and confined their violence to the home; they scored low on anger and depression measures and highest on a scale for social desirability.

Other studies (Fagan, Stewart, & Hansen, 1983; Snyder & Fruchtman, 1981; Walker, 1984) analyzed data from battered women. Their results varied: Walker (1984) and Fagan et al. (1983) found a positive correlation between violence toward strangers and the severity of woman battering. Snyder and Fruchtman (1981) divided battering relationships into five categories: sporadic violence within a fairly stable relationship, explosive relationships with injurious violence, severe unrelenting violence, extensive child abuse with infrequent wife abuse, and long histories of violence in the family of origin to the present. Shields and Hanneke (1983) interviewed 84 husbands and found that the "generally violent" men, the highest category of husbands, were more likely to have committed the most serious violence and to have more heavily abused alcohol and drugs.

Gondolf's (1988b) research tries to develop a behavioral typology of batterers based on the self-report of battered women admitted to the 50 Texas shelters during an 18-month period from 1984 to 1985 (N = 6,000). His findings are significant for debunking myths about batterers. When he cross-tabulated severity of violence with background variables such as race, education, income, and so on, he did not find that the most severely abusive and antisocial clusters of batterers were low-income or minority men. His results produced three clusters of batterer: the sociopathic batterer, the antisocial batterer, and the "typical" batterer.

The sociopathic batterer is extremely abusive, and probably sexually abusive, to his wife and children. His abuse would very likely include the use of a weapon. Gondolf (1988b) found that this batterer's response to abuse is extremely diverse and unpredictable; it includes blame, threats, and sexual demands. What is distinct about this batterer is that he is likely to be arrested for other violent crimes or for property- or alcohol-related crimes. The victims usually seek help in these cases by calling the police and obtaining legal assistance.

The antisocial batterer is also extremely physically and verbally abusive. Although his violence touches other parts of his life, he is less likely to have been arrested than the sociopathic batterer. His victim has also contacted the police for help.

The typical batterer conforms more to the prevailing clinical profiles of batterers. He is less likely to use a weapon and his abuse, in general, is less extensive and less severe than that of the antisocial batterer. This batterer is more likely to follow the cycle of violence and hence will apologize after abusive incidents. This batterer's general violence and arrests are much lower than the other batterers and therefore his victim is more likely to return to him.

Holtzworth-Munroe and Stuart (1994) used a different batterer typology formula and suggest three other categories of batterers: men who are highly dominating and narcissistic; men who tend to be impulsive, dependent on their partners, and highly jealous, controlling, and reactive; and men who are generally antisocial, negativistic, and defiant and who are generally violent and sadistic.

Gondolf's (1996) more recent research on batterers derives from samples taken from court-referred batterer treatment programs. He found that these batterers tend to be in their early 30s, men of color, and of lower socioeconomic status. Nearly half of Gondolf's sample from four different cities were not married and half were not living with the survivors. More than one third had a family history of violence or substance abuse. At least one third of the sample admitted to heavy alcohol use, and one fourth reported using other drugs in the previous year. Sixty-eight percent had other behavioral problems, in addition to domestic violence, such as fighting, drunk driving, and previous arrests. As for psychological findings, more than one fourth of the subjects would probably have been diagnosed as having a severe personality disorder, such as schizotypal, borderline, or paranoid, or a major mental disorder, such as depression. What is important to remember about these findings is that they reflect the population studied: those batterers who were referred to programs following arrest.

One other finding in the research is worth noting. Hotaling and Sugarman (1986) found that witnessing parental violence as a child or adolescent was a consistent risk marker for adult violence, whereas being abused as a child showed inconsistency as a risk marker. These findings suggest that paternal violence may be a stronger predictor of future violence than violence inflicted by the mother (Barnett, Fagan, & Booker, 1991; Hotaling & Sugarman, 1986).

Of course one of the most interesting findings to challenge the feminist construction of wife beating comes from the gay and lesbian domestic violence literature that documents that the rate of violence for gay or lesbian relationships is about the same as that for heterosexual couples (chapter 2). These studies seem to suggest that domestic violence may be as much related to issues of intimacy as they are about patriarchy.

ASSESSMENT OF THE THREAT OF THIS BATTERER

Despite everything we know about types of batterers, the accuracy and consistency of predicting violence remains a relatively young science. Only recently has computer software called MO-SAIC-20 (DeBecker, 1997) been developed for the purpose of assessing dangerousness in domestic violence cases. Available from Gavin DeBecker, Inc., MOSAIC-20 is "an artifical intuition system" that evaluates the dangerousness of a woman's situation as she reports it to the police (DeBecker, 1997). In essence, the computer program identifies those cases in which the danger of homicide is greatest. The Assessment of Threat method proposed here does not involve the use of MOSAIC-20 given that most practitioners will not have access to it; rather, it incorporates what we know about risk assessment in domestic violence cases. Threat assessment tools should only serve as guidelines, supplemented by trained judgment. Even MOSAIC-20 should only be used in conjunction with intuition and professional decision-making. As a tool, MOSAIC-20 can help quantify the data gathered during an assessment and make sense of it in relation to the danger posed by a given case.

The Assessment of Threat involves first and foremost an assessment of the batterer, from the battered woman's point of view, as well as a self-assessment of her own history. It often helps to use a current and past year calendar to help the battered woman get a sense of the range, frequency, and potential escalation in severity of abuse. Calendars can also serve the function of facilitating consciousness-raising in domestic violence cases.

The Assessment of Threat begins by returning to the Violence Tree. The practitioner should supplement the information gathered on the Tree with the following questions for the survivor:

1. Does the batterer have a criminal record? If so, for what crimes?
2. Does the batterer do other impulsive acts, such as crash his car or destroy property he cherishes?
3. Does the batterer have evidence of a mental health disorder (and/or previous psychiatric diagnosis), including

   - threatened or fantasized suicide?
   - acute or unusual depression with little hope for moving beyond it?
   - consumption of alcohol or drugs, elevating his despair, or ongoing substance abuse problem?

- obsession with the survivor or with controlling and regulating the survivor's contacts outside of the relationship?

4. Does the batterer have access to, obsession with, or demonstrated propensity to use weapons against the partner; threaten or fantasize homicide; possess or have access to weapons, including threatening to use or demonstrating a propensity to use household kitchen or other knives, scissors, and so on, in a threatening manner?
5. Does the batterer have difficulty maintaining consistent employment or is currently unemployed or is without other ties to the community?
6. Does the batterer have a childhood history of witnessing domestic violence?

Survivor Self-Assessment

Next, it is useful to have the survivor do a self-assessment. The following questions can help illuminate her history and will reveal a pattern of abuse and her reaction to it.

1. Does the survivor have a history of visits to the emergency room or to the doctor for domestic violence injuries?
2. Has the survivor visited a shelter?
3. Has the survivor requested the help of a therapist or clergy with a domestic violence–related problem?
4. Has the survivor requested the help of a friend or relative for a domestic violence–related problem?
5. Does the survivor have a history of thoughts of suicide or have a history of attempting suicide?
6. Does the survivor have a history of increased alcohol intake in anticipation of, during, or after an abusive incident?

Once the practitioner has gathered this information from the battered woman, she might decide that there are other people she needs to interview before completing the Survivor's Actions and Vulnerabilities Assessment. The issues presented when interviewing children and the batterer are described briefly below.

Interviewing Children

There is a long and complex literature on how to interview children, especially in child abuse cases. The following are guidelines only and should not be considered an exhaustive list of questions a practitioner might ask. Also the age of the child should be considered in terms of how a practitioner approaches the interview and what questions she should ask. If the child has experienced abuse directly, other issues might come into play, and the practitioner should be prepared for a more elaborate interview.

When interviewing children, be aware that their loyalties are divided. They may feel that they would rather tolerate their father's occasional outbursts of violence than what they perceive as their mother's "hysterical behavior." Often a woman's "hysterical behavior" is a response to domestic violence. A child's reluctance to report an abusive parent for fear of getting them in trouble is predictable and understandable. The practitioner should be prepared for this response by a child. In addition, the child will very likely identify with the abusive parent but might be having trouble differentiating between a person (his or her parent) and his or her action. This may manifest itself in a child's reluctance to answer questions about his or her parents' violence towards each other. To help create a safe space in which the child can share, the practitioner should interview each child separately and away from the parents.

Keeping these realities in mind, I suggest that the practitioner:

- Explain to the child that they did nothing wrong; that they are not in trouble.
- Explain that it is your job to help figure out what happened, so you need to ask a few questions.
- Ask the child to tell you everything the child saw and heard; be sure the child clearly identifies the participants.
- Many children will be sparse on details; be prepared to move to specific, focused questions.
- Ask directly if the child was touched in the process. Remember, children can be hurt indirectly, for example, when objects are thrown.

- Ask directly where the child was when the parties were "fighting."
- In closing, ask the child if they remember anything else or if there is something you forgot to ask.
- Be prepared to answer the child's questions honestly.
- Once you have determined what is going to happen, advise the child what will happen next.
- Thank the child for talking to you.

THE BATTERER'S ACTIONS AND VULNERABILITIES ASSESSMENT

When interviewing a batterer, it is useful to use the Batterer's Actions and Vulnerabilities Continuum to determine whether the practitioner believes he will reabuse and, if so, under what conditions (see Figure 7.3). This information could be gathered from the interview with the battered woman and the batterer, depending, of course, on his availability and whether or not it is safe for the practitioner to interview him (see Box 7.1). Official sources of information such as police reports and CPS records can also be helpful.

Should the practitioner have an opportunity to interview a batterer, the following domains should be covered to assist them in learning more about how he thinks and feels (San Diego Depart-

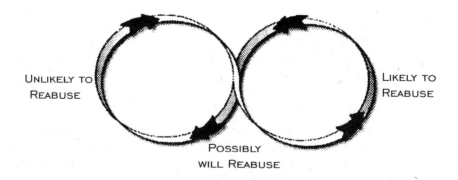

UNLIKELY TO
REABUSE

LIKELY TO
REABUSE

POSSIBLY
WILL REABUSE

FIGURE 7.3 Batterer's actions and vulnerabilities continuum.

ment of Social Services, 1996). It is useful to remember that in one study in which the batterer felt heard, he was much less likely to reabuse (Paternoster, Brame, Bachman, & Sherman, 1997). Therefore, when gathering information it is helpful to listen to him, without condoning what he has done, or his attitudes toward violence.

1. The practitioner may want to begin the interview with the abuser with questions about the batterer's current relationship and about his beliefs about the relationship.

   a. Ask him to describe his relationship with his wife or partner and with the family.
   b. Consider the following questions to help flesh out their violent dynamics.

   • What do you like/dislike about your wife or partner and family?
   • What do you do when you disagree?
   • What do you do when you are angry?

2. Next, the practitioner should assess the level of abuse, asking such questions as:

   a. Does anyone think your temper is a problem? If so, who?
   b. Have the police ever come to your home? When? Who called? Why did they call? What happened as a result?
   c. Have you ever had to forcefully touch someone?
   d. Have you ever been so angry you wanted to hurt someone?
   e. Have you ever stopped your wife or partner from leaving? What happened?

3. Next, it is helpful to inquire into his views of his own behavior and of violence in general. Such questions might include:

   a. When is it okay to hit your wife?
   b. How do you think your partner reacted when you (fill in the blank), (i.e., slapped her)?

    c. Who is responsible for the (fill in the blank), (i.e., broken table)?

4. Next, it is helpful to assess the risk to his children and his views on their witnessing of the domestic violence. These questions might focus on the following:

    a. Ask him to describe the children.

    b. What are his expectations of the children?

    c. How should they be disciplined?

    d. How are the kids affected when they see or hear you and your wife or partner fighting?

5. Finally, you should assess his willingness to address the violence. You might ask him:

    a. What will you do when the problems we identified come up again?

    b. What changes are you willing to make to:

- keep CPS out of your life?
- keep the police out of your life?
- keep your family safe?

It is useful to remember that batterers can be very charming. They may say that they are willing to change and yet have no intention of doing so. A practitioner should assess the seriousness of their commitment through action by placing them on the Batterer's Actions and Vulnerabilities Continuum (Figure 7.3).

A practitioner would mark "Unlikely to Reabuse" on the Batterer's Actions and Vulnerabilities Continuum if the alleged incident is not life threatening. Also pertinent to this assessment is whether (1) there have been other incidents of physical violence in their relationship, (2) the batterer has ties to the community and something to lose from criminal or other state intervention, and (3) there is no other criminal behavior or history of mental illness or substance abuse. If he hasn't previously abused her physically, he has ties to the community, and there is no other criminal behavior or history of mental illness or substance abuse,

Box 7.1 Safety Issues for CSWs, Clinicians, and Advocates

1. Recognize that although all batterers are potentially dangerous, not all will demonstrate that behavior with you. Clinicians and advocates are encouraged to trust their instincts but also heed these tips, which are useful in high-risk situations.
2. What is a high-risk situation is not always clear cut. The assessment of dangerousness is an infant science. Consider the following:
   a. What do you know about the batterer's history at this point?
      • Conduct a criminal records check; determine if courts or probation, and so on, are currently involved.
      • Review your findings from the Violence Tree, the Heart of Intimate Abuse, and the Assessment of Threat.
   b. Are you involved in confronting or negotiating any of the following potentially high-risk situations?
      • Victim is preparing to leave.
      • Children are going to be removed.
      • Batterer has just been released from jail and serious criminal charges are pending or batterer is being arrested (elevated if batterer has few "ties to the community").
      • Allegations regarding child abuse or neglect are being made directly to the batterer.
      • Batterer is inquiring directly about family's secret whereabouts.
      • History of alcohol use or abuse.
      • History of use of weapons.
3. Engage in active prevention planning; consider the following in your planning:
   a. Contact law enforcement if necessary.
   b. Do not meet alone with batterer; have him come to your office or other public place.
   c. Have a security officer accompany you to your car.
   d. Notify office security and coworkers of a potentially dangerous client visit.
   e. Explore multiple exits ahead of time.
   f. Know the procedure to follow in an emergency situation, in other words, how do you access help; is there a "call button" in the interview room?
   g. In an interview room, position yourself close to the door.
4. Should you find yourself in a dangerous situation:
   a. Again, trust your instincts. Many practitioners let the situation escalate too far before reacting or seeking help.
   b. Stay calm yourself. Use your active listening and allow for ventilation. Although you can validate angry feelings, you should also set some clear guidelines should behavior escalate.
   c. Assess your ability to provide control and be prepared to escape, if necessary.
   d. Notify the battered woman if you become aware that the batterer's anger is increasing.

the practitioner may designate him as unlikely to reabuse. Dutton (1995) reports, in a synthesis of the research in this area, that of the "10% of men who assault their wives once, 33% to 37% (3.3% of all men) do not repeat within a year" (Schulman, 1979; Straus et al., 1980). Schulman (1979) and Straus et al. (1980) found that 6.7% of men repeatedly assaulted their wives and 2.8% severely assaulted their wives.

If the practitioner thought, based on all the information gathered, it was possible that the batterer would reabuse, they would designate him as "Possibly Will Reabuse" on the Batterer's Actions and Vulnerabilities Continuum. Under these circumstances the practitioner would assess the batterer's ties to the community, whether he had some history of criminal behavior, or whether he had abused this or another intimate partner before. Whether he had a history of witnessing domestic violence in his family of origin might also be relevant.

Finally, the practitioner would mark "Likely to Reabuse" on the Batterer's Actions and Vulnerabilities Continuum if they felt certain that he would reabuse. Such factors as little or no ties to the community, a criminal record, and a history of mental illness and substance abuse would be relevant to consider. Also, the practitioner may want to learn more about whether there was a previous and serious history of physical or sexual abuse and whether or not this incident was life threatening. Inquiring into his interest in or possession of weapons is also important. It is critical that in assessing a future threat of violence, no one factor be determinant. In other words, it is possible that this incident may not be life threatening (emotional abuse or some minor form of destruction of property) and that this is evidence of what could come, even murder. Note too that a childhood history of witnessing domestic violence would be relevant to the analysis here. That kind of experience can give a batterer "permission" to abuse. Review the factors on the Assessment of Threat and all the information gathered from the interviews to better evaluate the dangerousness of this batterer.

Interviewing the batterer directly can help assess a different dimension of the violence. In this interaction, the practitioner can begin to understand the batterer's personal assessment of his violent behavior by asking questions that probe his relationship to and insight into his violence. Answers to these questions should help provide the CSW, advocate, or clinician critical insight into the batterer's functioning and the threat he poses to the battered woman.

Before completing the Batterer's Actions and Vulnerabilities Continuum, the practitioner should review the Threat Assessment, including data from interviews with the battered woman, the child, and the batterer and evidence secured from criminal or CPS records. The Assessment of Threat involves judgments that cannot be fully quantified through equations or decision-making models.

The interview of the batterer is designed to gather evidence that the practitioner then assesses and shares with the battered woman in light of the previous empirical work on batterers and their propensity for danger. But of course, none of the data gathered can fully predict what will happen. Some clinicians or advocates will err on the side of an "Authority-Oriented" intervention; others will err on the side of an "Empowerment-Oriented" response. Every clinician or advocate should know where they fall on the Continuum of Intervention (Figure 6.1) so that they are conscious of the sympathies they are likely to express when making judgments and determinations in cases involving intimate abuse.

SUMMARY AND REFLECTIONS

These systems strategies, coupled with the Affective Advocacy Model, should give practitioners working in any system the tools they need to assess the particulars of a given situation and to begin to tailor interventions that meet this survivor's unique needs. For each of the three systems addressed in this book (criminal justice, child protection, and health), chapters 8, 9, and 10 present models for rethinking domestic violence interventions in light of the approaches presented in this and the previous chapter. The case studies developed in the next three chapters are designed to bring to life both the Affective Advocacy Model and these Systems Strategies. Each case study is different, and each chapter presents different models of intervention. This gives practitioners the opportunity to choose which model works best based on their particular practice.

QUESTIONS

- ☐ Imagine reviewing the Violence Tree with a battered woman. What questions make you most uncomfortable?

- ☐ What are your own stereotypes of battered women? How have feminist or media images of battered women affected your own views?

- ☐ What scares you most about discussing the Survivor's Actions and Vulnerabilities Continuum with the battered woman? How will you respond when she admits that her strong identification with her culture prevents her from ever leaving her partner?

- ☐ What scares you most about interviewing children? What questions are you comfortable asking? What questions are you uncomfortable asking?

- ☐ What are the stereotypes you hold about batterers? What stereotypes do you need to leave behind in order to assess his future behavior on the Batterer's Actions and Vulnerabilities Continuum?

CHAPTER 8

Empowerment and Affective Strategies I: Meetings in Criminal Justice

---

> [F]or a woman who has been a victim of repeated physical abuse, degradation, and terroristic threats by a spouse or boyfriend, the thought of going to court may be so intimidating that no effort is made to get legal protection.
>
> (Roberts, 1996a, p. 101)

Battered women's interactions with the criminal justice system, particularly at the stage where the batterer is being prosecuted, can be emotionally devastating. The only empirical research done on prosecutors' attitudes toward battered women is speculative at best for understanding the experience of survivors who become involved in the prosecution of a domestic violence crime.

Rebovich (1996) reports that 33% of the prosecutors who responded to his survey claimed that more than 55% of their domestic violence-related cases involved "uncooperative" victims; 16% of respondents believed that between 41 and 55% of their victims were "uncooperative"; 26% of respondents believed that between 26 and 40% of their victims were "uncooperative." Only 26% of the prosecutors responding to Rebovich's survey reported that up to 25% of their cases involved "uncooperative" witnesses. It is also relevant that 92% of prosecutors surveyed reported that they used their subpoena power to force battered women to testify. In a related study, Buzawa, Austin, Bannon, and Jackson (1992) reported that victims were generally satisfied with police intervention (85%) when they followed their preferences. Together, these studies tentatively suggest that battered women may be dissatisfied when law enforcement (police or prosecutor) do not respect or else disregard their preference to avoid their involvement in the criminal justice process.

Survey results as well as anecdotal evidence from prosecutors suggest that victim preference is all too often rendered irrelevant in domestic violence cases. Rebovich's (1996) research reveals that 80% of the prosecutors he surveyed proceeded with the prosecution of a domestic violence case regardless of victim cooperation. Along these same lines, Teri Jackson's (1990) experience as a domestic violence prosecutor may be revealing. She started her prosecutorial tour in San Francisco wanting "to build [battered women's] self esteem so they would no longer tolerate abuse from anyone" (p. 561). In Jackson's words, "I assumed they would welcome and even embrace me as their savior from these horrible men . . . " (p. 561). After many unsuccessful attempts at playing "psychologist and social worker," Jackson decided to focus her attention on the goal of convicting the batterer.

Jackson makes several suggestions to prosecutors in her "Prosecutor's Brief" titled "Lessons Learned from a Domestic Violence Prosecutor." In their best light, these suggestions are disempowering; in their worst, they are manipulative, deceptive, and even dangerous. First, Jackson suggests that prosecutors serve the battered woman "with a subpoena or ask the judge to order her to appear for the next court date" (p. 561). Jackson seems completely unwilling to negotiate with the victim and unaware of the potential impact of such coercive action on a battered woman who may be enmeshed in an abusive dynamic. Refusing to tailor prosecutorial responses to individual women can have the effect of discouraging their participation altogether. Second, Jackson suggests letting the battered woman tell her story at some length, without interruption, to "reveal how cooperative or uncooperative the victim will be" (p. 561). Jackson seems uninterested in obtaining information from the victim which might help make her situation safer. Questioning a victim while she tells her story of abuse regarding the circumstances that might give rise to her reluctance to testify seems key—Jackson fails to seize this important opportunity. Jackson also suggests getting information from the victim about her contact with the defendant: "this information can be valuable later in laying a foundation for impeachment" (p. 561). Again, she seems unaware of the impact of such impeachment on the victim; she is obviously unfamiliar with the Ford and Regoli study (1993), which suggests that a battered woman who participates in the criminal justice process is least likely to experience repeat violence. Finally, Jackson recommends that prosecutors "be careful in what you say to the victim; it could be repeated to the defendant or his attorney . . . never discuss your personal feelings about the case" (p. 561). In my view, Jackson has gone much farther than refusing to play psychologist or social worker; this approach feels more like a calculated distance, one that is completely oblivious to the battered woman's history of violence and her possible future exposure to more abuse.

Donna Wills (1997), Head Deputy, Family Violence Division of the Los Angeles County District Attorney's Office, offers a similar sentiment:

> Aggressive prosecution of domestic violence offenders rejects the notion that victims should be given the choice of whether to press or drop charges. No human society can allow any citizen, battered woman or otherwise, to be beaten and terrorized while being held emotionally hostage to love and fear or blackmailed by financial dependence and cultural mores (p. 182).

This chapter begins with my observations of the criminal justice system and with support for my analysis. Next, I present a typical interaction in the criminal justice system between a Victim Advocate and a battered woman using an approach similar to that suggested by Jackson. I offer a brief critique of this method. Finally, I present an alternative interaction between a Victim Advocate and a battered woman that uses the Affective Advocacy and Systems Strategies method presented in chapters 6 and 7. I synthesize this interaction with my approach in a methodology that suggests the importance of implementing system-wide change that might affect how these dynamics unfold in criminal justice settings.

THE DYNAMICS OF CRIMINAL JUSTICE INTERACTIONS

Before proceeding to the case studies, it is important to highlight three correlative observations that underpin my empowering approach when considering how best to advise battered mothers on how to interact with the criminal justice system. The first is what assumptions we make about her. If a practitioner is working in the criminal justice system or has access to it, it is likely that the dominant view of law enforcement (including prosecutors) is that women in abusive relationships are too afraid to pursue charges against a batterer and hence are likely to refuse to cooperate in the arrest and prosecution of a perpetrator for fear of retaliation (Jackson, 1990; Wills, 1997). As I have revealed, these advocates will assume that the State must, without the support of the victim, take the necessary action against the batterer, including arresting, prosecuting, and punishing him. Using this paradigm as a prototype, battered women are too weak and submissive to act on their own behalf. My insight is that if law enforcement officers and prosecutors are unable to critically analyze the stereotypical assumptions they make about battered women, they will act according to these assumptions and fail to see the potential offered by criminal interventions to help a victim become empowered.

I begin with the assumption that battered women can make up their own minds about whether or not criminal action is the safest or most appropriate avenue given all the factors they must consider (Hart, 1996). I start not where the criminal justice system is but rather "where she is." I assume that the battered woman is not inherently intimidated by a court process (Newmark, Harell, & Salem, 1995) and that she may, if properly treated and primed, be willing to pursue charges against the batterer. Here the battered woman is seen as a typical survivor or victim who might be persuaded one way or another to take action against a perpetrator (Hart, 1996). As domestic violence scholars, practitioners, and policymakers, it is imperative that we examine our preconceived assumptions about battered women and be aware of the ways countertransference influences our methods of intervention in domestic violence cases.

The presence of children in an abusive relationship poses the most challenging and vexing questions when trying to devise empowering strategies for battered mothers. The problem is that CSWs, clinicians, or advocates may be unwilling to leave the children exposed to any level of domestic abuse while the battered woman struggles to break free from a man she loves, a man who supports her, or a man whom her children adore (when he isn't violent). Leaving is often a process for a battered woman and the question is what is the practitioner, a CSW, a clinician, or an advocate, willing to tolerate as the victim works through her issues.

Third, if the practitioner is working in the criminal justice system, it is helpful to know that testifying against the batterer is likely to make him angrier. According to Ford and Regoli (1993), her testimony, if of her own free will, can actually have the effect of keeping her safer. More recently, the research of Yegidis and Renzy (1994) suggests that perpetrators who were subjected to multiple stages in the criminal justice process were less likely to reoffend. The advantage of testifying against him is that, assuming he is convicted, the action becomes part of a record that can have an impact on future incidents of violence. In addition, all future counts of domestic violence are stacked up against that record.

It is also helpful to remember that the battered woman may not want to testify because she is finished with the batterer and may only want to get away from him with as little harm or contact as possible. If he is the father of her children, this is more complicated. But if he isn't, she may believe that refusing to testify means she is striking a bargain: he won't bother her and she won't testify against him. Only she can know whether such a bargain is realistic. What is important to remember is that if a battered woman doesn't want to testify, and you feel her reasons are based on sound judgment of the situation, then her refusal to testify should not be seen as noncooperation, rather, it could be interpreted as part and parcel of a bona fide safety plan.

CASE STUDY I: EMILY JONES MEETS ELAINE MONK, A VICTIM ADVOCATE

Emily Jones is an African American woman whose husband hit her several times in the face and was arrested for his crime last Friday. Emily and John have three children. She works part-time as a paralegal, and her husband is a postal worker. On the night of the incident, John was angry because Emily had come home late from the office. There has been a reorganization at work, and John has been under a lot of pressure lately. He is not usually physically abusive.

Elaine Monk has worked as a Victim Advocate for the City Attorney's office for several years now. She is tired of battered women who do not take responsibility for their lives. She is clear that she is there to help only those women who are ready to help themselves.

She reads Emily Jones's file that morning and is asked by the prosecutor to find out if Emily will testify against her husband. The City Attorney's office has a mandatory prosecution policy; they will proceed regardless of Emily's desire to prosecute or her willingness to testify. Elaine asks the court clerk who Emily Jones is, and she points her out.

Elaine:	Hi, I am a Victim Advocate for the City Attorney's office. How are you doing this morning?
Emily:	Terrible.
Elaine:	What's going on?
Emily:	I am really upset about this whole thing and I don't know what to do.
Elaine:	Why don't you tell me what happened and maybe I can help.
Emily:	I got this subpoena served on me and I don't have anything to say, so I don't know why I have to be here. I have three kids at home, I had to get my mother to watch the kids and I'll miss work if I don't get out of here soon.
Elaine:	Well, why don't you tell me what happened that night.
Emily:	Nothing happened. That's the point.
Elaine:	Well something happened that night otherwise we wouldn't be here. Why don't you tell me what happened.
Emily:	Nothing happened. The police came after I called 911 because John was just going crazy. But it's all over now, and he didn't hurt me or nothing.
Elaine:	That's not what the police report says. Will you testify as to what did happen that night?

Emily: I told you I have nothing to say about that night.

Elaine: Well, if you have nothing to say then we can't really do anything for you. There are victim assistance funds, but if you don't testify then you can't get the benefit of that money. Why don't you want to testify? Are you afraid?

Emily: No, I'm not afraid. I know what you will do to John—you'll throw him in jail. Then my kids will be without a father, he could lose his job, and then we'll really be in trouble.

Elaine: But your husband punched you in the face. He committed a crime; he needs to know he can't treat you that way.

Emily: He won't ever scare us like that again.

Elaine: Well, if you want to be sure, why not testify against him; that'll send the message home.

Emily: That's what you think.

Elaine: Well, it doesn't sound like there is much else for us to discuss, so you'll have to wait here until they call your case. If you need me, or you change your mind, I'll be here or in the next courtroom. Otherwise, you need to show up if you get a subpoena; you don't want to be in trouble too. I have some resources for you, if you want them, on how to contact shelters or counseling groups. I suggest that you contact these groups; they can help you escape the violence. Well, hope that helps. Bye, for now.

Emily: Bye.

Based on my experience, this interaction is typical of interactions between Victim Advocates working for prosecutors' offices and a victim to a domestic violence crime. In those instances where prosecutors' offices don't have Victim Advocates, this interaction is typical of a dialogue between a prosecutor and a victim in a domestic violence case.

Most prosecutors' offices who are committed to a mandatory prosecution stance have decided, as Rebovich's study suggests (1996), that the victim, if uncooperative, is dispensable to the case and that a strategy must be pursued that does not rely on her testimony. Indeed, around the country strategies are being developed and implemented that prosecute batterers for crimes as though they were "victimless" (Heisler, 1990). The only comparative situation is in murder trials, when the victim has died.

The interaction between Elaine and Emily is typical of what we might expect from a mandatory prosecution jurisdiction. Either Emily, as the victim, is willing to help by testifying or is viewed as hostile and "uncooperative." In the interaction above, Elaine is almost indifferent to Emily's safety, financial, familial, or emotional concerns. Although she suggests certain resources, she does not explore how victim assistance benefits or counseling might assist Emily or how Emily's friends or family might intervene. The entire interaction rests on whether or not Emily is willing to testify. The criminal justice system is seen as offering one and only one solution—a prosecution.

In the next interaction, using the skills outlined in chapters 6 and 7, Mark Nuñez, the Victim Advocate, is primarily concerned with building a relationship with Alicia Flores, the victim, so that he might help her both to address the violence in her life and to manage the criminal justice system's response to it. Testifying or not is secondary to his goal of helping the battered woman become aware of her options. The emotional subtext section of the dialogue helps the reader understand more about what's happening beneath the emotional surface.

CASE STUDY II: ALICIA FLORES MEETS MARK NUÑEZ, A VICTIM ADVOCATE

Alicia Flores is a Latina and 21 years old. She has a six-month-old child and is married to Martin. A couple of days ago, Martin and Alicia had a big fight, and the neighbors called the police. When they came, they saw that Mrs. Flores had a bruise and so they arrested Martin. Mrs. Flores was furious. She came downtown to straighten this whole thing out.

Mark Nuñez is a Latino who is fluent in Spanish. He is a Victim Advocate with the District Attorney's Family Violence Unit. He usually has the first contact with victims so that he can find out their history, learn more about the abuse, and determine whether they are willing to testify. He has several cases this morning. When he came into the courtroom, the clerk told him that Alicia Flores was waiting for him and was very anxious to talk with him.

Mark Nuñez locates Mrs. Flores in the courtroom, sitting in the waiting area. Their conversation is in Spanish.

Mark: Are you Mrs. Flores?
Alicia: Yes.

Emotional Subtext (MARK): *I sense that she seems absolutely terrified but is acting strong.*

Mark: My name is Mark Nuñez, and I am a Victim Advocate. I am here to help you through this process, to support you, and to offer you any help you may need or to answer any questions or concerns you may have. Whatever you tell me I will share with the prosecutor on your case.

Alicia: I've come to tell you and the judge that all the accusations and statements they have in the case against my husband are false. Do you know anything about my case?

Mark: Yes, I have a police report in the file.

Alicia: Oh.

Mark: Would you like to review the report with me?

Alicia: Sure.

Emotional Subtext (MARK): *I watched her read the report's first few lines. She immediately became uncomfortable and agitated. I knew, I could sense, that she was going to deny most or all of the report.*

Alicia: (pointing to the report) That's a lie. That never happened.

Mark: Why don't we go through the statements and I will underline everything that is untrue or incorrect.

Emotional Subtext (MARK): *I need very much to bond with her right now in her distress. I can do that by accepting that she believes this is a lie, that it didn't exactly happen the way it had been written down in the report, although I am full of doubts that these things didn't happen.*

They went through the document until almost the entire statement was underlined.

Emotional Subtext (MARK): *I am worried that my concealed disbelief is showing and that she will know that I really don't believe her even though I have outwardly done so. I do want to challenge her but not to the point that I alienate her; I sense that she needs so desperately to believe everything will be okay.*

Mark: As you may be aware, we will have to proceed with this case even though you have said that these events did not occur. The prosecutor will have to move forward even if you tell the judge that these are lies. I'm sorry. I know this is difficult for you.

Alicia: Yeah, I know.

Emotional Subtext (MARK): *Having little precious time left with Mrs. Flores, I am desperate to leave her with something. I feel helpless that she is so focused on wanting to tell the judge that nothing happened. I feel desperate to try and reach her, to reach the part of her that yearns for her own safety and the safety of her child. I have an idea.*

Mark: Do you have any fears about any possible violence from your husband once all of this blows over and you're back to normal and living again with him?

Alicia: No, nothing will ever happen again, everything will be just fine. We won't have any more problems. I have no fear, and there will be no future threats.

Emotional Subtext (MARK): *I know she is currently unmovable in her denial, but I've planted a seed. I'll try this.*

Mark: It is important Mrs. Flores, just in case, to have a friend or somewhere you can go that your husband will have no knowledge of, especially so you can be safe with your baby. This should be a safe place, a sacred place. Also, here is a list of phone numbers, including a number for a shelter, a place for Spanish-speaking women who are hurt by their husbands can go if they need to be safe. And remember, if you need me, come to me and we can talk some more. In the meantime, you should be here both today and tomorrow, so this case can proceed. I'll keep you posted.

Emotional Subtext (MARK): *I've planted the seed; that's the best I can do. Now we will wait and see. I have to go and talk to other victims now. It's so difficult to leave her like this.*

When Mark and Mrs. Flores meet later that day, she is weepy and distraught.

Emotional Subtext (MARK): *Maybe she has thought about what happened earlier, that is, about taking back her statement to the police. Maybe she has come to realize something; I'm not sure what yet.*

Mark: Hi Mrs. Flores. How are you?

Alicia: (crying) Nothing has changed. I told you earlier that my husband didn't hit me. All those underlined facts were untrue as I said (crying more).

Mark: Mrs. Flores, you seem very upset and that's understandable. It seems like maybe there is something you want to tell me.

Emotional Subtext (MARK): *I know the tears are her confession, the words her lies. I am sympathetic to her need to change her story and worry that her tears convey her fears.*

Mark: Tell me what you are feeling, and maybe if I know, I can help you manage whatever problem you have.

Alicia: I'm scared my husband will go to jail and that I won't have his income to support us. He is good to us. He tries to take care of us. He tries, he really does.

Mark: Okay, I hear you on this. (pause) Your husband is a good caretaker. (pause) How does he treat you otherwise?

Alicia: Well sometimes he is mean, but mostly he tries real hard. He is always sorry after an incident and that makes it much better.

Mark: But you seem afraid of him, and that's what worries me.

Alicia: Sometimes I am, but I'm more worried about how to put food on the table. Martin won't do anything too drastic. I know him.

Mark: Okay, well, let me take what you are saying into account. But I am worried about your safety and the safety of your child. Would you be willing to work with me to try and arrange for your safety and to arrange for you to get some benefits so you don't have to rely financially on your husband?

Alicia: Okay, maybe some more talking would help.

Mark: I have to go back to court now, but I will be back in a little while.

Emotional Subtext: I believe that by leaving her alone for a bit she can have a chance to reflect and to feel more comfortable being honest with me.

Mark: (returning after 15 minutes) Hi Mrs. Flores, how are you doing?

Alicia: Okay, but I'm still upset.

Mark: Do you want to talk more about it?

Alicia: It depends. What will happen if I talk to you? Will Martin get in more trouble?

Mark: He could, but you might also get what you need: some peace of mind and your safety. I can't promise that by talking everything will be okay. But some studies have shown that if you testify against your husband when he hurts you, that it can actually mean that you are safer in the long run. But only you are in a position to be able to judge that.

Alicia: Well, it is true that sometimes Martin goes crazy. But he doesn't mean to hurt anyone. He had a hard time as a kid; his father abandoned them after having beat up his mom a lot.

Mark: I have a diagram that might help you talk about what's been going on in your relationship. It's called a Violence Tree. Do you want to look at it with me?

Alicia: Okay.

Emotional Subtext (MARK): *I decide to proceed by having her look at the Violence Tree to get a sense of what she has been going through (Figure 7.1).*

Alicia: Yes well, he's done some or all of this, but I can't get into the details. I feel I have gotten him into enough trouble.

Mark: Okay, well maybe you can talk about what you love about Martin and the reasons you stick by him. To help us talk about some of those issues, let's look at the Heart of Intimate Abuse, another tool that might help you explain what you're feeling.

Emotional Subtext (MARK): *Well, if I can't get her to talk specifically about Martin's violence, maybe I can get Mrs. Flores to talk about her own experience of the relationship.*

Mark: (showing her the left side of the Heart of Intimate Abuse, Figure 2.3) What about Martin do you love?

Emotional Subtext (MARK): *I know that if I encourage her to talk about the positive dimensions of their relationship that she might feel more comfortable talking about the negative.*

Alicia: When he is happy and good to us, he is the best man I have ever known. He brings me flowers after work and even candy sometimes. He tells me how much he loves and needs me. I never felt loved by anyone before like I feel Martin cares about me.

Mark: How does Martin get along with your son?

Emotional Subtext (MARK): *I think I will just make my way down the Heart of Intimate Abuse and see how Mrs. Flores responds.*

Alicia: He loves our son. He is committed to our son. In fact, he has been working two jobs because of our son and wants to make sure he is brought up right.

Mark: Has all that pressure made things more difficult for Martin?

Alicia: Yeah, I am sure that the responsibility of the baby has increased Martin's stress, especially because he is now working two jobs. I am terrified that if this case goes ahead that he will lose his jobs. That would just make everything worse.

Mark: Has he ever hurt your son?

Alicia: No, Martin would never hurt our son; you can trust me on that.

Mark: The reason I am asking about your son is that many men who hurt their wives also hurt their children, either directly because they can't control themselves or indirectly, when the child gets caught in the "crossfire." What I mean by that is that if and when he hits you, he could hit your son by accident. You need to be very, very careful that if you feel Martin is going to be violent that you avoid him, and you be sure to protect your son as well.

Alicia: Oh no, Martin wouldn't do that.

Mark: (still working with The Heart of Intimate Abuse) What role do you think religion, culture, or race plays in your relationship with Martin?

Alicia: Oh, we're Catholic, and I would never do anything that would jeopardize my faith. My parents were both born in Mexico and they believe in lifelong marriage. They have been through a lot and they've stuck by each other. I would do the same.

Mark: Have you told your parents about what's been going on with Martin?

Alicia: Oh no, I could never tell them what was going on. They'd really disapprove.

Mark: Have you told anyone?

Alicia: I talked to my priest about how Martin makes me feel sometimes; he says I should just try and do better.

Mark: How did you feel when he said that?

Alicia: I felt I needed to do what he said.

Emotional Subtext (Mark): *I need to make a note that I could talk with the priest about this case, if Mrs. Flores thought that was a good idea.*

Mark: Are you afraid of Martin?

Emotional Subtext (Mark): *I'm asking this question because I actually think she may be ready to respond.*

Alicia: Sometimes. He gets so crazy sometimes I don't know what he will do next. It makes me scared and really sad.

Mark: What do you do to protect yourself during those times?

Alicia: Well once I went to a friend's house to stay. But that got Martin madder. Usually, I just bear through it and it finally ends and then he feels all sorry and everything.

Mark: I know you said that Martin takes good care of you financially. Do you work?

Alicia: No, I don't work. I take care of the baby and Martin works. He doesn't really want me to work and I am happy to stay home and take care of the baby.

Mark: Why doesn't he want you to work?

Alicia: He likes me to be home most of the day so he knows where I am.

Mark: (referring to the right side of the Heart of Intimate Abuse) Do you see the other side of this heart? Here it describes how men who are abusive can try and control their wives' actions. One example of that is to tell them not to work. Is it like that?

Alicia: Yeah, sometimes Martin can get pretty uptight, but I can handle it.

Emotional Subtext (Mark): *I am tempted to go back to the Violence Tree, but I don't want to feel like I am pressuring her to tell me things that we can use against her husband. So instead, I think I will be more direct and ask her what she wants to do with this case.*

Mark: Mrs. Flores, given what we have talked about, what do you think you want to do with this case?

Alicia: What do you mean?

Mark: Do you think you want to testify, or do you want to deny what you said in the police report.

Alicia: I can't go through with any testimony.

Mark: As I said before, there is some evidence that if you testify it can make you feel stronger, and Martin could feel there are legal repercussions to his violence, and it may actually have some impact. I can't promise that though. You are the only person who would know whether you and your son would be safer if you testified or not.

Alicia: I just don't think I could do it to him.

Mark: It sounds like you will stay with him, is that right?

Alicia: Oh yes. I love Martin. He could do whatever; I will always stick by him.

Mark: Do you think it would help if I talked to your priest? Maybe he would be willing to talk with Martin.

Alicia: That might help, but you probably don't have time to do that.

Mark: And we need to come up with a Personal Safety Plan for you and your son, just in case you need to escape (Appendix II). A Personal Safety Plan just allows you to plan for the possibility that Martin could get mad again.

Alicia: I don't think I'll need that. But if you think I do, I guess I'll do it. What do you think will happen to Martin?

Mark: Chances are he will be found guilty, even if you don't testify, because of the evidence the police gathered when they went to the house the night of the incident. Since this is his first offense, he will probably get a little jail time and will have to attend a batterer's treatment group. Would you like some counseling referrals for yourself? They usually involve groups of women from your home country and neighboring countries who are in a similar situation, many of them have kids, and you talk about what's been happening in your relationship.

Alicia: I don't think so, but if you give me the number I will call if I need to.

The interaction continues as Mark spends some time developing a Personal Safety Plan and discussing Mrs. Flores' eligibility for special benefits that would help support her and her son, should she choose to pursue them.

SUMMARY AND REFLECTIONS

The criminal justice system, like child protection and health care, demands a specialized approach to battered women, depending on the kind of interaction, and the two people engaged in the sharing process. Below, I present a Checklist of Interactional Guidelines, which is also a review of the Affective Advocacy and Systems Strategies methods presented in chapters 6 and 7. This Checklist can help Victim Advocates, or other advocates in the criminal justice system, keep track of the guiding principles in these interactions. In this next section, I briefly compare and contrast the two Victim Advocates' approaches, Elaine Monk and Mark Nuñez, and how their interactions with survivors measure up against the Checklist.

CHECKLIST OF INTERACTIONAL GUIDELINES

1. *Reflect on the violence in one's own life.* Before taking a job in domestic violence, it would be expected, using an empowerment approach, that Elaine and Mark would have reflected on the violence in their own lives. Elaine seems to be looking outward, not inward, is frustrated, and is judgmental of women who are not yet ready to confront their violent lovers or to testify against them. Mark, on the other hand, seems to understand that responding to violence in one's life is a process and realizes that each interaction helps one work through that violence until a course of action becomes clear.

2. *Accept the battered woman "as she is."* Elaine seems frustrated by her perception that Emily is unwilling to "cooperate" in the way Elaine needs her to cooperate. Mark sees Mrs. Flores' resistance or reluctance as an opportunity to connect, to make a dent in her denial, and to plant the seeds for change.

3. *A Feeling-Driven approach.* Asking a battered woman how she feels enables an advocate to understand why a survivor is doing what she is doing. Elaine seems to find Emily's feelings irrelevant; Mark seems attuned to Mrs. Flores' concerns and uses them to move the conversation to new plateaus.

4. *Shared suffering.* Although a sense of shared suffering is not inherently relevant to these interactions, had Elaine had a history of abuse, she could have shared that with Emily. Similarly, if Mark had felt the need to share his own family history, the intervention might have benefited from it. Sharing a history of suffering can be transformative for a victim who may otherwise feel isolated from other people's abuse.

5. *Transference and countertransference.* These interactions were somewhat brief and therefore failed to tease out, in any significant sense, the transference and countertransference issues that might be operating. Superficially, it felt as though Elaine's interaction with Emily reinforced Elaine's underlying negative attitudes toward battered women and therefore brought her countertransference issues to the surface. Elaine's collective experience with other survivors, which seemed to frustrate her, seemed to be projected onto Emily. Emily was no longer her own battered woman but a composite of all of Elaine's clients who wouldn't cooperate.

The interaction with Mark was critical because it was an opportunity for Mrs. Flores to connect with a sensitive man who listened. This had a positive effect on her receptivity to Mark's interpretation of her experience, and to his input into what she might consider doing. Mark, unlike Elaine, did not come to the interaction with preconceived assumptions about Mrs. Flores and therefore was less susceptible to countertransferences that would hinder Mrs. Flores' responses to him.

6. *When to share and when not to share.* Although neither Elaine nor Mark shared their personal stories, had they chosen to, the time and nature of that sharing would have been critical.

7. *What happened.* Although neither Elaine nor Mark were terribly successful at eliciting what happened from the battered women themselves, Mark used both the Violence Tree and the Heart of Intimate Abuse to learn more about Mrs. Flores' history. These visual aids can help move dialogue along and help elicit responses from victims that respect their perspective.

8. *Assess the battered woman.* The Heart of Intimate Abuse allowed Mark to assess Mrs. Flores' vulnerabilities (financial, religious, and emotional) and to try to respond in concrete ways through information on benefits, an offer to call her priest, and

counseling referrals. Elaine made no specific inquiries into Emily's vulnerabilities, nor did she seem interested in them.

9.   *Threat posed to the battered women and her children.* Elaine did not pursue this question with Emily at all; Mark pursued the threat from Martin to their son only briefly when they looked at the Violence Tree. Mark did try to present arguments to Mrs. Flores to encourage her to testify against Martin, so as to reduce the likelihood of future violence; he did so in a way that encouraged her to action. It seemed Elaine pursued Emily on this front but did not explicitly share with Emily the safety benefit she might have gained from giving testimony.

FINAL THOUGHTS

> We have virtually no appropriate measures to tap
> and document the strengths of women who are in or
> have been in violent and threatening relationships.
>   Angela Browne
>   (Barnett, Miller-Perrin, & Perrin, 1997, p. 212)

Interactions with the criminal justice system involve many competing interests. Usually, practitioners in the system have unidimensional demands that force them to focus their interactions with battered women not on the most pressing issues of action and vulnerability but on their willingness or unwillingness to testify. In Case Study I, we witness how that focus can alienate the survivor and serve little or no other purpose. In Case Study II, we saw how such an interaction can be broadened to encompass the dual interests of both the system and the battered mother's overall or long-term safety concerns and interests.

In the next chapter, we examine how CPS interventions can empower battered women, even in a mandatory reporting environment.

QUESTIONS

❐ How does the method suggested by Jackson for interviewing and working with battered women undermine an approach that is designed to empower the victim?

❐ How could the interaction between Elaine and Emily be improved to encompass a more empowering approach?

❐ How would you have changed the interaction between Mark and Mrs. Flores?

❐ How is the criminal justice system unique in its use of the Affective Advocacy and Systems Strategies method? What specific issues are more or less relevant to criminal justice interactions?

CHAPTER 9

Empowerment and Affective Strategies II: Meetings in Public Child Welfare

This was one of many violent altercations, which must inevitably have affected the child even though he has not yet been physically injured.

Judge P. F. Kremer
(*In re Jon N., a Minor v. Fred N.*, 1986, p. 322)

The public child welfare system poses unique challenges to the CSW who is committed to using empowerment strategies for intervening in cases involving domestic violence. Because CSWs and other advocates and clinicians who work with children are mandated reporters, the dynamic between the practitioner and the battered mother is not protected from outside institutional influence. Although in health care such mandates are just beginning to evolve, in public child welfare they are now well established.

The public child welfare system has been criticized by domestic violence advocates on two fronts. The first charge is that public child welfare agencies have blamed battered women for the abuse by their partners through the use of "failure to protect" statutes (see chapter 4) (Enos, 1996). The second charge is that CPS agencies have been indifferent to domestic violence, exposing battered women and their children to abuse by failing to intervene (see chapter 4) (Callahan, 1993). In the context of a case study, this chapter relies on the many tools presented in chapters 6 and 7 that help the CSW investigating an allegation of domestic violence and child abuse to explore and respond in an empowering and supportive way, a method that avoids, as much as possible, blaming the battered woman for the violence of her abuser while simultaneously focusing on critical safety issues for both her and her child(ren).

Presented herein are interviews between a CSW and a child, a battered mother, and a batterer. "Susan's reflections" are designed to help the reader follow the method she is using to interact with each family member.

CASE STUDY: CSW SUSAN MARTIN MEETS THE NGUYENS

Huong Nguyen is the child of Vietnamese immigrants. She is 26 years old and married to Viet Nguyen, also of Vietnamese descent. They were both born in the U.S. They have a son together, Dannie, who is 8 years old. They were married 3 years after Dannie was born and have been married 5 years. Huong was hoping to finish college but got pregnant with Dannie. At that point she dropped out of school, married Viet, and became a professional hairdresser. Viet works at a computer assembly plant. Huong went to college in the United States and is still taking a few college courses. They live in a duplex apartment. CPS was called when Dannie's teacher at school noticed that he had a bruise over his left eye.

Susan Martin has been a CPS worker for 10 years. She was assigned the case because domestic violence was suspected; the teacher suspected intimate abuse because the mother has been seen with bruises, especially around the eyes. Susan has been trained in how to intervene in cases of domestic violence when there is an allegation of child abuse.

Susan decides to interview Dannie first. Her theory is that Dannie might share with her the fact that his father is violent. Susan goes to the school to meet him. Dannie is pulled out of class to talk to her.

Susan: Hi Dannie. My name is Susan and I am from Child Protective Services. (pause) I talk to a lot of kids. Today I am going to talk to you. I was told that you had a bruise on your eye, and I'm here to see that you are okay. Before I ask you how you're doing, I just want to let you know that you didn't do anything wrong and that you aren't in any trouble. (pause) How are you doing today, Dannie?

Dannie: Okay.

Susan: Does your eye hurt?

Dannie: Oh, not really. It looks worse than it is.

Susan: What happened?

Dannie: I was playing with my dog, and I hit my eye on the corner of the table. That's all.

Susan: Really?

Dannie: Yeah, that's all.

Susan: How do your parents get along?

Dannie: They get along fine. Why?

Susan: Someone who knows your mother tells me that there may be some problems at home. Do you ever see your parents fighting?

Dannie: Sometimes, yeah. My dad gets real mad.

Susan: And does he ever hit your mommy?

Dannie: Sometimes.

Susan: What does your mommy do?

Dannie: She starts crying and locks herself in the bathroom.

Susan: When was the last time your parents were fighting?

Dannie: Last night.

Susan: What happened?

Dannie: Dad hit mom with the phone book.

Susan: What did your mother do?

Dannie: She ran into the bathroom.

Susan: Where were you when this was going on?

Dannie: I was in my room when the fighting started and came out to watch what was going on.

Susan: Does your bruise have anything to do with your parents fighting?

Dannie: No.

Susan: And then what happened?

Dannie: Nothing . . . my mom was upset.

Susan: Kids really can't stop parents from fighting, but some kids tell me they wish it could be different. If it could be different, how would you like it to be? What would be your wish?

Dannie: I wish my dad wouldn't get so mad.

Susan:	Dannie, can you tell me anything else about your parents fighting, or about what happened last night?
Dannie:	No, there's nothing else to tell.
Susan:	Okay, well thanks Dannie for talking to me. It really helps. Maybe we will talk again soon.
Dannie:	Bye.
Susan:	Bye.

Susan's Reflection: *In this interaction Susan gets some information from Dannie that will be helpful to her interaction with Dannie's mother. She knows now that his parents are fighting and that there is some physical violence. She thinks that Dannie may be hiding that his black eye happened when his parents were fighting, but she can't be sure. She believes that she can pursue this further with Dannie's mother.*

Susan Martin arrives at Huong Nguyen's house around 11 a.m. She wants to find her at home alone, and she wants plenty of time to talk.

I. Affective Advocacy.   In the first part of the interview, Susan will use her Affective Advocacy skills to connect with Huong Nguyen. She will be honest about why she is there and about her reporting requirements. In addition, she will convey her interest in and concern for Huong.

Susan	(knocking on the door of the apartment).
Huong:	Who is it?
Susan:	Susan Martin from Child Protective Services.
Huong:	Who are you?
Susan:	I am here to talk to you about the bruise Dannie got on his eye the other night.
Huong:	Oh?
Susan:	Can I come in?
Huong:	I guess so.
Susan:	Hi, I am from Child Protective Services (handing her a business card and showing her a badge). We investigate whether or not child abuse is occurring in a family.
Huong:	Oh, why would you come here? Dannie fell when he was playing with the dog.
Susan:	Yes, that's what he told me, I saw him already at school.

Huong: You talked to Dannie?

Susan: Yes, I had a chance to talk with him at school.

Huong: What did he say?

Susan: That he got the black eye playing with the dog. But it also seems there may be more going on here.

Huong: What do you mean?

Susan: I understand you may be fighting with your husband. I see you also have bruising and swelling around your eye, which I would like to talk about. I have two questions: Is it safe for you to talk to me? And, are you willing?

Huong: I don't know.

Susan: Well, before you decide, I want to tell you that my job at Child Protective Services is to investigate any suspicion of child abuse. We also try our best to strengthen families and keep them safe. We also have this new program that recognizes that when parents fight—either verbally or physically—this often has an effect on the children. We are especially interested in working with mothers who may be experiencing some problems with their husbands or partners. What you tell me is important to me. I see a lot of families with this kind of problem, and I myself had some violence in my history. I am aware that because you are Vietnamese and I am not, that there are differences between us. My job is to help you with whatever is going on here, if anything, in a way that is sensitive to your needs. But I need to be honest with you. If it turns out that Dannie is exposed to serious harm, we will have to work together to protect him, to take care of him, to be sure he is not going to get hurt, if you are willing. If not, I may have to intervene without your help. But I will only do this if you are unwilling to take action to protect Dannie. Can I count on your help?

Huong: (crying) Why are you saying all this to me?

Susan: Because Huong, may I call you Huong?

Huong: Yes.

Susan: Because Huong, I am worried about you and your little boy.

Huong: Oh.

Susan: How do you and your husband get along? What is his name?

Huong: His name is Viet, and we get along fine most of the time.

Susan: So there are some good things about Viet. (pause) What happens when you fight?

Huong:	Oh, sometimes he gets a little physical, but mostly it is nothing.
Susan:	I take getting "a little physical," very seriously Huong. Can we talk more about your feelings about this?
Huong:	There's nothing to say really. It makes me really sad, but what can you do?
Susan:	I know a lot about getting help for people who are going through this, but let's talk more about whether or not you are safe.
Huong:	What will happen to Viet if I tell you things?
Susan:	I guess it depends on how difficult things are. Hopefully, my being involved can help make things better, not worse.

II. What happened and what's happening. At this point, Susan wants to find out what happened during the most recent incident and what's been happening in general.

Susan:	Do you want to tell me what happened when you got that bruise?
Huong:	Viet threw a phone book at me the other night, and I hit my eye.
Susan:	How did he throw it at you?
Huong:	He just threw it at me because he was mad.
Susan:	What happened after he threw the phone book at you?
Huong:	I hit my eye on the door and then I went into the bathroom and started crying.
Susan:	Did Dannie get hit during that time?
Huong:	No, he hit his eye when he was playing with the dog. Viet wouldn't hurt Dannie.
Susan:	Where was Dannie when the fight happened?
Huong:	He was upstairs in his room. He may have heard us fighting, but he didn't see what happened.

Susan's Reflection: *It is unclear at this point whether or not Huong is being honest about what happened to Dannie. Susan will need to figure out, with more information, whether or not Dannie is at risk for abuse or if witnessing the domestic violence is enough to take some action. Several factors will be relevant to this consideration. Susan is an "Empowerment-Oriented" practitioner (see chapter 6), but she is also affected by agency policy. She is currently working in a less restrictive CPS agency environment which means that she has more latitude to continue her assessment with this family over a period of time. Susan used to work in a more restrictive* *environment in which her mandate was to remove the child(ren) from the home if there was any threat to child safety. She is aware that the more restrictive the agency policy, the more difficult it is to be an empowerment-oriented practitioner. An Affirmative Action Plan for CSWs is a form that can help guide how CSWs might proceed in a case, depending on whether they are working in a more or less restrictive CPS environment (see Appendix III for Sample Affirmative Action Plans for CSWs).*

Susan continues her conversation with Huong and moves toward helping her make the connection between her abuse and its impact on Dannie.

Susan: I'm sure Dannie knows what is going on, indeed, most kids do know what happens when their parents are fighting. It upsets them, and they often say they feel its their fault. How do you think it affects Dannie?

Huong: I just assumed it didn't bother him because he never mentioned it.

Susan: Yeah, kids know. Witnessing your father hitting your mother can be as devastating as experiencing the violence yourself. It is hard for kids, and the studies show that many kids who grow up in households where there was some abuse are abusive to their partners when they grow up. Also, kids feel badly because they can't stop it or protect you. It makes kids feel powerless or having to choose between the two of you. When they grow up in this environment, it's easy to see how they could repeat the pattern when they become adults.

Susan's Reflection: *Here Susan begins the dialogue about Dannie and the impact the violence may be having on him. She is starting to call the problems "violence," preparing Huong for the Violence Tree (Figure 7.1), which Susan will introduce.*

Susan: I wonder if you would be willing to look at this diagram with me. The Tree describes the different kinds of problems people have in their families. I wonder if you could share with me whether any of these things have happened in your relationship with Viet.

Huong: Oh yeah. He is always yelling at me; he spit at me once, and sometimes he throws things at me, as I said. He has punched me once too.

Susan:	Do you notice under the "child abuse" category that there is something called "witnessing" (referring to the Tree)? That's when children see the violence between their parents—the position at my agency is that witnessing is a form of child abuse.
	Can you see how the abuses are connected through the branches? The abuses are painfully interconnected, as verbal abuse can lead to physical abuse, or emotional abuse can lead to sexual abuse. Also, you can begin to understand the origins of the violence, maybe stemming back to childhood.

III. Assessing This Battered Woman. Once Susan has become clearer about what's happening between Huong and Viet, and the implications of what's happening in Dannie's life, she can move to the next stage in the interview, which is to assess the battered woman. She begins by starting to contemplate the Survivor's Actions and Vulnerabilities Continuum (Figure 7.2). She realizes quickly that she needs more information and moves the dialogue to questions about the Heart of Intimate Abuse (Figure 2.3).

Susan:	I'm wondering if we could talk more about what's been going on with Viet. This Heart of Intimate Abuse diagram can help us talk about the ways you feel unsafe in your relationship and also what your perception of Viet's issues are. Are you willing to discuss it with me (showing her the Heart)?
Huong:	Okay.
Susan:	I am wondering how you feel about Viet.
Huong:	He is my husband. We have been together a long time and gone through a lot together, especially family stuff. He has been very good to me. He takes good care of us, and he loves us very much.
Susan:	Do you love him?
Huong:	Oh yes.
Susan:	It sounds like he can be wonderful to you. How does he take care of you?
Huong:	(smiling) He buys us nice things and takes us to nice restaurants. He cooks for us and we go to the park together. We have a nice time together.
Susan:	I wonder if you tolerate some of the hard parts of your relationship because you want Dannie to have his father around.

Huong: No question. Dannie needs his father! He idolizes him; he totally adores him. Plus his father plays baseball and things that I can't do.

Susan: How do you think your being Vietnamese in the U.S. influences what you tolerate from Viet?

Huong: Oh, we are very connected. Our culture is very important to us. Both our parents live nearby, and we see them every weekend. Being together is very important.

Susan: Do your parents know that Viet has punched you or thrown things at you?

Huong: Yeah. They have seen my bruises. But my dad did it to my mom, and his dad did it to his mom. That's the way it is. That's the way men and women get along.

Susan: Did you see your father hit your mother?

Huong: Yes.

Susan: How did it make you feel?

Huong: I hated it more than anything. I'd go into my room crying when he would get started. It was awful. But that's how we lived.

Susan: How would your parents feel if you took some time away from Viet?

Huong: Oh they would be very upset and angry. This is the way marriage should be.

Susan: Are you afraid of Viet?

Huong: No, not really. He is very small, and I know that I could defend myself if I needed to. I don't feel he is threatening, but it is upsetting.

Susan: How do you support yourself?

Huong: Viet makes most of the money. We need his money to live. I bring in some extra cash during the days, when I'm not in school, as a hairdresser.

Susan: Should we talk a bit about what you think makes Viet get angry (pointing to the right side of the Heart of Intimate Abuse). Do you think he loves you?

Huong: Oh yes, there is no question that Viet loves me.

Susan: How does he express that love?

Huong: By doing nice things for us.

Susan: Did he ever share with you his own history of witnessing violence in his family? Did you share with him yours?

Huong: Oh yeah, no question. When we first got together it was like we were brother and sister. Everything he had gone

through I'd gone through, and vice versa. Sometimes the
parallels were crazy. That's when things were really nice.
He was so good to me then.

*Susan's Reflection: Susan knows that one dynamic that often binds a
battered woman to a man is his own childhood history of violence. It is
helpful to learn the extent to which Viet shared his own history with Huong,
as this often makes the battered woman more sympathetic to his violence.*

Susan: Does he ever use Dannie to scare you?

Huong: Sometimes. If I talk about taking some time for myself, after
one of these things happen, he immediately says that he
will take Dannie away from me and not let me see him. I
can't be without my Dannie.

Susan: What role do you think Vietnamese culture has played in
his abuse.

Huong: He is a macho guy. He thinks he is entitled to do what he
wants in the world, and especially in his family. This is his
little kingdom.

Susan: Do you think he uses his culture or his manhood as an
excuse for being physical with you?

Huong: Yeah, I guess so. I never thought about it in that way.
He always says he is a Vietnamese man and that's what
Vietnamese men do. But I don't think it is right.

*Susan's Reflection: Susan senses with this comment that Huong is
starting to open up; that she is starting to touch her own strength. She wants
to reinforce her openness.*

Susan: What you just said makes sense to me Huong. You are
right, it isn't right. A woman is entitled to live her life free
of threat and violence. Can you see that?

Huong: Well, a little. But then I remember how hard he had it as
a kid and then I get all worried about him. He can't live
without us, he needs us.

Susan: I'm not sure where to go from here. It sounds like you
believe that what Viet does isn't that serious, and at the
same time, you feel you don't deserve it.

Huong: Yeah.

Susan: And how do you feel about Dannie living with this kind of
thing?

Huong: Yeah, I guess I see that it isn't good for him if he sees it.

Susan's Reflection: Susan again refers to the Survivor's Actions and Vulnerabilities Continuum to determine what Huong might do. She assesses what Huong's reasons are for staying. Her sense is that Huong is very embedded in this relationship. She loves Viet, there is a deep cultural connection, and she thinks Viet is a good father to Dannie. Next, Susan contemplates what resources she might be able to connect Huong with and what action Huong is willing to take. Her sense is that Huong might go only so far as encouraging Viet to get counseling. Susan feels comfortable with developing a Personal Safety Plan (Appendix II), just in case; she hopes Huong will be willing to make one. She still needs to assess Viet and his level of threat.

IV. Assessing the Batterer.   Now that Susan has a sense of where Huong is in relation to the Heart of Intimate Abuse, she can better read how Huong is interpreting Viet's violence. Now she must turn to assess Viet's threat.

Susan:	Would you consider getting Viet some help, maybe some counseling?
Huong:	Oh he would never do that.
Susan:	I know a group near here that is located in the Chinese Cultural Center. It is a good group counseling arrangement and they have special Vietnamese groups for men like Viet, most of whom are younger and living through what they learned in their families.
Huong:	I think it would be great if he is willing.

Susan's Reflection: Susan begins this part of the assessment by evaluating Huong's willingness or openness to change. Susan senses that Huong is not ready to take any more drastic action than getting Viet counseling and she, in turn, has assessed that she feels comfortable monitoring this situation. Working in a less restrictive CPS environment gives her an opportunity to keep an eye on this family—rather than to take the more drastic (and probably unnecessary) step of removing Dannie. Unless things get dramatically worse, Susan's sense is that Huong will stay with Viet. Before she makes her final assessment, she wants to learn more about Viet's threat.

Susan:	Maybe we should use my calendar so you can give me a sense, Huong, of the number and kinds of incidents we talked about when we went through the Violence Tree. In the last year, how many times has Viet physically hurt you?

Huong: Oh it has been two or three. It happens every 4 or 5 months, or so. You just happened to come on a bad day.

Susan: Does Viet have a criminal record?

Huong: Oh God no.

Susan: Has Viet ever been arrested?

Huong: No.

Susan: Has Viet destroyed things in the house or other property?

Huong: No.

Susan: Has he ever threatened suicide, or has he threatened to kill you?.

Huong: No.

Susan: Does he have access to any weapons?

Huong: No.

Susan: Does he drink or take any drugs?

Huong: No.

Susan: How long has he had his current job?

Huong: He's been at this company 6 years.

Susan's assessment is that Viet is not dangerous but that he is occasionally violent. She would place him as "Likely to-Reabuse" on the Batterer's Actions and Vulnerabilities Continuum (Figure 7.3); she is almost certain he will reabuse, especially without an intervention, but doesn't feel it would be life threatening.

Her tentative assessment is that Huong and Viet will stay together and that Viet would benefit, given that his violence may be susceptible to outside intervention, from group treatment. Huong seems to agree with that. Susan has residual worries about Dannie, who is witnessing the abuse; after all, Viet's violence is probably related to his own family history. She will need to interview Viet before her assessment is complete. Lastly, she will need to consult with her supervisor to ensure that she hasn't missed anything, that her actions are consistent with agency policy, and that her supervisor supports the plan. Susan will continue to monitor the situation, and if Dannie is injured again, she will challenge Huong very directly, especially now that they have established a connection. She will also develop a Personal Safety Plan with Huong just in case she needs one.

IV. Plan of Action.   To help finalize her decision on what action she and Huong should take, Susan reviews the Affirmative Action Plan; she is employed in a county that uses a less restrictive approach (Appendix III). Her options, given that she believes this case is a low to medium risk, depend on what Huong is willing to do. It is helpful first to review the Personal Safety Plan to get a better sense of what action Huong is willing to take.

Susan: Given that Dannie is living here and given Huong, that you have shared with me that Viet has been pretty consistently violent, I need to know that you and Dannie are going to be safe. Would you be willing to develop a Personal Safety Plan with me?

Huong: Well, what's that?

Susan: That's where we plan where you will go if Viet gets violent again. I am worried that Dannie will get in the line of fire, that is, that he will accidentally get hurt when Viet gets angry or violent, and I am worried about your safety. You are just as important as your child. Can you understand that?

Huong: Yeah, but if I leave Viet will get more mad. I can tell you that.

Susan: Yeah, the studies do show that when you leave, he might get angrier. But you also need to protect yourself and your son, and that is a good reason to leave. Planning how and when you leave is important. Do you have a place you can go if you need to?

Huong: Well, I can't go to my parents. Maybe I could go to my girlfriend's house.

Susan: Does Viet know her?

Huong: No, not really; we are friends from the beauty shop.

Susan: Okay, that's good.

They proceeded to go through all of the sections in the Personal Safety Plan and also filled out the Social Support Inventory Forms (Appendix II). The Social Support Inventory will help Susan assess Huong's willingness to act and also the availability of resources in her life, both emotional and material. Susan and Huong talk about her willingness to call the police if she needs to, and she seems to feel comfortable doing so if the violence escalates.

Susan's Reflection: *Susan concludes that Huong is willing to protect Dannie and is willing to encourage Viet to go to batterer's treatment. These are the department's conditions for the child remaining in the home. Many* *agencies formalize this arrangement with a behavioral contract, rather than court intervention. Given that Huong is willing to do these things and that she feels Viet is a low to medium threat risk at this time, Susan will monitor the situation by continuing an ongoing assessment and ensuring that Viet is enrolled in and attending treatment. Huong also agrees that it would do her some good to talk with other Vietnamese women about these issues. Susan does not require her to attend counseling at this time. She is encouraging Huong to take that step on her own. Another equally valid CSW approach might be to require Huong to attend the women's group, on the assumption that she deserves (and needs) support and a chance to find out how other women manage the abuse (for a more complete discussion of these treatment issues, see chapter 4).*

Susan closes the interview by giving Huong her pager number and by reassuring her that with some intervention, she hopes that Viet's violence will lessen. Susan agrees to return that evening to talk to Viet about the treatment and about her involvement in the case. She reassures Huong that she will be available and that now that Susan is involved there might be an escalation of the abuse. That's where the Personal Safety Plan comes in, and her willingness to call the police. Huong suggests what time she should return, and Susan agrees.

At the designated time, Susan returns to talk with Viet. Susan knocks after listening at the door to determine if the situation seems threatening and to be sure that it is safe for her to enter. After determining that it isn't threatening, Susan knocks on the door.

Susan:	(knocking) Hello—
Viet:	Hello. Who is it?
Susan:	My name is Susan Martin. I am from the Department of Child Protective Services. Are you Viet Nguyen?
Viet:	Yes.
Susan:	Can I come in?
Viet:	What do you want?
Susan:	I want to talk to you about what's been going on with Huong and Dannie.
Viet:	(opening the door) What do you mean, what's been going on.
Susan:	Child Protective Services monitors child abuse and domestic violence cases. I am here because I was alerted that your son had a black eye. When I arrived to talk to your wife, she too had a black eye. It seemed to me that it was not

	self-inflicted and we need to talk about your involvement in this situation.
Viet:	And . . . why are you here?
Susan:	Because by law, I assess and intervene in cases involving child abuse and domestic violence.
Viet:	There is no child abuse here, so you can leave.
Susan:	Well, the truth is that if Dannie is seeing you hit your wife, this is called "witnessing" of domestic violence and that is a form of child abuse.
Susan:	Do you want to sit down with me, Mr. Nguyen, and discuss what's been going on? The other choice is that we bring the police into this discussion. I cannot leave without discussing the situation. Would you rather do this with me or with me and the police?
Viet:	You.

Susan's Reflection: Susan needs to assess his threat and also wants to get a sense of what his insight is into his own violence.

Susan:	How do you think you and your wife have been getting along?
Viet:	We get along fine. Sometimes we fight, but everyone fights.
Susan:	But not everyone fights physically.
Viet:	Well my parents did and their parents did. That's how it is in the Vietnamese community.
Susan:	It may be that some members of your community find it acceptable. But it isn't okay; indeed, it is against the law to hit your wife.
Viet:	It is?
Susan:	Yes. It is a crime. You could go to jail or even prison for domestic violence crimes.
Viet:	Well, she makes me so mad sometimes; it is very frustrating.
Susan:	If Huong is making you mad, you need to discuss it without violence. I am also worried about Dannie. As a children's social worker, I am concerned and will be monitoring Dannie. This means I will also monitor what you are doing and your involvement. Dannie's witnessing of you and your wife fighting can be devastating for him. Do you think there is a risk that Dannie will be hurt when you are being violent toward Huong?
Viet:	No, Dannie is always in his room if we are fighting.

Susan: Well, you have a point, it may start out that way. Most kids I talk to tell me they come out and watch the fighting. They even try to protect their moms. Sometimes what they hear is just as frightening as what they see. (pause) I want to be honest with you; Child Protective Services tries first to keep families together, when it's safe for everybody. When that is not possible, we can and do take action. Are you willing to work with me to keep your family together?

Viet: Huong told me that you wanted me to go to some classes. I'm not sure what's involved with that.

Susan: There is a batterer's treatment group at the Chinese Cultural Center down the street and I want you to start attending. In fact, I will require that you attend as a condition of Dannie and Huong staying here. I will get weekly reports of your progress. If anything happens again, and I feel I need to intervene, I may ask Huong and Dannie to leave the house, and the police may also get involved. So you need to know I am serious about monitoring the situation.

Viet: I guess I am willing to go.

Susan's Reflection: Based on all the interviews, Susan is somewhat satisfied that Viet does not pose a high risk to Huong and that he is willing to participate in treatment, even if reluctantly. There is at least some anecdotal evidence that pressure from the criminal justice system, or even the threat of intervention, can be enough to get compliance from a law-abiding Asian American man (Yung, 1997). Susan will keep a close eye on the situation, talking to Huong every couple of days (as necessary) for the next 2 or 3 weeks and also checking in with Viet and Dannie. Susan will take more drastic action if Viet's violence escalates or if he does not comply with the treatment program's demands.

TYPES OF BATTERER TREATMENT PROGRAMS

This case study raises questions about types of batterer treatment programs and their effectiveness. Practitioners should be familiar with the kinds of treatment programs that are available, and how to assess their effectiveness for their particular client.

Most batterer treatment programs are mandated or are designed to last at least one year. It is important to carefully evaluate programs because there are certainly differences among them (see Box 9.1). Some programs focus only on extinguishing physi-

---

Box 9.1 BATTERER TREATMENT PROGRAM PHILOSOPHIES*

Cognitive-Behavioral and Psychoeducational Models

- Violence stems from learned behavior, either through witnessing or as victims of child abuse. Or it can be learned or reinforced when battering has no legal or social consequences (Tolman & Bennett, 1990).
- Violence is also seen as an anger control problem (Scalia, 1994).
- Therapy works on unlearning violent behavior and on controlling anger and stress (Adams, 1988).
- CRITIQUE: When treatment is not combined with sociocultural explanations, it fails to consider gender dynamics, including issues of power and control, which legitimize violence against women. When treatment occurs in group settings, it fails to address individual differences between batterers (Moore, Greenfield, Wilson, & Kok, 1997). Treatment approaches, including confrontation, can mimic the batterer's abuse and reinforce negative styles (Scalia, 1994).

Profeminist Model

- Violence reinforces the power and control of men over women and ensures that the imbalance will be maintained (Bograd, 1988; Yllö & Straus, 1990).
- Violence can be physical or emotional. Intimidating acts are also common as the batterer attempts to maintain power and control. The batterer bears sole responsibility for the abuse and its consequences (Adams, 1988; Bograd, 1988, 1992).
- Therapy involves education as well as challenges to sexist attitudes and behaviors and forces batterers to confront all controlling behaviors (Adams, 1988).
- CRITIQUE: Treatment discourages joint counseling, which the battered woman might view as necessary for keeping the relationship together. This approach is less sympathetic to family origins of violence, which the battered woman might want to explore with the batterer.

---

cally violent battering patterns without addressing the cultural and social structural supports that underpin the battering of women and the acceptance of battering. These include hierarchical social relationships based on gender, linguistic structures that objectify women, and gender socialization that keep women in subordinate positions.

Box 9.1 *(continued)*

Insight Model

- Problems are intrapsychic and stem from early developmental difficulties (Adams, 1988).
- Therapy focuses on the past and how it is affecting present behavior (Whitfield, 1987).
- Therapy works on building the self-esteem of a fragile human being, redefining masculinity, fathering, and coparenting, and addressing fears of intimacy (Carden, 1994; Whitfield, 1987).
- CRITIQUE: Insight Model does not address structural problems such as inequality in a relationship. Batterers are not held strictly accountable for their violence (Pence & Shepard, 1988; Whalen, 1996).

Interactional or Systems Theory

- Problems stem from the dynamics in a couple or family; responsibility for violence in a relationship is therefore shared (Erchak, 1984; Neidig, 1984).
- Assigning blame for the violence undermines individual power and misplaces culpability (Neidig, 1984).
- Joint therapy is necessary because "it truly does take two to quarrel" (Cook & Frantz-Cook, 1984; Deschner, 1984; Neidig & Friedman, 1984).
- The therapy works on both people to change his/her contribution to the problems, including violence (Adams, 1988).
- CRITIQUE: Systems Theory is overly concerned with preserving the relationship, never dealing with the power imbalance often endemic to it (Bograd, 1984).

*Often, treatment programs will combine philosophies to address the shortcomings of particular approaches. For example, many treatment programs integrate behavioral, cognitive, and feminist approaches (Saunders, 1996). Some practitioners advocate for the use of insight techniques when providing a cognitive-behavioral treatment modality (Scalia, 1994).

The research of Prochaska, Diclemente, and Norcross (1992) conducted on addictive behavior reveals that relapse is the rule, rather than the exception. According to Prochaska et al. (1992), people naturally change within a stage paradigm. Precontemplation usually involves no intent to change in the foreseeable future; the person seeks treatment only under pressure; he is resistant to recognizing or modifying a problem. The Contemplation stage involves a growing awareness of the problem; the person starts thinking about change but is not yet committed to action. In the Preparation stage, the person intends to take change action that he has unsuccessfully attempted in the past. The Action stage involves the modification of behavior, and the Decision-making stage involves the person working to prevent relapse, to consolidate his gains. This "Action" work becomes the work of a lifetime.

For treatment to be effective, it is often helpful to match the client to his stage of change (Dutton, 1995). Some batterers might find themselves entrenched in the Precontemplation and Contemplation Stages if they have been unreflective of their violence and are resistant to change. For batterers who have a long uncontrolled history or for "sociopathic" batterers, reflection and change is even more difficult (Saunders, 1996).

ARE BATTERERS' COUNSELING PROGRAMS EFFECTIVE?

Whether batterers' counseling programs are truly effective at reducing intimate abuse remains unclear. Reviews of the research on batterers' treatment are numerous (Eisikovits & Edleson, 1989; Gondolf, 1991, 1997a; Rosenfeld, 1992; Tolman & Bennett, 1990). These reviews indicate that there is cessation of violence in a substantial portion of those batterers who complete treatment (60% to 80%); there is a less impressive reduction in verbal abuse and verbal threats. Gondolf (1997a) reports several methodological shortcomings of these studies, which compromise the validity and reliability of these findings, including: battered women's response rates (30% to 45%), short-term follow-up after treatment (generally 6 months), reliance on self-report measures, lack of control groups, event-oriented outcomes, effect of intervening variables such as victim services, and "completer" subjects that fail to account for dropouts and other noncompliant subjects (Gondolf, 1997a). Some theories advanced by Gondolf (1997a) try to explain the positive findings of these studies, including: the participant's motivation (Rosenfeld, 1992), differences in personality traits among batterers (Saunders, 1996), program structure and community linkages (Edleson & Tolman, 1992), and social context (Gondolf, 1997b). The greatest problem with batterer treatment is that the majority of programs experience high drop-out rates, ranging between 40–60% in 3 months (DeMaris, 1989; Gondolf, 1990; Pirog-Good & Stets, 1986).

Group treatment for batterers has been the primary method employed in this country (Dutton, 1995). Group treatment provides batterers with an opportunity to practice new skills and to receive reinforcement from the treatment coordinator (Dutton, 1995). Batterers also have an opportunity to discuss and share feelings with other group members. They receive feedback on cognitive distortions and denial from members in the group who are at various stages of awareness (Dutton, 1995). The increased feedback can augment the batterer's own perceptions of the situation. Batterers have an opportunity to role play family dynamics through male and female pairing of group therapists, where they can argue with the opposite sex without a partner actually being present. Group members support each other and provide humor, camaraderie, and friendship, and, most importantly, they reinforce nonabusive behavior.

Recent studies have questioned the effectiveness of these methods which often rely on a combination of philosophical approaches (see Box 9.1) (Browne, Saunders, & Staecker, 1997; Carden, 1994; Jennings, 1987; Moore, et al., 1997; Saunders, 1996; Scalia, 1994; Schubmehl, 1991). The most widely used model is the feminist-cognitive behavioral intervention, also known as the psychoeducational power and control intervention, which is offered in a group setting. The debate focuses on whether a confrontational approach concerned, almost exclusively, with changing behavior rather than increasing insight with the batterers' abusive styles, is efficacious for all types of abusers. The question is whether a one-size-fits-all approach to treatment is working.

Saunders (1996) examined this issue by analyzing the interaction of abuser traits with treatment models. He found that men with antisocial traits had better outcomes when they received feminist cognitive-behavioral treatment, whereas men with dependent personalities had better outcomes in insight-oriented or "process-psychodynamic" groups. Dutton, Bodnarchuk, Kropp, Hart, and Ogloff (1997) found in a study of post-treatment recidivism that elevations on personality disorder profiles (borderline, antisocial, and avoidant) were the strongest predictors for whether men would reabuse after treatment. Together these studies suggest the importance of pre-treatment screening to ensure that the batterer's particular personality and other traits are detected and specifically addressed when determining which treatment is appropriate.

Although not all batterers batter for the same reasons, some issues are common themes to consider when assessing the appropriateness of a treatment program. The first is power. Most batterers have a need for control and often believe that if a partner is independent, the batterer has lost control. Batterers often set rules for the relationship and then force their partner to adopt those rules (Dutton, 1995).

A second common theme is related to issues of intimacy. We have learned that pregnancy often leads to increased abuse (McFarlane & Parker, 1994). Pregnancy requires a shift in roles—to mother and father—and the batterer may feel trapped by the partner's increased need for affection and support.

Another issue is how batterers deal with arousal and whether or not it leads to aggression (Dutton, 1995). Batterers often have difficulty thinking through the consequences of their behavior at the time their anger is aroused. An issue that often arises in treatment is their ability and willingness to subject arousal to cognitive control.

A final issue is the batterer's belief system and whether or not the batterer is willing to work on cognitive restructuring (Dutton, 1995). Batterers often hold beliefs about their female partners based on sexism or old family patterns. The issue is whether they are willing to change.

The studies indicate that men underreport their violence (Dutton, 1986). One extended study of court-mandated treatment (Dutton, 1986) found that both husbands and wives reported less violence following the treatment, although their specific reports often differed. The reasons for the variance in the rating of the husband's violence by husband and wife include the fact that the batterer may not view or recognize his actions as violent. The batterer may be invested in his denial or minimization.

The question about a treatment program's ability to guarantee safety or reduce risk is an important one and should be considered. Although incidents of violence do decrease post treatment, they still persist. Treatment possibly reduces the risk but does not guarantee a battered woman's safety. It may also indicate that minimization and denial will continue to persist once treatment has begun.

Batterer treatment programs have increased in number, and courts sometimes require batterers to enter these programs. The goals of a treatment program should include specifically addressing the unique features and traits of this batterers' abuse pattern and improving protection for the victim who chooses to remain in the relationship. More tailored treatment, including culturally oriented approaches which are closely monitored, can reinforce the community's commitment to a battered woman's safety and well-being.

The following are some factors to consider when evaluating treatment programs for batterers.

1.   Determine the program's orientation and suitability for a particular batterer. Since batterers differ concerning the etiology of the abuse and the nature of the violence, the program needs to be tailored to this batterer's specific characteristics (Saunders, 1996). For some batterers, certain treatments may never be effective, or culturally sensitive treatment may be necessary (Edleson, 1996). Consult the Violence Tree, the Heart of Intimate Abuse, and the Assessment of Threat for the issues operating in assessing this offender.

2.   Make sure that the program is certified.

3.   Check to see if the program keeps records of short-term and long-term recidivism rates. A program that is concerned with its effectiveness over a long period of time is one that is itself reflective and change oriented.

4.   Ask about the program's willingness to provide written progress reports to you. Tell them that you will get a signed client release.

5.   Find out what constitutes compliance, progress, and grounds for termination.

SUMMARY AND REFLECTIONS

Reasons why these 11 women had not disclosed the abuse they experienced to social workers may have

included the control rather than care nature of the
social services' involvement.

(Mullender, 1996, p. 97)

When a CSW intervenes in a family, their whole world is shattered.
How that interaction unfolds is everything. Even in the face of
growing caseloads, CSWs must be cognizant of their power and
use it in ways that ameliorate, rather than exacerbate, the violence. What is strikingly obvious from the interactions traced in
this chapter is that domestic violence training is needed to prepare the CSW for the unique issues posed by the intersections
of domestic violence and child welfare.

Some people reviewing this case study may feel that Susan
Martin did not do enough. Chances are that these practitioners fall
on the "Authority-Oriented" side of the Continuum of Intervention
(Figure 6.1). "Empowerment-Oriented" practitioners will probably
be able to see how this kind of interaction, one that does not rob
Huong Nguyen of her power over and within her family but rather
reinforces it, can contribute to her own sense of strength and to
a rebalancing of control in their abusive relationship.

Huong was not, of her own volition, leaving Viet on the day of
this interview. She had not yet reached a breaking point, nor did
she feel "enough was enough" (Fischer & Rose, 1995). Had Susan
Martin measured the violence as a high risk or life-threatening,
she would have tried to persuade Huong to action. She may or
may not have been successful. If she had been successful, Susan
might have placed Huong and Dannie at Huong's girlfriend's
house, depending in part on the availability of shelter beds for
a Vietnamese woman and her son. Susan may also have required
her to obtain a restraining order. Susan may have had Viet arrested. These interventions may or may not have exacerbated
Viet's violence, may or may not have ameliorated it. All the time,
Susan would be aware that Huong was far from ready to leave
Viet, that she had many vulnerabilities to face before such drastic
action could be imagined.

Susan is aware, both because she has reflected on these issues
and lived and breathed them through her work, that she will not
end the violence in Huong's life. She must help Huong act on her
own behalf and on behalf of Dannie and help her imagine a life

without Viet's violence. She must help to unravel years of conditioning in which both she and Viet were taught to believe that violence was inevitable in an intimate relationship and that there was nothing they could do about it. Susan Martin established enough of a connection with this family, and particularly with Huong, to help navigate through this unchartered territory together.

In the next chapter we explore case studies from the health care system and expose a method for empowering battered women, even when mandatory reporting is required.

QUESTIONS

❏ If you are a CSW, would you interview Dannie before or after you interviewed Huong? What are the merits of each?

❏ What are the advantages and disadvantages of warning Huong of your mandated reporting status?

❏ What Affirmative Action would you take in this case:

- if you are working in a less restrictive CPS agency environment?

- if you are working in a more restrictive CPS agency environment?

❏ Where do you fall on the Continuum of Intervention in this case? Do you agree with Susan Martin's approach? What would you have done differently?

CHAPTER 10

Empowerment and Affective Strategies III: Meetings in Health Care

> . . . I knew that if I was to tell them what actually happened that they would call the police and . . . they couldn't guarantee me that they would be there 24 hours to protect me from this maniac. So, therefore, I wasn't taking a chance on my life. . . . What [I would have] preferred [would have been for it] to be my choice. Well I need help, can you call the police? Or if, um, this happened to me but I don't want the police involved, can you please treat me and keep my confidentiality . . .
>
> Participant, Battered Women Focus Group
> (Mooney & Rodriguez, 1996, p. 97)

Domestic violence in health care practice poses a different set of challenges from those we have explored in the criminal justice and child protection systems. Mandatory reporting, whatever form it may take, further clouds a relationship between doctor and patient, a relationship that is already fraught with tension and misunderstanding (Waitzkin, 1991). Feminist complaints about the interactions between male doctors and female patients abound (Lewin & Olesen, 1985; Lorber, 1984). It is domestic violence, possibly more than any other issue, that poses the greatest challenge to health care professionals as they open Pandora's box.

With the increase of women physicians and the emerging emphasis on family practice, some doctors may be more willing to embrace the issue of intimate abuse, to see it as within their medical purview. Without their help, interventions will remain exclusively in the criminal justice domain, a realm that most battered women will very likely avoid. In addition, dentists, nurses, physician's assistants, and medical social workers must be prepared to address intimate abuse in the health care setting. Although many health care professionals may still "look the other way," this chapter is designed to guide willing practitioners through the morass of these interactions, with the intent of empowering battered women in the process.

This chapter presents two case studies. The first case study, set in a hospital emergency room, involves a nurse and a doctor and a battered woman. The second case study, set at an HMO, involves two interviews. The first is an interview between a nurse and a doctor and a battered woman. The second interview is between a doctor and a batterer.

Before proceeding to the case studies, it is useful to review some of the issues that are likely to underpin these interactions, such as mandatory reporting, dual relationships (where the physician treats both the battered woman and the batterer), and the ever-vexing problem of the practitioner's countertransference in relation to the issue of domestic violence.

Mandatory reporting, of one kind or another, is instituted in one form or another, in all states except three (see chapter 5). In a mandatory reporting situation health practitioners know what they have to do. If they suspect domestic violence, they must contact law enforcement. The issue, under these circumstances, is how to tell the victim they have a duty to intervene and to help manage her reaction. Most importantly, the health care practitioner must prepare the battered woman for the danger which might be triggered by the report and in doing so should develop a Personal Safety Plan (Appendix II). Because some form of mandatory reporting of domestic violence has been instituted in nearly every state, Case Study I explores how such a breach of confidentiality may be handled sensitively in an interaction with a battered woman.

The second vexing problem that is likely to arise in domestic violence cases is how health practitioners should respond when the batterer is known by the physician either because he appears at the emergency room or because he is a patient in the same practice. Some researchers in the area have argued that it may be inappropriate to treat both a wife and a husband if they are in a battering relationship and that there is a "conflict of interest" (Herbert, 1991). Others have argued that both the battered woman and the batterer can benefit from intervention by the health care practitioner (Ferris, Norton, Dunn, Gort, & Degani, 1997). These issues are addressed in Case Study II, in which the family physician confronts the batterer, at the request of her patient, the battered woman.

As is critical for all practitioners working in domestic violence, health care personnel should become aware of where they fall on the Continuum of Intervention (see chapter 6). Some health care practitioners, either because of their own experience of violence or because of their reflections on it, believe that intervention from outside agencies should only be appropriate if the battered woman is incapable of "managing" the situation on her own. Hence, in their minds, most battered women should be given options and assistance but should not be forced to respond in a way that a professional demands. This approach is usually adopted by an "Empowerment-Oriented" practitioner (Figure 6.1). Other professionals might believe that all battered women suffer from some form of Battered-Woman Syndrome and that outside intervention, regardless of the victim's protestations, is necessary and advisable. I have referred to this approach as "Authority-Oriented" (Figure 6.1). As health care practitioners, it is helpful to reflect on these divergent approaches and to know where you fall on this continuum. Are you able to make the long-term investment in empowerment that allows the battered woman to guide when and how professional intervention occurs? Are you comfortable taking that risk? It is helpful to remember that where you fall on the continuum often differs, depending on any given case.

This chapter proceeds by exploring these questions through the case studies presented. Case Study I explores how health care personnel can navigate an interaction with a battered woman who presents with a stab wound when a mandated report is made. In Case Study II, the battered woman and her husband are patients in the same family practice. The battered woman tells the family practitioner and her nurse that she has sustained multiple injuries from her battering husband, who is also a patient in the practice. A subsequent interview with the batterer is also presented.

CASE STUDY I: JOYCE MACK MEETS EMERGENCY HOSPITAL STAFF

Joyce Mack presents to the emergency room with a knife wound to her leg. She is a white woman and by profession an Executive Assistant in a corporation. Ms. Mack tells the presenting nurse, Nurse Hawkins, that she accidentally stabbed herself with a kitchen knife when she was cooking dinner for her live-in lover. The story is suspicious to the nurse, who alerts the attending physician that the story "doesn't add up."

Dr. Stern is the Attending Physician on duty at the hospital. He is aware of his duty to report an incident of violence if there is a deadly weapon involved. Joyce Mack's injury is not too terribly severe. It is a superficial wound, but nevertheless it involves a "deadly weapon." He has had some contact with domestic violence victims as an Attending Physician and has attended several trainings on how to intervene in domestic violence cases (see Box 10.1). He is aware from the nurse that the patient's story is dubious. He wants to work closely with the nurse, who is a woman, to ensure that Joyce Mack feels as comfortable as she can given that he will have to alert law enforcement to her injury.

Dr. Stern and Nurse Hawkins meet Joyce Mack as she is lying on a gurney.

Doctor:	Hi, My name is Dr. Stern. I am the Attending Physician on duty tonight and want to find out how you are doing. Nurse Hawkins tells me that you stabbed yourself with a knife while you were cooking. Can I examine it?
Joyce:	Sure. It was so stupid of me, I can't believe I did it. Do you think it will be okay?
Doctor:	(examining Ms. Mack) The wound looks superficial, which

Box 10.1 Mandatory Reporting Jurisdictions: Steps for Intervention

1. Assess wounds and injuries.
2. Treat wounds and injuries.
3. Assess duty to report (depending on the state).
4. Be direct that you suspect abuse.
5. Tell victim that you must report.
6. Tell victim that what she tells you will be told to the police.
7. Attempt to discuss the violence (Violence Tree, Heart of Intimate Abuse).
8. Call the police.
9. Develop Personal Safety Plan.
10. Schedule follow-up appointments.

	means that it doesn't look like it penetrated any vessels. You're lucky because there are some important arteries in your leg that can cause a lot of trouble. How long ago did you get a tetanus shot?
Joyce:	Oh, years ago I would think.
Doctor:	Okay, well I would like to give you a tetanus shot and then give you a few stitches and close up the wound. We will schedule an appointment 3 days from now to take the stitches out and to make sure the wound is healing properly. We will also send a record of your visit to your family physician.
Joyce:	Okay. How long do you think I will be here tonight? My friend is at home waiting for me, and I need to get back.
Doctor:	We should have you out of here in a couple of hours. But there's something else we need to talk about.
Joyce:	What's that?
Doctor:	The nurse and I were talking about how this injury occurred. (Pause) We are concerned that the knife wound wasn't an accident but rather was something else that may have happened.
Joyce:	What do you mean?
Nurse:	You said that you accidentally stabbed yourself when you were cooking. However, the position of the wound is such that you couldn't have really stabbed yourself in that way. May I call you Joyce?

Joyce: Sure.

Nurse: Joyce, we are suspecting that maybe something else is going on, especially because I noticed that you also had some bruising on your arm. (Pause) Did you and your friend have a fight?

Joyce: No. What bruising? What are you talking about?

Nurse :   (pointing to the bruises) Here, on your arm, that is fresh bruising. It seems like those were inflicted by someone else, as maybe was the knife wound. Did you and your friend fight tonight?

Joyce: No, as I said, it happened as I said.

Doctor: Would you like me to leave the room so you can talk about this with Nurse Hawkins? Would you feel more comfortable with me outside?

Joyce: No, I have nothing to hide from you or from anyone.

Doctor: Well, let me tell you the situation we are in. The law in this state provides that if we suspect that a wound is caused by a "deadly weapon" we must report it to the authorities.

Joyce: This wasn't a deadly weapon, it was a kitchen knife for God's sake.

Doctor: This is an awfully large cut for a kitchen knife. Was it a large knife?

Joyce: It was a fairly large knife, I was cutting raw chicken with it.

Doctor: Joyce, I am hoping that you can be honest with me. Either way I will have to have the authorities intervene in this situation, but neither Nurse Hawkins nor myself can be sure that these wounds are self-inflicted. The bruises suggest otherwise, and even the stab wound, in the place it is on your leg, doesn't make sense.

Joyce: What will happen to me?

Doctor: Well, the police will come by the hospital and want to interview you and then they will go by the house and interview your friend.

Joyce: What will happen to my friend?

Doctor: He might get arrested, depending on what the evidence turns up. Are you sure you don't want to tell me anything more about what happened tonight?

Joyce: (Upset) No.

Dr. Stern leaves the room, hoping that if the nurse has a chance to talk with Joyce, that Joyce will soften and maybe even reveal her secret. He is 99% certain that the injuries were not caused by her accident, as she claims, and therefore he feels he is in a reporting situation. He doesn't necessarily believe in the mandatory reporting law, sees the negative consequences of it, and wishes he didn't have to report. But he feels compelled. He calls the police, knowing that there will be some lead time before they arrive.

Dr. Stern then delivers the medical treatment Joyce needs. After the medical procedure is completed, Nurse Hawkins and Joyce Mack have a chance to talk.

Nurse: Joyce, maybe it would help if we explored how you and your friend get along. What's your friend's name?

Joyce: His name is Stephen, Stephen's his name.

Nurse: How do you get along?

Joyce: We get along okay. We get along great. We have been together 7 years now and we have the usual fights but nothing big.

Nurse: What kind of fights are the usual fights?

Joyce: You know, over money and over his not working. Sometimes we fight about the kids.

Nurse: Do you have kids together?

Joyce: No, I have kids with another man; they don't live with me, but they often come and visit.

Nurse: Were they there tonight?

Joyce: No.

Nurse: Joyce, do you love Stephen?

Joyce: Oh yes. He has been good to me in the past; he is just going through a really bad time right now because he isn't working. Usually, he makes sets for the movie industry, and everything is quiet right now and there isn't any work.

Nurse: What are the wonderful things Stephen has done or does for you?

Joyce: He fixes my car, he makes me breakfast in bed, and he makes me jewelry. See, he made me this beautiful silver bracelet.

Nurse: What are some of the harder things about your relationship?

Joyce: He has been really angry for the last few months; really grumpy. He yells at me when I leave for work and when I get back. He doesn't want me going out with my friends, and he is afraid I am laughing at him behind his back.

Nurse: Has he threatened to hurt you in any way or to commit suicide?

Joyce: Oh no, he loves me too much to do that sort of stuff.

Nurse: Maybe you would be willing to look at this diagram that we call the Violence Tree (Figure 7.1) with me. But before we do, you need to know that if you tell me things, I will have to share them with the police.

Joyce: Then I guess we shouldn't even get to talking because I won't tell you a thing; not if it will get Stephen in trouble.

Nurse: I understand. This reporting law makes it difficult for health professionals to work with people who may be in dangerous situations. But before I go, I'd like to share some resources with you in case you need a place to be safe.

Nurse Hawkins leaves Joyce with referrals to shelters, hotlines, and women's counseling groups. To give closure to their time together, Nurse Hawkins wants to reassure Joyce that she is there for her and that whatever happened she could count on her and Dr. Stern for their support if she needed it.

Nurse: Joyce, I sense that you were nearly ready to share with me what was going on in your relationship, that there were some things happening that were hard for you and that you were worried about.

Joyce: (tearful) Yeah.

Nurse: I know this reporting thing can be really hard, and I am sorry for the impact it will have on your relationship. But sometimes police intervention in the earlier stages of violence in a relationship can be really helpful, or sometimes it can make things worse. I just want you to know that I and Dr. Stern are here for you. He is a good doctor and cares about his patients. The only reason we are making the report is because the law requires us to. Don't be afraid to come back; I can help you negotiate the system and help you get services you may need. I want you to feel that I will be here for you and that if you need to come back to the hospital at any time that you can. If I am not here, all the staff are trained in this kind of intervention, and they will all be sensitive to what you need.

I think that before you leave the hospital tonight we should spend a little time developing a Personal Safety Plan (Appendix II), so that if something happens between

you and Stephen, you will have a plan for what to do.
Would you mind doing that with me?

Joyce: I don't think I need to, but if you feel I should, and as long
as I'm sitting here, okay.

They develop a Personal Safety Plan without ever discussing what
happened.

Nurse: There is one more thing. This is the Heart of Intimate Abuse
(handing her the diagram) (Figure 2.3). You may want to
take this diagram with you and think about how the dynamics on the heart are affecting your relationship. This may
help you understand what's going on better, both in terms
of your own vulnerabilities and Stephen's as well. If you
want to come back and talk about it, I would be happy to
do so. Or, I could help you get a counselor, who wouldn't
otherwise be bound to report the domestic violence and
who could talk with you about what's been going on.

Joyce: Okay.

Before Nurse Hawkins says goodbye, she gets Dr. Stern.

Dr. Stern: I heard that you and Nurse Hawkins had a chance to talk
and that she was able to reassure you that if you need to
come back to the emergency room for anything that you
should feel comfortable doing so. Please, don't ever feel
afraid of coming here.

Joyce: (with trepidation) Okay.

Nurse: Okay for now. We have scheduled an appointment for a
few days from now so that we can check the wound and
check back in with you. I will be here at the time you are
scheduled to return, and so will Dr. Stern.

Dr. Stern and Nurse Hawkins leave the room.

CRITICAL ANALYSIS

This interaction reflects the impossibilities posed by a mandatory
reporting situation. If the health care practitioner hopes to keep
channels open with a victim, it is important to be honest and up

front about reporting requirements. If the practitioner is dishonest or withholding about her status as a mandated reporter, she may alienate Joyce forever. Honesty leaves the door open, allowing Joyce to return to the practitioner in the spirit of the safety they cultivated. There is no doubt that the nurse's decision to warn Joyce that their conversation was not confidential stifled this interaction. The decision to warn Joyce of her reporting duties can be interpreted in two ways. First, that it was a mistake to disclose her status as a reporter because Joyce may have revealed the abuse to Nurse Hawkins. Another interpretation is that Nurse Hawkins' honesty is good long-term planning; when Joyce is really ready to share, she will do so from a position of strength and resolve. Dr. Stern's decision to have some closure with Joyce was important so that the doctor and the nurse could be seen as aligned. If Joyce returns to the emergency room and meets Dr. Stern without Nurse Hawkins, she can remember that they were both part of an honest and supportive interaction that Joyce can count on in the future.

Two other components of this interview should be highlighted. First, Nurse Hawkins was able to convince Joyce to do a Personal Safety Plan, without ever admitting that the violence occurred. This enabled Joyce to be prepared for future incidents of violence. This is particularly key given that Nurse Hawkins and Dr. Stern could not predict how Stephen might react to police intervention (Ferris et al., 1997). Second, it is important to schedule a follow-up visit with the patient to learn more about what happened. If she misses that visit, a follow-up call should be made. Ensuring that the patient makes contact with the family physician is also important, so that consistent care can be monitored.

CASE STUDY II: THE GOODYS MEET THE FAMILY PRACTITIONERS

This case involves Dr. Janet Rubin, who works as a family practitioner in an HMO in a state that does not mandate reporting of a domestic violence crime. Dr. Rubin's nurse is Nurse Darrell. Dr. Rubin and Nurse Darrell have known the Goodys for a long time. At various points, both the doctor and the nurse have suspected

---

Box 10.2 Nonmandatory Reporting Jurisdictions: Steps for Intervention in a Dual Relationship

1. Be direct if you suspect domestic violence.
2. Use language that won't alienate the survivor, like "problems" and "tensions." Introduce "violence" and "abuse" slowly.
3. Use the Tree of Violence and the Heart of Intimate Abuse to explore what's been happening in the relationship. Discuss her vulnerabilities.
4. Assess the threat.
5. Present the options: call the police, treatment, discuss the matter with the abuser.
6. How does she want you to proceed?
7. Reassure the battered woman that health practitioners' contact with the batterer should not induce consequences.
8. Keep in contact and keep the Personal Safety Plan current.

---

an abusive relationship but never had any evidence of it (see Box 10.2). Jackie Goody is a white woman and a lawyer in a small law firm; she is working hard to make partner in the firm. Her husband, Jeffrey Goody is also white and a physician in private practice. Mostly, his medical care is handled by his associates in the practice. For yearly physicals, however, he always comes to Dr. Rubin. The Goodys have two children, ages 12 and 14 who are also treated by the HMO pediatrics department. Jackie Goody presents to Nurse Darrell on this day with a black eye and other bruises, which she tries to hide.

Jackie: (taking off her sunglasses) I just want you to check out this black eye that I got yesterday when I accidentally walked into the door. How does it look to you?

Nurse: Quite honestly, Jackie, it looks like this wasn't an accident. It looks like you got punched in the eye.

Jackie: (laughing nervously) Why do you say that?

Nurse: Because I know what happens when you walk into a door and when you get punched in the eye. This looks like you were punched in the eye. (pause) Jackie, let me be honest with you. Janet and I have suspected that you and your husband haven't been getting along, but we never had any evidence of it. (pause) Is that what happened?

Jackie: (looking shocked) Why do you say that?

Nurse: I don't know. We have suspected it because the few times you have come into the clinic together we have sensed tension; we have sensed his anger and his impatience with you. We have sensed your unhappiness. And a couple of times now you have had injuries we couldn't explain away. Remember the black and blue marks on your legs that you attributed to rollerblading? We suspected then but were very uncertain. Now that we seem to have some pattern of "excuses," it seems more obvious.

Jackie: Yeah, well a lot has been happening. It is really awful.

Nurse: Why don't I get Janet so we can discuss this together.

Jackie: Okay.

Nurse Darrell returns with Dr. Janet Rubin.

Janet: Nurse Darrell has been telling me that there have been some problems between you and Jeffrey. She shared with you our suspicion. As painful as it will be, I am pleased that we can talk about it. I've been worried the last couple of times you've come in.

Jackie: Yeah, it has been getting worse. The more stress Jeffrey is under, the more excited he gets.

Janet: Tell us what happened when you got this black eye.

Jackie: Well, we just started fighting last night about how much time I was spending at the office, and when I wouldn't tell him that I'd spend less time there, he just hauled off and punched me in the eye.

Janet: What happened next?

Jackie: I started to cry and then he felt really guilty and tried to comfort me. I asked him to leave me alone and he left.

Janet: Where were the kids when all this was happening?

Jackie: Oh they were asleep at the time. They never see us fighting, we always do it after they're asleep.

Janet: Let's talk a little bit more about what you've been through, before we talk about the children. Do you want to review with us the Tree of Violence?

Jackie: What's that?

Nurse: It helps us understand more about what's been going on between you and Jeffrey and to learn more about the interconnections of the kinds of problems you may be experiencing.

Jackie: Okay.

Together they go through the Violence Tree, and Jackie reveals that nearly all the abuses described on the Tree have happened to her.

Jackie: Wow, that's scary. He has done nearly every one of those things to me. He even forced me to have sex with him one night when I wouldn't make love to him and he really wanted it.

Nurse: Have you had any thoughts about leaving Jeffrey?

Jackie: Oh yeah, all the time. But whenever I threaten, he gets even worse. So, I just stop, it passes, and then he acts up again.

Nurse: It is true that when you plan to separate, or even threaten it, that some men become even more angry and aggressive. That doesn't mean you can't leave, it just means that if you are planning it, you have to do it safely. Are you serious about leaving?

Jackie: Sometimes I am, and other times I just can't see myself doing it.

Nurse: Some women find it helpful to reflect on the many reasons why they stay in relationships that are violent. This other diagram, called The Heart of Intimate Abuse, can help us do that together. Do you want to talk about it?

Together they discuss the reasons Jackie stays in the abusive relationship using The Heart of Intimate Abuse as their guide. It emerges that the primary reason she stays is for the children.

Nurse: It's so hard when you have children to make decisions about leaving a relationship. Of course I'm sure they love their father. But they also know he is mean or even violent to you. There is no question that they have either seen him be violent, or they have heard him.

Jackie: No, they have always been asleep.

Janet: Jackie, I know it is hard to hear, but there is no question that the children know what's been going on. I bet if you asked them, they would tell you.

Nurse: A lot of battered women stay in an abusive relationship for the children, thinking divorce is the worst thing. Others leave when they realize that studies show that children exposed to domestic violence experience symptoms similar and sometimes worse than children who have been directly abused. You may want to think about that when thinking about what you want to do. And you may want to join a support group of women who are in similar relationships and hear their stories.

Jackie: I had no idea.

Janet: We should talk about how violent you think Jeffrey is. Does he have access to a weapon?

Jackie: No, not beyond his fist.

Janet: Does he have an alcohol or drug problem?

Jackie: No.

Janet: Has he threatened to kill you or to commit suicide?

Jackie: No.

Janet: How often has he been physical?

Jackie: Not that often; this black eye is the worst it has been. Usually it is just a push or a shove, or he spits at me. There was the time he forced himself on me sexually.

Janet: Does it feel like things are getting worse?

Jackie: No, not really.

Janet: What would you like to do about it?

Jackie: I don't know; I certainly don't want him to get into trouble, and I don't want anything to happen to him.

Nurse: The studies show that having him arrested and taking the case through the criminal justice system can really help in the cases involving men who have "ties to the community." Ties mean employment, a high status job, and so on, that is, that they have something to lose.

Jackie: I definitely don't want him arrested.

Janet: Do you want me to talk with him?

Jackie: Yeah, I think that might help. And I think I would prefer that to getting the police involved. I'll keep it in the back of my mind that it might help if I involve the police, but I'll hold onto that option until after you've talked to him.

Janet: Okay, well, I know he is coming in next week. Should I wait until then?

Jackie: Yeah, next week is fine.

Nurse: There is one other thing. We will probably recommend that Jeffrey attend a batterer's treatment group before we would take any more aggressive action, like calling the police. I assume that's the kind of intervention you'd want us to suggest.

Jackie:	Oh yeah, I don't want the police involved at this point.
Nurse:	Is there anything else you would like us to recommend.
Jackie:	Well, I have thought about going to counseling with Jeffrey. Do you think it would help?
Nurse:	Couples counseling can get tricky when there is violence involved because the counseling can trigger issues that get the abusive partner angry and then it can leave the woman unprotected. We usually recommend couples counseling only if the woman feels comfortable that the violence has stopped (at least for a period of time), and she has a separate therapist to whom any new incidents of violence can be comfortably reported. No matter what, the therapist must be trained in domestic violence practice (for a fuller discussion of couples counseling, see p. 207). Do you want us to mention couples counseling to Jeffrey?
Jackie:	No, I think I want to wait until after you talk with him. I will discuss couples counseling with him myself.

Before they end their time together, Jackie and Nurse Darrell develop a Personal Safety Plan, just in case Jeffrey becomes angry and wants to retaliate when he learns that Dr. Rubin knows. Nurse Darrell follows up with Jackie the next day to see how she is doing. Jackie reports that she is looking forward to hearing what happens when Dr. Rubin talks to Jeffrey.

Jeffrey arrives the following Wednesday for his scheduled yearly checkup. Before they go into the examining room, Janet invites Jeffrey into her office. Janet and Nurse Darrell had discussed who should lead the conversation with Jeffrey, and they both agreed that because Jeffrey was a doctor it made sense for Janet to lead that conversation and to do it alone.

Janet:	Hi Jeffrey. How are you?
Jeffrey:	Fine, Janet. How are you doing?
Janet:	I am doing well. There is something I need to discuss with you. (pause) I saw Jackie last week and treated her for a black eye. (pause) It was clear to me that her injury was not due to her "running into a door" as she had suggested but rather was due to an injury. (pause) I suspected that there had been problems in your relationship and confronted her with my suspicion that you had hit her.
Jeffrey:	Well, none of it is my fault. Jackie has been working so hard lately that I've had to take care of the kids and everything else. I'm sick of it; she got what she deserved.

Janet: Jeffrey, you and I have known each other a long time. We did a residency together. Do you really feel that Jackie deserves to be hit?

Jeffrey: Well, she deserves to be put in her place; I'm sick and tired of having all the responsibilities and of trying to hold the family together.

Janet: Jeffrey, you do realize that hitting your wife is a crime and that you could go to jail for this crime.

Jeffrey: That's absurd. I'm not going to jail for this.

Janet: If we were in California, I would, as a healthcare professional, have to report this abuse, and you would be arrested.

Jeffrey: Yeah, but we aren't and that is absurd.

Janet: Jeffrey, I assume you will take what I am saying seriously. It sounds like you need to get in a batterer's treatment group. You gave your wife a black eye, and she had other bruises. I have suspected this abuse before. (pause) You need to deal with this problem, which is separate and distinct from Jackie's working too hard. (pause) Those "marital" problems you can deal with, once you start addressing your problem with violence. But if you don't deal with that, or you refuse to, I may have to take more aggressive action.

Jeffrey: What are you implying?

Janet: I have recourse Jeffrey. I will have the police, or even child protective services intervene if I need to. You need to get treatment, and if you refuse, I will take more aggressive action.

Jeffrey: What are these "treatment groups"?

Janet: There are many in our area. They serve both professional and nonprofessional men. This is not a problem that only poor people suffer from. There will be doctors and lawyers in this group, and you will see what happens when the courts get involved in a case. A group treatment model is the preferred method of treatment (see chapter 9). I will give you a referral. Should we do your checkup now?

Jeffrey: Okay.

After her exam, Janet takes Jeffrey into her office once again.

Janet: I assume you have thought about what we talked about.

Jeffrey: Yeah.

Janet: Will you call the referral I have given you?

Jeffrey: Yeah.

Janet: I will check back with you tomorrow and will assume you have made arrangements. I will also call Jackie and reassure her that you will not punish her for my discovering your abuse. Do we understand each other?

Jeffrey: Yes.

The appointment ends and Janet calls Jackie at her office. She reports what was said to Jeffrey and that he reluctantly agreed to attend the batterer's treatment. Janet shares that she did threaten to take additional steps to intervene if Jeffrey doesn't follow through on the treatment and that she agreed to call him tomorrow to see that he had taken some action. Janet also underscored that the discovery of the abuse was her own and that there should be no repercussions to Jackie. Janet reminded Jackie of her Personal Safety Plan and they agreed to talk daily, at least briefly, for at least 2 weeks.

CRITICAL ANALYSIS

This interaction reflects the possibilities of domestic violence intervention offered to health care professionals practicing in family medicine. It is an optimistic option, when one considers the pace with which a family practice is run. Domestic violence, however, like any health care emergency, merits this kind of attention. Lives are literally at stake.

A dual relationship, rather than posing barriers to intervention, presents opportunities for the physician, a nurse, or a social worker to improve the violence in battered women's lives. Janet and Nurse Darrell have now generated enough of a connection with Jackie to ensure, at a minimum, an ongoing dialogue regarding her abuse while also holding Jeffrey accountable for his violent actions.

What is clear from this interaction is that a direct approach works, especially when there is a previous relationship established with the patient. In addition, such tools as the Violence Tree and the Heart of Intimate Abuse can help facilitate conversations with battered women who might otherwise be reluctant to reveal their experience with violence. Assessing the threat when you are proposing a risky intervention is also critical to helping to ensure the battered woman's safety. Personal Safety Planning and consistent contact is the necessary back-up when the infant science of Threat Assessment fails the battered woman.

Similarly, contact with the batterer should be directed toward an outcome. An interaction like this one is probably only possible with someone like Jeffrey Goody, who has strong ties to the community and a lot to lose by Janet's disclosure of his abuse. Janet's threat is real to someone like Jeffrey Goody and therefore is truly threatening. It is important to be sure that the batterer not be allowed to excuse his battering or to blame the battered woman. Janet does an excellent job of reinforcing her intolerance for his abuse.

WHEN IS COUPLES COUNSELING APPROPRIATE?

This interaction raises the issue of couples counseling for the treatment of domestic violence. It is useful to examine this issue, at least briefly, in light of the empowerment approach that is suggested.

In general, feminist advocates have opposed couples counseling on the assumption that when domestic violence is present in a relationship, the relationship is fraught with a power imbalance that irreparably controls the therapy (Dobash & Dobash, 1992). Advocates for this position argue that if the dynamic of the relationship involves control exhibited by the batterer, that control is likely to pervade the counseling process, which would only exacerbate the destructive dynamic between the battered woman and her batterer (Dobash & Dobash, 1992).

Some scholars and clinicians, however, have suggested that couples counseling may have a positive effect, even a recidivist effect on the battering relationship (Geller, 1998; Wylie, 1996). An innovative program in New Jersey, for example, reveals that intensive treatment that involves men's and women's groups, as well as couples groups, can successfully change people's lives. The Institute for Family Services in Somerset reports that 75% of their court-mandated clients never repeat the offense (Wylie, 1996).

My position is that there are some cases in which couples counseling may not be appropriate, but I am not completely opposed to it as a treatment modality. If couples counseling is requested by the batterer while trying to avoid specific offender treatment, it is inappropriate insofar as it places the batterer in a position of having the power to determine where the battered woman will go by requiring her to attend the treatment. Reenacting the destructive controlling dynamic only reinforces his right to abuse and should be avoided at all costs.

I believe, however, that couples counseling could be appropriate with a therapist experienced in working with issues of domestic violence and cognizant of the power dynamics that are often involved in abusive relationships. The therapist should still make independent assurances that the woman will disclose any new incidents of violence and that the batterer will be held accountable. Couples treatment may be particularly appropriate if used in addition to separate treatment for each client to ensure that the battered woman has a safe place to express herself and to exhibit her fear.

Therapists trained in couples counseling should be aware of several potential problems of couples treatment. First, that a session could actually increase a battered woman's danger insofar as something in the session could "set him off" (Dobash & Dobash, 1992). Second, that the therapy could lead to the development of alliances that could act unconsciously to reinforce the batterer's excuses for being violent. Couples counseling is very delicate indeed; in one session a therapist aligns with one partner; in another session, the other. In a violent relationship, this delicate balance can become life threatening if not attended to by the therapist. In couples counseling it becomes critical that the alliances are strictly monitored.

To do couples counseling in an abusive relationship, the therapist should feel, on balance, that her work with this couple could actually lessen the possibility of abuse, rather than exacerbate it. The therapist should consider such questions as Would the survivor feel comfortable reporting new incidents of abuse? Would the perpetrator self-report new incidents of abuse? Could the therapist ensure that the perpetrator's old and new acts of violence would not be minimized? Would the therapist be willing to report reportable incidents of abuse?

Should the therapist feel that these issues could be addressed and that she is qualified to do such counseling, proceeding with couples work is particularly appropriate if the battered woman feels it is a desired modality. The therapist might also consider, given the success of the Institute for Family Services Somerset program, couples group work (Wylie, 1996).

SUMMARY AND REFLECTIONS

> Everything we know about domestic violence rests upon respecting the autonomy of the victim. . . . We've been working for the last 25 years to empower victims to make their own decisions in their own best interests.
>
> Janet Nudelman, 1996
> (Roan, 1996, p. 1)

Domestic violence poses challenges to health care workers when interacting with victims and batterers. Case Study I reveals the difficulty posed by mandatory reporting, the stifling of expression, rather than eliciting it. Moreover, it takes the power away from the battered woman, rather than handing it back to her.

Case Study II, on the other hand, inspires opportunities for intervening in domestic abuse in an empowering way; in this case the battered woman moves from a relative position of weakness to a position of strength. Dr. Janet Rubin pressures the batterer, on behalf of Jackie Goody, and she does so according to Jackie's direction.

In the next chapter, we explore what systems change might be necessary to realize a more comprehensive empowering paradigm for battered women and their children.

QUESTIONS

❒ Where do you stand on the Continuum of Intervention (see chapter 6) in relation to mandatory reporting? Would you tend to be Empowerment vs. Authority Oriented? Do you lean toward involving the police regardless of the battered woman's concerns? Do you lean toward the battered woman's preference even if you can't be sure that it will keep her completely safe?

☐ Do you agree with how the nurse and doctor in Case Study I handled their mandatory reporting duty? What would you change about the interaction?

☐ Did you think the interviews with the battered woman and the batterer in Case Study II were appropriate in light of the patient's right to confidentiality?

Part IV

Future Interventions

CHAPTER 11

An Empowerment Model for Battered Women and Their Children

> The first principle of recovery is the empowerment of the survivor. She must be the author and arbiter of her own recovery. Others may offer advice, support, assistance, affection, and care, but not cure. Many benevolent and well-intentioned attempts to assist the survivor flounder because this fundamental principle of empowerment is not observed. No intervention that takes power away from the survivor can possibly foster her recovery, no matter how much it appears to be in her immediate best interest. In the words of an incest survivor "Good therapists were those who really validated my experience and helped me to control my behavior rather than trying to control me."
>
> (Herman, 1997, p. 133)

As this book has argued, many battered women's advocates believe that the heart of intimate abuse lies in the systems that "should" redress it. They contend that criminal justice, public child welfare, and health care personnel must act decisively when intervening, because battered women are incapable of preventing batterers from battering (Jacobson et al., 1994). Although this is no doubt true, we must also acknowledge that none of these systems, no matter how aggressive they become, will ever fully protect a woman from her abuser. Ultimately, the battered woman is left to find strategies that escape him, that elude his efforts to find her, and that cope with the reality that he is the father of her children. Together with these systems, a battered woman must be integral to any strategy designed to stop or mitigate the violence in *her and her children's* lives.

The belief that the State must act decisively has led us toward mandatory arrest and prosecution policies, allegations of "failure to protect," and mandatory reporting. These approaches rely on the unspoken assumption that battered women are too weak or too damaged to act on their own and their children's behalf. These policies assume that the only way to eradicate domestic violence is through interventions that take the responsibility away from the battered woman and hold the batterer accountable for his abuse. This unidimensional approach has taken the battered woman out of the intimate abuse equation. It has led some battered women back to their abusive relationships and has driven some battered women further underground. When the State mimics the violence the battered woman endures at home, she is likely to return to the abuse with which she is most familiar.

There is no question that some battered women benefit from state intervention that acts unilaterally, and without their input. I believe that trained domestic violence practitioners should have the skills to identify Hedda Nussbaum and women like her—those women who have completely lost their way to the violence. But even Hedda Nussbaum, years later, seems to have recovered her lost voice (Russo, 1997). For those of us who think we can distinguish between those who can and cannot act on their own behalf, those who can and cannot be empowered, we are implored to design strategies to determine who is who, to test their effectiveness, and to help other practitioners do the same.

Endemic to these abusive policies are the unexamined beliefs that drive them. We know so little about violence and yet we pretend to know so much. We spew, spit, and judge without reflecting on our own abuses and the violence we ourselves inflict and endure. Arnold Schwartznegger films and the Persian Gulf war contribute to our tolerance for some, but not other, violences. We are all abusive in ways we repress and reject. When we project those judgments onto the battered women with whom we work or on behalf of the women for whom we lobby, write legislation, or represent, the results are devastating. We essentialize, stereotype, and isolate. We pretend we have it together, and they do not.

I am not suggesting that when you yell at your child for sticking his hand in the toilet or you chastise your spouse for making a mess that you are a batterer, in that sense. Instead, I am suggesting that if we are really serious about eradicating violence, then we should start with ourselves. We should see the strength in our resistance to abuse and the pity in our acceptance of it. We should acknowledge how difficult it is to address abuse, even more so in its subtlest forms, and hence come to appreciate the challenges battered women face. Most importantly, we should sympathize with their commitment to love, family, culture, religion, and race and their fear and financial dependence and recognize ourselves in them.

From this point of view, a new agenda emerges. This book has argued that we need new strategies for working with a battered woman that recognizes her and that reifies her strength in the context of her experience. We need to find ways to see the clues and nurture the hints. We must capture, in the moments we meet with her, a connection she can cherish that acknowledges who she is and who she could be. We must embrace her for who she is, who she has become and help her imagine what could be. We must do so with the patience she demands. We must be patient, knowing that she and her children could die. A dying that, under current practice, prevails.

The differences among battered women must be acknowledged and embraced. All the studies reveal that there is no essential battered woman and that each must be taken on her own ground, in her own story. Race, culture, religion, and family of origin are relevant, but not determinative, features of every survivor's narrative. We must see them for who they are.

Davis and Srinivasan (1995) in their article titled "Listening to the Voices of Battered Women: What Helps Them Escape Violence," discuss their findings of nine focus groups conducted in seven cities in a midwestern state. Of the 55 women who completed brief demographic questionnaires, 87% had at least one child. Approximately 10% of the participants were women of color. They posed the question, "What helps battered women get out of abusive relationships and survive and grow once they are outside these relationships?" Six principles were derived from the women's responses:

1. Draw on the woman's knowledge of what is right and what is wrong with her life.
2. Give the woman information about resources that can enable her to leave and eventually to live without her abuser.
3. Mobilize the resources of family and friends.
4. Listen without judging.
5. Provide suggestions while supporting the woman's right to make her own choices.
6. Offer groups with other women who have had similar experiences so that the battered woman can move beyond her sense of self-blame and can nurture the hope that change is possible (Davis & Srinivasan, 1995, pp. 64–67).

This book presents a practice strategy that recognizes the voice of battered women and challenges the criminal justice, child protection, and health care systems that all too often ignore or reject them. The conceptual tools introduced in this book, especially The Heart of Intimate Abuse and the Violence Tree, are specifically designed to help us have the conversations with battered women from their ground, in lexicons they can understand.

RETHINKING SYSTEMS APPROACHES

What still plagues this equation is the reality that the criminal justice, child protection, and health care systems are on a collision course with the empowerment of women. Chapters 3, 4, and 5 reveal that the systems themselves, and the machinery that drives them, are all too often larger than the CSWs, advocates, and clinicians who work within them.

Previously, I have argued that institutions and their corresponding ideologies must be reformed to ensure that all battered women needing services are welcome irrespective of the nature or status of their relationships (Mills, 1996a). Although this proposal needs to be developed further in future work, I recommend that we consider implementing an additional system for addressing intimate abuse by establishing a Domestic Violence Commission. The commission, with local coordinating offices nationwide, could be battered women's shelters, hotlines, and so on that are deputized to take complaints and help battered women take action. Employees at these commissions would be trained to acknowledge the shifting uncertainty of a survivor's experience as she grapples with a multitude of conflicting loyalties. Their purpose would be to provide battered women who would otherwise never contact law enforcement, child protection, or health care systems with a panoply of options and with information and support (Geffner, 1997).

I suggest that a federally funded and locally administered Domestic Violence Commission could serve as a national clearinghouse for battered women seeking assistance. This new institution could be integral to the collaborative efforts currently being undertaken in communities by CSWs, advocates, and clinicians known as Domestic Violence Councils or Advisory Boards. The Commission could draw on existing relationships with law enforcement, child protection, and health care to carry out their respective functions. But also, the Commission could provide additional resources, both financial and institutional, to agencies that are willing to reach out to battered women in nonjudgmental and empowering ways that do not dictate how they should respond to the violence in their lives. I am suggesting that this approach will attract battered women whom we otherwise neglect using current strategies that mandate intervention.

Developing this idea further, I suggest that this Domestic Violence Commission could take a form similar to that of the United States Equal Employment Opportunity Commission (EEOC), which provides oversight and coordination of all federal regulations, practices and policies affecting equal employment opportunity. Numerous federal statutes now govern domestic violence practice. It makes sense that a federal commission could help oversee and monitor, legally, fiscally, and programmatically, services for battered women. Because a Domestic Violence Commission would have less of an investigatory function and instead be a kind of clearinghouse, drawing on existing resources to ensure their prompt response, it could hopefully avoid the pitfalls and administrative slowdowns for which the EEOC is so famous (Subcommittee on Employer and Employee Relations, 1995).

I suggest too that the Domestic Violence Commission offices, scattered throughout the United States as are Social Security or welfare offices, could help battered women file domestic violence complaints in informal, confidential, and private settings. Those offices could be located in hospital emergency rooms, in police stations, on hotlines, in legal services, and so on. These offices, in turn, could monitor and ensure responses by the systems that became involved in the cases initiated by the victim. The current practice of helping to protect the battered woman from the repercussions of a complaint should be used to allay her well-founded fears that she will be seen as blameworthy for the consequences the batterer reaps from his violence.

Restraining orders and other legal remedies would be available if they were desired. Other measures, depending on the woman's requests, would be available to ensure her safety (shelter stays for either the victim or the perpetrator, and house surveillance, including monitoring devices, are just a few examples). Depending on the remedy she sought, she would have a choice of financial assistance (welfare, credit, alimony, or a job), assistance with other government benefits (including welfare and housing), and child care. Ongoing related criminal or civil actions, only if and when she was ready to file and physically and emotionally prepared to proceed, could be heard in a unified domestic violence court similar to the Unified Court in Hawaii by judges who are trained in the complexities of adjudicating these cases.

This commission could advance domestic violence policy by empowering the battered woman herself to design a course of action she feels would eradicate violence from her life. A flexible remedy menu and time line that respects the uncertainty generated by conflicting loyalties is just what the battered woman seeks when she finally feels ready to act. Drawing on existing agencies that embrace a nonjudgmental philosophy but connecting them further to additional federal resources is one way to encourage systems that currently serve battered women to adopt a more reflexive posture.

ENVOI

Two years ago, I was standing in front of the Wash and Fold on Bethnal Green Road in East London, chatting with a friend. Out of the corner of the eye we both saw a mother scolding her child, the usual thing. When she was done, she spanked him. And then the surprising part happened. Her son hit her back. I remember feeling "Good for him." I identified strongly with his desire to fight back, with the injustice and humiliation of his mother's violence. Until I realized that quite possibly, he was a batterer in the making.

Knowing Brenda Aris and the other women at Frontera Prison, having been a victim myself, and having spent years interviewing and working with battered women, one has to ponder what might bring an end to the intimate abuse that batters women. No doubt, the intergenerational transmission of violence is one powerful factor. We must remind ourselves, however, that we don't know enough yet to contemplate with any certainty what might end violence. Hence, I turn our attention to healing it.

How do we recover? Martha Minow poses this question when she ponders the meaning of "vengeance and forgiveness" in the context of survivors of such atrocities as the Holocaust, apartheid, and Bosnia (Minow, 1997). Describing legal responses to genocide and torture, Minow acknowledges the significant limitations of legal responses that all too often fail. Minow exposes the heart of the dilemma; that is, how do we "honor" victims and still "demonstrate that perpetrators cannot get away with the wrongs they have done" (p. 4).

This question seems particularly vexing in the context of intimate relationships that are so ripe for violence. Goldner, Penn, Sheinberg, and Walker (1990) have argued that the alliance between men and women is so powerful that it can result in a kind of "fatal attraction." They argue that we falter as practitioners when we do not recognize the powerful ties that bind. If we neglect these ties, their research suggests, the couple will fortify themselves against the world's judgments. "Thus, unless this powerful bond is given its due, the relationship will not be visible in all its aspects, and the couple's bond will become a secret coalition against all outsiders . . . " (p. 359).

All intimate relationships exhibit dimensions of traumatic bonding and forms of violence (Dutton, 1995; Goldner et al., 1990; Painter & Dutton, 1985). For me, the heart of intimate abuse is finding ways to heal the wounds so evident in this traumatic bonding. Based on my own recovery and the work of people who are dying (Levine, 1984), I am convinced that the path of forgiveness, rather than vengeance, will ultimately serve the function of interrupting the cycle of the violence that plagues us. As Viktor Frankl, (1984) a Holocaust survivor, reflected,

> We must never forget that we may also find meaning in life even when confronted with a hopeless situation, when facing a fate that cannot be changed. For what then matters is to bear witness to the uniquely human potential at its best, which is to transform a personal tragedy into a triumph, to turn one's predicament into a human achievement. When we are no longer able to change a situation—we are challenged to change ourselves (p. 135).

Pursuing forgiveness over vengeance is not a simple mandate. Batterers, according to some victims, deserve to be punished. Victims deserve to heal from that punishment. Other battered women, like many other survivors, just want to put the trauma behind them. This may take the form of forgiving themselves for having been complicit or for having stayed as long as they did. The path to healing for the battered woman has to include the possibility that she will want to do this forgiveness work for herself and so she can move on.

Currently, systems approaches tend to push battered women towards revenge or towards mimicking the violence experienced. The alternative approaches elaborated in this book offer the possibility of a greater flexibility and the likelihood of a longer-lasting and deeper healing. These approaches advocate a process of understanding that potentially allows a battered woman to break patterns of violence and to move on to healthier and more fulfilling relationships. With most, if not all, of our efforts at reform being geared toward vengeance, some battered women may be hindered from pursuing this path of personal growth. I suggest that we reflect on this limitation of prevailing strategies, on the larger goal of healing abuse, and on a system that all too often renders its victims invisible.

In sum, we need strategies and systems that respond to the survivor's need for flexibility and help her work through her personal ways of knowing, being, and relating so that she can learn in her own mind and soul to distinguish between violence and healthy expressions of intimacy. In this vein, interventions for battered women, in any system, must take account of the dynamic and contingent nature of violence as it manifests between intimates. That the law is distant and itself violent, abstract, and abusive, requires that we envision a more reflexive system, one that requires practitioners to reflect on how they consciously or unconsciously inflict state-legitimized violence by forcing interventions on battered women.

Practitioners too should focus their attention on how they, either personally or institutionally, hold themselves above violence, contributing to erroneous assumptions that they can eradicate violence in women's lives. Violence can only be eradicated when we make an effort to understand its undercurrents in each of us. An important aspect of this personal and collective understanding is to recognize that the patriarchy battered women's advocates so loathe is strengthened, not weakened, when systems are violent in the ways I have described. Ironically, in their current form, the criminal justice, child welfare, and health care systems all too often model the very violence they claim to eradicate.

Preliminary research, as I have argued throughout this book, suggests that empowerment strategies for survivors, strategies that they design and put into action, help them reduce incidents of domestic violence in their lives. A Domestic Violence Commission that draws on engaging and empowering strategies and models and treats the battered woman with all her attending complexity should be initiated to respect her unique conundrum. By providing a nonjudgmental approach to the problem of domestic violence and by not imposing assumptions about the battered woman on them, the Commission, and its attending practitioners, can incrementally empower a survivor to confront the violence in her life as she explores the emotional, cultural, and financial loyalties to which we all, to one degree or another, are bound.

For me, the heart of intimate abuse lies in its mystery. As with love, the contour of that space is profoundly personal. When you meet a battered woman and you have engaged her, you are exploring that intimate domain. Hold it as though it was precious, as though it was your only child, as though it was your beloved. Hold it without judgment and with an insight she may have repressed. See through her eyes: the wedding day, the first picnic, family vacations; the first fight, the slammed door, the rape. And together, you might, just by chance, begin to replace the clinging images with possibility, with light, and with a sense of something different. Whatever it takes, no matter how long, navigate delicately in this precious space and together, I believe, you can get there.

Appendixes

CPS Risk Assessment in California

Form	Counties	Explicit Reference to Domestic Violence	Possible Implicit Reference to Domestic Violence
Los Angeles Risk Assessment Form	Los Angeles, San Bernardino, San Francisco, San Mateo, Tulare, and San Joaquin (child under 5)	Spousal Abuse	N/A
Fresno Risk Assessment Form	Alameda, Butte, Colusa, Glenn, Humboldt, Kern, Lake, Lassen, Madera, Marin, Merced, Nevada, Plumas, Riverside, Sacramento, San Diego, San Joaquin (child over 5), Santa Clara, Solano, Sutter, Trinity, Ventura, Yolo, and Yuba	None	History of Abuse/ Neglect in Family
State Risk Assessment Form	Alpine, Amador, Calaveras, Del Norte, Imperial, Inyo, Kings, Mariposa, Mono, Modoc, San Benito, Sierra, Siskiyou, Sonoma, Stanislaus, and Tuolumne	None	History of Abuse

(continued)

APPENDIX I *(continued)*

Form	Counties	Explicit Reference to Domestic Violence	Possible Implicit Reference to Domestic Violence
No Form: "State" Model Training	El Dorado	N/A	N/A
No Form: "Fresno" Model Training	Contra Costa, Mendocino, Monterey, Napa, Orange, Placer, Santa Barbara, and Tehama	N/A	N/A
No Form: Own Training	Fresno and Shasta	N/A	N/A
Own Form	Santa Cruz	No	No
Online Risk Assessment	San Luis Obispo	No	No

(Mills, 1998a, p. 138)

Appendix II

A Personal Safety Plan

If you don't have some of this information, now is the time to get it. IMPORTANT! KEEP THIS INFORMATION IN A SAFE AND PRIVATE PLACE WHERE ____(NAME)____ CANNOT FIND IT!

1. **Important phone numbers:**

   Police: **911** or _____

   Domestic Violence Hotline: 1-800-978-3600

   My attorney: _____ Other: _____

2. **I can call these friends or relatives in an emergency:**

   Name: _____ Phone: _____

   Name: _____ Phone: _____

3. **These neighbors will call the police if they hear me being battered:**

   Name: _____ Phone: _____

   Name: _____ Phone: _____

4. **I can go to these places if I have to leave my home in a hurry:**

   Name: _____ Phone: _____

Address: _____

Name: _____ Phone: _____

Address: _____

5. I have given copies of the documents checked below to a friend for safekeeping:

[—]   My birth certificate

[—]   My children's birth certificates

[—]   My social security card

[—]   My children's school records

[—]   My children's medical records

[—]   Bank books

[—]   Welfare identification

[—]   My passport or green card

[—]   My children's passports or green cards

[—]   Insurance papers

[—]   My lease agreement or mortgage payment book

[—]   Important addresses and telephone numbers

[—]   Other: _____

[—]   Other: _____

[—]   Other: _____

6. The following are hidden in a safe place:

[—]   An extra set of car keys

[—]   Some extra money

[—]   An extra change of clothes for me and my children

[—]   _____

[—]   _____

SAFETY MEASURES WHILE YOU'RE IN AN ABUSIVE RELATIONSHIP

If you are living with the person who is hurting you, here are some things you can do to ensure your and your children's safety.

1.   Have important phone numbers memorized—friends and relatives whom you can call in an emergency. If your children are old enough, teach them important phone numbers, including when and how to dial 911.

2.   Keep this Personal Safety Plan in a safe place—where your batterer won't find it but where you can get it when you need to review it.

3.   Keep change for pay phones with you at all times.

4.   If you can, open your own bank account.

5.   Stay in touch with friends. Get to know your neighbors. Resist any temptation to cut yourself off from people, even if you feel like you just want to be left alone.

6.   Rehearse your escape plan until you know it by heart.

7.   Leave a set of car keys, extra money, a change of clothes, and copies of the following documents with a trusted friend or relative.

- You and your children's birth certificates
- Your children's school and medical records
- Bank books
- Welfare identification
- Passports or green cards
- Your social security card
- Lease agreements or mortgage payment books
- Insurance papers
- Important addresses and telephone numbers
- Any other important documents

SAFETY AFTER YOU HAVE LEFT THE RELATIONSHIP

Once you no longer live together, here are some things you can do to enhance the safety of you and your children.

1. **Change the locks**—if you're still in your home and your former partner is the one who has left.

2. **Install as many security features as possible in your home.** These might include metal doors and gates, security alarm system, smoke detectors, and outside lights.

3. **Inform neighbors that your former partner is not welcome on the premises.** Ask them to call the police if they see someone loitering about your property or watching your home.

4. **Make sure the people who care for your children are very clear about who does and does not have permission to pick up your children.**

5. **Obtain a restraining order.** Keep it near you at all times and make sure friends and neighbors have copies to show the police.

6. **Let your coworkers know about the situation**—if your former partner is likely to come to your work place to bother you. Ask them to warn you if they observe that person around.

7. **Avoid the stores, banks, and businesses you used when you were living with your former partner.**

8. **Get counseling.** Attend workshops. Join support groups. Do whatever it takes to form a supportive network that will be there when you need it.

(Adapted from Los Angeles Domestic Violence Council, 1996)

SOCIAL SUPPORT INVENTORY, PART I

Social support networks are an important and critical factor in a battered woman's ability to recover from violence. This inventory will

- help her identify her sources of support,
- help her identify where she may have been isolated, and
- help her identify where she may want to target her network efforts.

The information on this inventory may also become part of her safety and action plan.

NAME: _____

Directions. List as many people you can think of in each category. First, list your personal allies and resources, then you can also list people in organizations who might be considered professional helpers. Remember to think of people you can easily reach by phone and in the neighborhood. Do these individuals know about your situation? If not, can you tell them?

Note: On these inventories, references to the first person (you and I) refer to the client.

List the names and relationship of adults whom

1. *You feel really care about you and listen to you:*

   Name: _____   Relationship: _____

   _____   _____

   _____   _____

2. *You count on for advice or information on personal matters or resources:*

   Name: _____   Relationship: _____

   _____   _____

   _____   _____

3. *You depend on when you need help:*

   Name: _____   Relationship: _____

   _____   _____

   _____   _____

4. *You can count on for favors:*

   Name: _____   Relationship: _____

   _____   _____

   _____   _____

SOCIAL SUPPORT INVENTORY, PART II

1. Were you able to list personal social support allies in all categories?
2. Of those listed, which can you count on to be part of your safety plan?

   - A key issue may be whether or not the batterer would have access to you or the children if you were to temporarily live with the person.
   - Also, consider: *what other resources* can I count on from this person, other than a place to live? List them as a resource on Part III.

3. If not, is there value in trying to develop supports in the *general areas* where you have none or few?

   - Companionship: What do you need?
   - Advice and information: What do you need?
   - Practical assistance: What do you need?
   - Emotional support: What do you need?

4. How would you go about developing supports?

   - Plan for developing support and alliances in the identified areas.

SOCIAL SUPPORT INVENTORY, PART III

The following list (Table A.1) is one that battered women need to consider in developing a safety and action plan. This can also serve as a checklist to help her take stock of where she is, if independent survival is her goal. The list can also help practitioners work with battered women in considering realistic options.

TABLE A.1

RESOURCE	I Have This/ Identify Resource	I Need to Develop
Housing		
Material Goods & Resources		
Cash on Hand/Finances		
Employment		
Education/Job Training/Skills		
Transportation		
Social Support		
Legal Assistance/Protection		
Child Care		
Health Care/Mental Health Care		

(Adapted from Mills & Friend, 1997)

Appendix III

Sample Affirmative Action Plans for CSWs

SAMPLE AFFIRMATIVE ACTION PLAN FOR CSWs : LESS RESTRICTIVE APPROACH

- An Affirmative Action Plan is necessary when the CSW has determined that domestic violence is present, and there is risk of threat. The remaining parent becomes the focus of the CSW's interventions.
- *REMEMBER: Avoid blaming the victim for the actions of the abuser. The parents share responsibility for the safety of the children.*
- Always try to make a Personal Safety Plan (Appendix II) with the victim, regardless of her level of cooperation.
- Ask yourself, have you done all that you can to assist the victim *and* ensure that the batterer is held accountable for his violence?

Once you have done an Assessment of Threat (chapter 7) and completed a Personal Safety Plan, you will be developing a plan of action. This includes eliciting from the victim what she thinks would help her and her child(ren) become more safe. Ask her to explain her reasons because they may not be obvious. Please note that many of the identified social supports are also strengths and should be factored into your Risk Assessment.

ASSESSMENT OF THREAT

An Assessment of Threat is always appropriate when safety for the mother and child is at issue (use the Violence Tree (Figure 7.1) and the Assessment of Threat).

1. First, consider access to her and her child(ren)

   - Does he live there; is he ex- or current partner?
   - Is he a current legal custody holder?

2. How dangerous is the batterer (refer to Assessment of Threat)? Given that the clinical prediction of dangerousness is not always reliable, CPS workers are encouraged to evaluate this in collaborative decision making. Include your supervisor.
3. What needs to be done to ensure safety?

Victim is willing to:	CPS worker options include:
Do nothing to change the situation	(1) remove the children and/or (2) continue ongoing assessment*
Obtain a restraining order (presumes police report and potential arrest of the batterer)	continue ongoing assessment (includes compliance with restraining order)*
Leave the home and go to a shelter (includes getting a restraining order)	(1) depending on the shelter, children may be able to go with mother* and (2) ongoing assessment
Leave the home and go to a safe friend/family home (includes getting a restraining order)	(1) children may go with the mother* and (2) ongoing assessment*

In every case, the victim:

1. should fill out a Personal Safety Plan that describes what she needs to respond to in a crisis; she should be encouraged to use it.
2. should be given additional resource material according to her needs and at the discretion of the CPS worker.
3. should be advised that any assessment is prelimenary and needs to be discussed with a supervisor and, in some cases, an administrator. If there is a need to separate the mother and remove the child(ren), the police may need to be involved.

(continued)

APPENDIX III *(continued)*

4. deserves to be evaluated on her own terms, weighing and balancing the battered woman's strengths against the risks to the child. Some things are hard to itemize and weigh, but this assessment process should help both the victim and the CPS worker think in a concrete, logical, and organized fashion about these complex issues. Training and experience are components of professional judgment; these are critical components of an assessment.

If the children are to remain with the mother and she goes to a relative/friend, assess all parties for risk of child abuse. In a less restrictive agency, ongoing assessment includes a range of options, including voluntary family maintenance. When children "go with mothers," consider requesting an accelerated hearing and release to the mother or other relative (available in some juvenile court jurisdictions) (Adapted from Mills & Friend, 1997).

SAMPLE AFFIRMATIVE ACTION PLAN FOR CSWS: MORE RESTRICTIVE APPROACH

- An Affirmative Action Plan is necessary when a CSW has determined that domestic violence is present, and there is risk of threat. The remaining parent becomes the focus of the CSW's interventions.
- *REMEMBER: Avoid blaming the victim for the actions of the abuser. The parents share responsibility for the safety of the children.*
- Always try to make a Personal Safety Plan with the victim, regardless of her level of cooperation.
- Ask yourself, have you done all that you can to ensure that the batterer is held accountable for his violence?

Once you have done an Assessment of Threat and completed a Personal Safety Plan, you will develop a plan of action. This includes eliciting from the victim what she thinks would help her and her child(ren) become more safe. Ask her to explain her reasons, because they may not be obvious. Please note that many of the identified social supports are also strengths and should be factored into your Risk Assessment. If the children are to remain with the victim and she goes to a relative/friend, assess all parties for risk of child abuse.

LOW RISK

An Assessment of *low risk* is appropriate if the batterer does not have access to the battered woman and/or family members. (Is he living there or not? Is he an ex- or current partner? Does he have legal custody?) Use the Violence Tree and the Assessment of Threat as a guide for your individual assessment of dangerousness.

Victim is willing to:	*CPS worker options include:*
Do nothing to change the situation	*(1) continue ongoing assessment*
Obtain a restraining order (presumes police report and potential arrest of the batterer)	*(1) continue ongoing assessment (includes compliance with restraining order)*
Leave the home and go to a shelter (includes getting a restraining order)	*(1) depending on the shelter, children may be able to go with mother, and (2) ongoing assessment*
Leave the home and go to a safe friend/family home (includes restraining order)	*(1) children may go with the mother, and (2) ongoing assessment*

HIGH RISK

An Assessment of *high risk* is appropriate if the batterer has access to the victim and/or family members; use the Violence Tree and the Assessment of Threat as a guide for your individual assessment of dangerousness.

Victim is willing to:	*CPS worker options include:*
Do nothing to change the situation	*(1) remove the children*
Obtain a restraining order (no arrest is made due to victim's choice and no good reason)	*(1) remove the children*

(continued)

APPENDIX III *(continued)*

Make a police report that results in the batterer's arrest (includes obtaining a restraining order)	*(1) leave children with the mother, and (2) continue ongoing assessment (includes compliance with restraining order)*
Leave the home and go to a shelter (includes getting a restraining order)	*(1) depending on the shelter, children may be able to go with mother, and (2) ongoing assessment*
Leave the home and go to a safe friend/family home (includes getting a restraining order)	*(1) children may go with the mother, and (2) ongoing assessment*

In every case, the victim:

1. should fill out a Personal Safety Plan that describes what she needs to respond to in a crisis; she should be encouraged to use it.
2. should be given additional resource material according to her needs and at the discretion of the CPS worker.
3. should be advised that any assessment is preliminary and needs to be discussed with a supervisor and, in some cases, an administrator. If there is a need to separate the mother and remove the child(ren), the police may need to be involved.
4. deserves to be evaluated on individual and case merits (strengths/risks). Some things are hard to itemize and weigh, but this assessment process should help both the victim and CPS worker think in a concrete, logical, and organized fashion about these complex issues. Training and experience are components of professional judgment; these are critical components of an assessment (Adapted from Mills & Friend, 1997).

References

References

Adams, D. C. (1988). Treatment models of men who batter: A profeminist analysis. In K. A. Yllö & M. Bograd (Eds.), *Feminist perspectives on wife abuse* (pp. 176–199). Newbury Park, CA: Sage Publications.

Aguirre, B. E. (1985). Why do they return? Abused wives in shelters. *Social Work, 30*, 350–354.

Aitken, L., & Griffin, G. (1996). *Gender issues in elder abuse.* London, England: Sage Publications.

Allen, P. G. (1986). Violence and the American Indian woman. In M. C. Burns (Ed.), *The speaking profits us: Violence in the lives of women of color* (pp. 5–7). Seattle, WA: Center for the Prevention of Sexual and Domestic Violence.

Allert, C. S., Chalkley, C., Whitney, J. R., & Librett, A. (1997, January–March). Domestic violence: Efficacy of health provider training in Utah. *Prehospital and Disaster Medicine, 12*(1), 52–56.

American Humane Association. (September 1994). The link between child abuse and domestic violence. *Child protection leader,* 1–2.

American Medical Association. (1992). Physicians and domestic violence: Ethical considerations. *Journal of the American Medical Association, 267*, 3190–3193.

Aron, L., & Olson, K. (1997a). *Efforts by child welfare agencies to address domestic violence: The experiences of five communities.* Washington, DC: Urban Institute.

Aron, L., & Olson, K. (1997b). Efforts by child welfare agencies to address domestic violence. *Public Welfare, 55*(3), 4–13.

Barnett, O. W., Fagan, R. W., & Booker, J. M. (1991). Hostility and stress as mediators of aggression in violent men. *Journal of Family Violence, 6*, 219–241.

Barnett, O. W., & Fagan, R. W. (1993). Alcohol use in male spouse abusers and their female partners. *Journal of Family Violence, 8*, 1–25.

Barnett, O. W., & LaViolette, A. D. (1993). *It could happen to anyone: Why battered women stay.* Newbury Park, CA: Sage Publications.

Barnett, O. W., & Miller, C. (1984, August). *A classification of wife abusers on the BEM sex-role inventory.* Paper presented at the Second National Conference for Family Violence Researchers, Durham, NH.

Barnett, O. W., Miller-Perrin, C. L., & Perrin, R. D. (1997). *Family violence across the lifespan.* Thousand Oaks, CA: Sage Publications.

Bartasavic v. Mitchell, 471 A.2d 833 (1984).

Berk, R. A., Campbell, A., Klap, R., & Western, B. (1992). A Bayesian analysis of the Colorado Springs spouse abuse experiment. *Journal of Criminal Law and Criminology, 83*(1), 170–200.

Berkowitz, L. (1983). The goals of aggression. In D. Finkelhor, G. Hotaling, & M. A. Straus (Eds.), *The dark side of families* (pp. 166–181). Beverly Hills, CA: Sage Publications.

Billings, A. G., & Moos, R. H. (1983). Comparisons of children of depressed and nondepressed parents: A social environmental perspective. *Journal of Abnormal Child Psychology, 11*(4), 463–486.

Bograd, M. (1984). Family systems approaches to wife battering: A feminist critique. *American Journal of Orthopsychiatry, 54,* 558–568.

Bograd, M. (1988). Feminist perspectives on wife abuse: An introduction. In K. A. Yllö & M. Bograd (Eds.), *Feminist perspectives on wife abuse* (pp. 11–26). Beverly Hills, CA: Sage.

Bograd, M. (1992). Values in conflict: Challenges to family therapists' thinking. *Journal of Marital and Family Therapy, 18*(3), 245–256.

Bokunewicz, B., & Copel, L. C. (1992). Attitudes of emergency nurses before and after a 60-minute educational presentation on partner abuse. *Journal of Emergency Nursing, 18*(1),24–27.

Borch-Jacobsen, M. (1991). *Lacan: The absolute master* (D. Brick, Trans.). Stanford, CA: Stanford University Press.

Bowker, L. H. (1983). *Beating wife beating.* Lexington, MA: Lexington Books.

Bowker, L. H. (1993). A battered woman's problems are social, not psychological. In R. J. Gelles & D. R. Loseke (Eds.), *Current controversies on family violence* (pp. 154–165). Newbury Park, CA: Sage Publications.

Bowker, L. H., Arbitell, M., & McFerron, J. R. (1988). On the relationship between wife beating and child abuse. In K. A. Yllö & M. Bograd (Eds.), *Feminist perspectives on wife abuse* (pp. 158–174). Newbury Park, CA: Sage.

Bowman, C. (1992). The arrest experiment: A feminist critique. *Journal of Criminal Law and Criminology, 83*(1), 201–208.

Browne, K., Saunders, D. G., & Staecker, K. M. (1997, May–June). Process-psychodynamic groups for men who batter: A brief treatment model. *Families in Society: The Journal of Contemporary Human Services,* 265–271.

Brownell, P., & Abelman, I. (1998). Elder Abuse: Protective and empowerment strategies for crisis intervention. In A. Roberts (Ed.), *Battered women and their families* (2nd ed.) (pp. 313–344). New York: Springer.

Brownell, P., & Congress, E. P. (1998). Application of the culturagram to empower culturally and ethnically diverse battered women. In A. Roberts (Ed.), *Battered women and their families* (2nd ed.) (pp. 387–404). New York: Springer.

Brownell, P. (1998). Women, welfare, work and domestic violence. In A. Roberts (Ed.), *Battered women and their families* (2nd ed.) (pp. 291–309). New York: Springer.

Bryant, W., & Panico, S. (1994). Physicians' legal responsibilities to victims of domestic violence. *North Carolina Medical Journal, 55,* 418–421.

Buzawa, E., Austin, T., Bannon, J., & Jackson, J. (1992). Role of victim preference in determining police response to victims of domestic violence. In E. Buzawa & C. Buzawa (Eds.), *Domestic violence: The changing criminal justice response* (pp. 255–269). Westport, CT: Greenwood.

Buzawa, E., & Buzawa, C. (1993). The scientific evidence is not conclusive: Arrest is no panacea. In R. J. Gelles & D. R. Loseke (Eds.), *Current controversies on family violence* (pp. 337–356). Newbury Park, CA: Sage Publications.

Buzawa, E., & Buzawa, C. (1996). *Domestic violence: The criminal justice response* (2nd ed.). Thousand Oaks, CA: Sage Publications.

Cahn, N. (1991). Civil images of battered women: The impact of domestic violence on child custody decisions. *Vanderbilt Law Review, 44,* 1041–1097.

Callahan, M. (1993). Feminist approaches: Women re-create child welfare. In B. Wharf (Ed.), *Rethinking child welfare in Canada* (pp. 172–209). Toronto, Canada: McLelland & Stewart.

Campbell, J. C. (1992). "If I can't have you, no one can": Power and control in homicide of female partners. In J. Radford & D. E. H. Russell (Eds.), *Femicide: The politics of woman killing* (pp. 99–113). New York: Twayne Publishers.

Carden, A. D. (1994). Wife abuse and the wife abuser: Review and recommendations. *The Counseling Psychologist, 22*(4), 539–582.

Carlson, B. (1996). Children of battered women: Research, programs, and services. In A. Roberts (Ed.), *Helping battered women: New perspectives and remedies* (pp. 172–187). New York: Oxford University Press.

Carlson, B. (1997). Mental retardation and domestic violence: An ecological approach to intervention. *Social Work, 42,* 70–89.

Carlson, B., & Maciol, K. (1997). Domestic violence: Gay men and lesbians. In *Encyclopedia of social work supplement.* Washington, DC: NASW Press.

Carmen, E., Rieker, P., & Mills, T. (1984). Victims of violence and psychiatric illness. *American Journal of Psychiatry, 141,* 378–383.

Chambliss, L., Bay, R. C., & Jones, R. F. (1995). Domestic violence: An educational imperative. *American Journal of Obstetrics & Gynecology, 172*(3), 1035–1038.

Chaudhuri, M., & Daly, K. (1992). Do restraining orders help? Battered women's experiences with male violence and the legal process. In E. Buzawa and C. Buzawa (Eds.), *Domestic violence: The changing criminal justice response* (pp. 227–252). Westport, CT: Greenwood.

Cohen, S., De Vos, E., & Newberger, E. (1997). Barriers to physician identification and treatment of family violence: Lessons from five communities. *Academic Medicine, 72*(1), S19–S25.

Commonwealth Fund, Commission on Women's Health. (1993). *Survey of women's health.* New York: Author.

Cook, D. R., & Frantz-Cook, A. (1984). A systematic treatment approach to wife battering. *Journal of Marital and Family Therapy, 10*(1), 83–93.

Corse, S. J., Schmid, K., & Trickett, P. K. (1990). Social network characteristics of mothers in abusing and nonabusing families and their relationships to parenting beliefs. *Journal of Community Psychology, 18*(1), 44–59.

Corsilles, A. (1994). Note: No drop policies in the prosecution of domestic violence cases: Guarantee to action or dangerous solution. *Fordham Law Review, 63,* 853–881.

Crenshaw, K. (1991). Mapping the margins: Intersectionality, identity politics, and violence against women of color. *Stanford Law Review, 43,* 1241–1299.

Davidson, H. A. (1995, Summer). Child abuse and domestic violence: Legal connections and controversies. *Family Law Quarterly, 29*(2), 357–373.

Davis, L. V., & Srinivasan, M. (1995). Listening to the voices of battered women: What helps them escape violence. *AFFILIA, 10*(1), 49–69.

Davis, L. V., & Hagen, J. L. (1992). The problem of wife abuse: The interrelationship of social policy and social work practice. *Social Work, 37,* 15–20.

Davis, P. (1994, February 9). Woman pleads guilty in death of son, 2: Fairfax mother admits she lied about husband's killing of boy. *The Washington Post*, pp. D1–D2.

DeBecker, G. (1997). *The gift of fear: Survival signals that protect us from violence.* New York: Little Brown.

DeMaris, A. (1989). Attrition in batterers counseling: The role of social and demographic factors. *Social Service Review, 63,* 142–154.

Deschner, J. (1984). *The hitting habit: Anger control for battering couples.* New York: Free Press.

Dobash, R. E., & Dobash, R. P. (1979). *Violence against wives: A case against the patriarchy.* New York: The Free Press.

Dobash, R. E., & Dobash, R. P. (1992). *Women, violence and social change.* New York: Routledge.

Dohrn, B. (1995). Symposium: Domestic violence, child abuse, and the law: Bad mothers, good mothers, and the state: Children on the margins. *University of Chicago Law School Roundtable, 2*(1), 1–12.

Dunford, F. (1992). The measurement of recidivism in cases of spouse assault. *Journal of Criminal Law and Criminology, 83*(1), 120–136.

Dutton, D. G. (1986). The outcome of court-mandated treatment for wife assault: A quasi-experimental evaluation. *Violence and Victims, 1*(3), 163–175.

Dutton, D. G. (1995). *The domestic assault of women: Psychological and criminal justice perspectives.* Vancouver, Canada: UBC Press.

Dutton, D. G., Bodnarchuk, M., Kropp, R., Hart, S., & Ogloff, J. (1997). Client personality disorders affecting wife assault post-treatment recidivism. *Violence and Victims, 12*(1), 37–50.

Dutton, D. G., & Golant, S. (1995). *The batterer: A psychological profile.* New York: Basic Books.

Echlin, C., & Marshall, L. (1995). Child protection services for children of battered women. In E. Peled, P. Jaffe, & J. L. Edleson (Eds.), *Ending the cycle of violence: Community responses to children of battered women* (pp. 170–185). Thousand Oaks, CA: Sage Publications.

Edleson, J. L. (1996). Controversy and change in batterer's programs. In J. Edleson & Z. Eisikovits (Eds.), *Future interventions with battered women and their families* (pp. 154–169). Thousand Oaks, CA: Sage Publications.

Edleson, J. L., & Tolman, R. (1992). *Intervention for men who batter: An ecological approach.* Newbury Park, CA: Sage Publications.

Eisikovits, Z. C., & Edleson, J. L. (1989). Intervention with men who batter: A critical review of the literature. *Social Service Review, 37,* 385–414.

Eliot, G. (1871/1992). *Middlemarch.* New York: Bantam Books.

Ellard, J. H., Herbert, T. B., & Thompson, L. J. (1991). Coping with an abusive relationship: How and why do people stay? *Journal of Marriage and the Family, 53,* 311–325.

Enos, V. P. (1996). Recent development: Prosecuting battered mothers: State laws failure to protect battered women and abused children. *Harvard Women's Law Journal, 19,* 229–266.

Erchak, G. M. (1984). The escalation and maintenance of spouse abuse: A cybernetic model. *Victimology: An International Journal, 9*(2), 247–253.

Fagan, J., Stewart, D., & Hansen, K. (1983). Violent men or violent husbands? Background factors and situational correlates. In D. Finkelhor, G. Hotaling, & M. A. Straus (Eds.), *The dark side of families* (pp. 49–67). Beverly Hills, CA: Sage Publications.

Faludi, S. (1991). *Backlash.* New York: Crown.

Family Violence Prevention Fund. (1997). *The health care response to domestic violence: Policy recommendations* [On-line]. Available: http://www.fvpf.org/fund/the_facts/health_response.html

Fantuzzo, J., & Lindquist, C. (1989). The effects of observing conjugal violence on children: A review and analysis of research methodology. *Journal of Family Violence, 4*(1), 77–94.

Felder, R., & Victor, B. (1996). *Getting away with murder: Weapons for the war against domestic violence.* New York: Simon & Schuster.

Ferraro, K., & Pope, L. (1993). Irreconcilable differences: Battered women, police, and the law. In N. Z. Hilton (Ed.), *Legal responses to wife assault: Current trends and evaluation* (pp. 96–123). Newbury Park, CA: Sage Publications.

Ferris, L. E., Norton, P. G., Dunn, E. V., Gort, E. H., & Degani, N. (1997). Guidelines for managing domestic abuse when male and female partners are patients of the same physician. *Journal of the American Medical Association, 278*(10), 851–857.

Finkelhor, D. (1983). Common features of family abuse. In D. Finkelhor, G. Hotaling, & M. A. Straus (Eds.), *The dark side of families: Current family violence research* (pp. 17–30). Beverly Hills, CA: Sage Publications.

Finkelhor, D., & Yllö, K. A. (1987). *License to rape: Sexual abuse of wives.* New York: Free Press.

Fiore, F. (1989, December 26). A battered wife wins acquittal in murder case. *Los Angeles Times,* p. B1.

Fischer, K., & Rose, M. (1995). When "enough is enough": Battered women's decision making around court orders of protection. *Crime & Delinquency, 41,* 414–429.

Fleck-Henderson, A., & Krug, S. (1997). Memo to Linda Mills and Colleen Friend.

Ford, D., & Regoli, M. (1993). The criminal prosecution of wife assaulters: Process, problems, and effects. In N. Z. Hilton (Ed.), *Legal responses to wife assault: Current trends and evaluation* (pp. 127–164). Newbury Park, CA: Sage Publications.

Frankl, V. (1984). *Man's search for meaning.* New York: Pocket Books.

Frisch, L. (1992). Research that succeeds, policies that fail. *The Journal of Criminal Law and Criminology, 83*(1), 209–216.

Frisch, M. B., & MacKenzie, C. J. (1991). A comparison of formerly and chronically battered women on cognitive and situational dimensions. *Psychotherapy, 28*, 339–344.

Geffner, R. (1997). An interview with Robert Geffner. In O. W. Barnett, C. L. Miller-Perrin, & R. D. Perrin (Eds.), *Family violence across the life span: An introduction* (pp. 275–276). Thousand Oaks, CA: Sage Publications.

Geller, J. (1998). Conjoint therapy for the treatment of partner abuse: Indications and contraindications. In A. Roberts (Ed.), *Battered women and their families* (2nd ed.) (pp. 76–96). New York: Springer Publishing.

Gelles, R. J. (1997). *Intimate violence in families* (3rd ed.). Thousand Oaks, CA: Sage Publications.

Gelles, R. J., & Straus, M. A. (1987). Is violence toward children increasing: A comparison of 1975 and 1985 National Survey Rates. *Journal of Interpersonal Violence, 2*, 212–222.

Ginorio, A., & Reno, J. (1986). Violence in the lives of Latina women. In M. C. Burns (Ed.), *The speaking profits us: Violence in the lives of women of color* (pp. 13–16). Seattle, WA: Center for the Prevention of Sexual and Domestic Violence.

Gold, E. R. (1986). Long-term effects of sexual victimization in childhood: An attributional approach. *Journal of Consulting and Clinical Psychology, 54*, 471–475.

Goldberg, H. (1984). The dynamics of rage between the sexes in a bonded relationship. In L. Barnhill (Ed.), *Clinical approaches to family violence.* Aspen, CO: Aspen Family Therapy Series.

Goldberg, W. G., & Tomlanovich, M. C. (1984). Domestic violence victims in the emergency department. *Journal of the American Medical Association, 251*, 3259–3264.

Goldner, V., Penn, P., Sheinberg, M., & Walker, G. (1990). Love and violence: Gender paradoxes in volatile attachments. *Family Process, 29*(4), 343–364.

Gondolf, E. W. (1985). Anger and oppression in men who batter: Empiricist and feminist perspectives and their implications for research. *Victimology: An International Journal, 10*, 311–324.

Gondolf, E. W. (1988a). The effect of batterer counseling on shelter outcome. *Journal of Interpersonal Violence, 3*, 275–289.

Gondolf, E. W. (1988b). Who are those guys? Toward a behavioral typology of batterers. *Violence and Victims, 3*(3), 187–203.

Gondolf, E. W. (1990). An exploratory survey of court-mandated batterer programs. *Response, 13*(3), 7–11.

Gondolf, E. W. (1991). A victim-based assessment of court-mandated counseling for batterers. *Criminal Justice Review, 16,* 214–226.

Gondolf, E. W. (1996, November). *Characteristics of court-mandated batterers in four cities: Diversity and dichotomy.* Paper presented at the annual meeting of the American Society of Criminology, Chicago, IL.

Gondolf, E. W. (1997a). Batterer programs: What we know and need to know. *Journal of Interpersonal Violence, 12*(1), 83–98.

Gondolf, E. W. (1997b). Expanding batterer program evaluation. In G. K. Kantor & J. Jasinski (Eds.), *Out of darkness: Contemporary research perspectives on family violence.* Thousand Oaks, CA: Sage Publications.

Goode, W. (1971). Force and violence in the family. *Journal of Marriage and the Family, 33*(4), 624–636.

Goodyer, I. M. (1990). Family relationships, life events and childhood psychopathology. *Journal of Child Psychology and Psychiatry and Allied Disciplines, 31*(1), 161–192.

Gordon, L. E. (1996). Mental health of medical students: The culture of objectivity in medicine. *The Pharos,* Spring, 2–10.

Hackler, J. (1991). The reduction of violent crime through economic equality for women. *Journal of Family Violence, 6,* 199–216.

Hamberger, L. K., & Hastings, J. E. (1986). Personality correlates of men who abuse their partners: A cross-validation study. *Journal of Family Violence, 1*(4), 323–341.

Hamilton, B., & Coates, J. (1993). Perceived helpfulness and use of professional services by abused women. *Journal of Family Violence, 8*(4), 313–324.

Hammond, N. (1986). Lesbian victims and the reluctance to identify abuse. In K. Lobel, for The National Coalition Against Domestic Violence Lesbian Task Force (Ed.), *Naming the violence: Speaking out about lesbian battering* (pp. 190–197). Seattle, WA: Seal Press.

Hanna, C. (1996). No right to choose: Mandated victim participation in domestic violence prosecutions. *Harvard Law Review, 109,* 1850–1910.

Harlow, C. (1991). *Female victims of violent crime.* Washington DC: Bureau of Justice Statistics.

Hart, B. (1988). Beyond the duty to warn: A therapist's "duty to protect" battered women's children. In K. A. Yllö & M. Bogard (Eds.), *Feminist perspectives on wife abuse* (pp. 334–348). Beverly Hills, CA: Sage Publications.

Hart, B. (1992). Battered women and the duty to protect children. In State codes on domestic violence: Analysis, commentary, and recommendations. *Juvenile Family Court Journal, 43*(4), 79–80.

Hart, B. (1993). Battered women and the criminal justice system. *American Behavioral Scientist, 36,* 624–638.

Hart, B. (1996). Battered women and the criminal justice system. In E. Buzawa & C. Buzawa (Eds.), *Do arrests and restraining orders work?* (pp. 98–114). Thousand Oaks, CA: Sage Publications.

Harvard Law Review Association. (1993). Developments in the law—Legal responses to domestic violence: VI. Battered women and child custody decisionmaking, *Harvard Law Review, 106,* 1597–1620.

Hasselt, V. N., Morrison, R. L., Bellack, A. S., & Hersen, M. (Eds.). (1988). *Handbook of family violence.* New York: Plenum.

Hazen, A., Miller, S., & Landsverk, J. The Impact of Family Violence on Children. Presentation at 1995 San Diego Conference on Child Maltreatment. San Diego, CA.

Heisler, C. (1990). Evidence and other information sources. In N. Lemon (1996), *Domestic violence law: A comprehensive overview of cases and sources* (pp. 563–565). San Francisco, CA: Austin & Winfield.

Henderson, L. (1988). The dialogue of heart and head. *Cardozo Law Review, 10(1/2),* 123–148.

Herbert, C. P. (1991). Family violence and family physicians: Opportunity and obligation. *Canadian Family Physician, 37,* 385–390.

Herman, J. (1997). *Trauma and recovery.* New York: Basic Books.

Herr, C., Grogan, E., Clark, S., & Carson, L. (1998). Developing services for lesbians in abusive relationships: A macro and micro approach. In A. Roberts (Ed.), *Battered women and their families* (2nd ed.) (pp. 365–384). New York: Springer.

Hershorn, M., & Rosenbaum, A. (1985). Children of marital violence: A closer look at the unintended victims. *American Journal of Orthopsychiatry, 55*(2), 260–266.

Hester, J., & Pearson, C. (1993). Domestic violence, mediation, and child contact arrangements: Issues from current research. *Family Mediation, 3*(2), 3–6.

Hester, J., & Radford, L. (1992). Domestic violence and access arrangements for children in Denmark and England. *Journal of Social Work and Family Law, 1,* 57–70.

Hilton, Z. (1992). Battered women's concerns about their children witnessing wife assault. *Journal of Interpersonal Violence, 7*(1), 77–86.

Hirschel, J. D., & Hutchison, I. (1992). Female spouse abuse and the police response: The Charlotte North Carolina experiment. *Journal of Criminal Law and Criminology, 83*(1), 73–119.

Hofeller, K. H. (1982). *Social, psychological and situational factors in wife abuse.* Palo Alto, CA: R & E Research Associates, Inc.

Holtzworth-Munroe, A., & Stuart, G. L. (1994). Typologies of male batterers: Three subtypes and the differences among them. *Psychological Bulletin, 116,* 476–497.

Holy Bible. Revised Berkeley Version (1977 Edition). National Tennessee Gideons International. Grand Rapids, MI: Zondervan Publishing.

Horsburgh, B. (1995). Recent development: Lifting the veil of secrecy: Domestic violence in the Jewish community. *Harvard Women's Law Journal, 18,* 171–217.

Horton, A. L., & Johnson, B. L. (1993). Profile and strategies of women who have ended abuse. *Families in Society: The Journal of Contemporary Human Services, 74,* 481–492.

Hotaling, G., & Sugarman, D. (1986). An analysis of risk markers in husband to wife violence: The current state of knowledge. *Violence and Victims, 1,* 101–124.

Hyman, A., & Chez, R. A. (1995). Mandatory reporting of domestic violence by health care providers: A misguided approach. *Women's Health Issues, 5*(4), 208–213.

Hyman, A., Schilinger, D., & Lo, B. (1995). Laws mandating reporting of domestic violence: Do they promote patient well-being? *Journal of the American Medical Association, 273*(22), 1781–1787.

In re Farley, 469 N.W.2d 295 (Mich. 1991).

In re Heather A., 52 Cal. App. 4th 183 (1997).

In re Jon N., 179 Cal. App. 3d 156 (1986); 224 Cal. Rptr. 319 (1986).

Jackson, H., & Nuttall, R. (1996). *Childhood abuse: Effects on clinicians' personal and professional lives*. Thousand Oaks, CA: Sage Publications.

Jackson, T. (1990). Lessons learned from a domestic violence prosecutor. In N. Lemon (1996), *Domestic violence law: A comprehensive overview of cases and sources* (pp. 561–562). San Francisco, CA: Austin & Winfield.

Jacobson, N. S., Gottman, J. M., Waltz, J., Rushe, R., Babcock, J. C., & Holtzworth-Munroe, A. (1994). Affect, verbal content and psycho-physiology in the arguments of couples with a violent husband. *Journal of Consulting and Clinical Psychology, 62*, 982–988.

Jaffe, P. (1986). Impact of police charges in incidents of wife abuse. *Journal of Family Violence, 1*, 137–149.

Jaffe, P., Wilson, S. K., & Wolfe, D. A. (1986). Specific assessment and intervention strategies for children exposed to wife battering: Preliminary empirical investigations. *Canadian Journal of Behavior Science, 18*, 356–366.

Jaffe, P., Wolfe, D. A., & Wilson, S. (1990). *Children of battered women*. Newbury Park, CA: Sage Publications.

Jaffe, P., Wolfe, D. A., Wilson, S., & Zak, L. (1986). Similarities in behavioral and social maladjustment among child victims and witnesses to family violence. *American Journal of Orthopsychiatry, 56*(1), 142–146.

Jennings, J. L. (1987). History and issues in the treatment of battering men: A case for unstructured group therapy. *Journal of Family Violence, 2*(3), 193–219.

Johnson, I. M., Crowley, J., & Sigler, R. T. (1992). Agency response to domestic violence: Services provided by battered women. In E. C. Viano (Ed.), *Intimate violence: An interdisciplinary perspective* (pp. 191–202). Bristol, PA: Taylor & Francis.

Johnson, J. (1996, April 27). A new side to domestic violence; arrests of women have risen sharply since passage of tougher laws. Critics say some men manipulate the system; others say female abusers have long been overlooked. *Los Angeles Times*, p. A1.

Jones, A. (1994). *Next time she'll be dead: Battering and how to stop it*. Boston, MA: Beacon Press.

Jones, J. T. R. (1996). Battered spouses' damage actions against non-reporting physicians. *DePaul Law Review, 45*, 191–262.

Jung, C. G. (1966). *The practice of psychology: Essays on the psychology of transference and other subjects* (R. F. C. Hull, Trans.). New York: Pantheon.

Keilitz, S. (1994). Legal report: Civil protection orders: A viable justice system tool for deterring domestic violence. *Violence and Victims, 9*, 79–84.

Kurz, D. (1987). Emergency department responses to battered women: Resistance to medicalization. *Social Problems, 34*(1), 69–81.

Kurz, D. (1993). Physical assaults by husbands: A major social problem. In R. J. Gelles & D. R. Loseke (Eds.) *Current controversies on family violence* (pp. 88–103). Newbury Park, CA: Sage Publications.

LaBell, L. S. (1979). Wife abuse: A sociological study of battered women and their mates. *Victimology: An International Journal, 4,* 257–267.

Lee, M. Y., & Au, P. (1998). Chinese battered women in North America: Their experiences and treatment. In A. Roberts (Ed.), *Battered women and their families* (2nd ed.) (pp. 448–482). New York: Springer Publishing.

Lerman, L. (1992). The decontextualization of domestic violence. *Journal of Criminal Law and Criminology, 83*(1), 217–240.

Levine, S. (1984). *Meetings at the edge: Dialogues with the grieving and the dying, the healing and the healed.* New York: Anchor Books Doubleday.

Levy, D. (1996, September 9). Doctors study fitness of spouse-abuse laws. *USA Today,* p. 1D.

Lewin, E., & Olesen, V. (Eds.). (1985). *Women, health, and healing.* New York: Tavistock.

Lie, G., & Gentlewarrior, S. (1991). Intimate violence in lesbian relationships: Discussion of survey findings and practice implications. *Journal of Social Service Research, 15,* 41–59.

Lie, G., Schlitt, R., Bush, J., Montague, M., & Reyes, L. (1991). Lesbians in currently aggressive relationships: How frequently do they report aggressive past relationships? *Violence and Victims, 6,* 121–135.

Lindsey, D. (1994). *The welfare of children.* New York: Oxford University Press.

Littleton, C. (1989). Women's experience and the problem of transition: Perspectives on male battering of women. *University of Chicago Legal Forum, Vol. 1989,* 23–57.

Littleton, C. (1993). Women's experience and the problem of transition. In M. Minow (Ed.), *Family matters: Readings on family lives and the law* (pp. 261–272). New York: New Press.

Lockhart, L. L., White., B. W., Causby, V., & Isaac, A. (1994). Letting out the secret: Violence in lesbian relationships. *Journal of Interpersonal Violence, 9,* 469–492.

Lorber, J. (1984). *Women physicians: Careers, status and power.* New York: Tavistock.

Los Angeles County Department of Public Social Services. (1992). *Elder and dependent adult abuse reporting* [Booklet]. Los Angeles, CA: Author.

Los Angeles County District Attorney's Office, Family Violence Division. (1996). *Pledge to victims* [Brochure]. Los Angeles, CA: Author.

Los Angeles Domestic Violence Council. (1996). *It shouldn't hurt to go home* [Booklet] (pp. 16–17). Los Angeles, CA: Author.

Loulan, J. (1987). *Lesbian passion.* San Francisco, CA: Spinsters/Aunt Lute.

Mahoney, M. (1991). Legal images of battered women: Redefining the issue of separation. *Michigan Law Review, 90,* 1–93.

Mama, A. (1996). *The hidden struggle: Statutory and voluntary sector responses to violence against black women in the home.* London, England: Whiting and Birch, Ltd.

Margulies, P. (1996). The violence of law and violence against women. *Cardozo Studies in Law and Literature, 8*(1), 179–202.

McFarlane, J., & Parker, B. (1994). Abuse during pregnancy: An assessment and intervention protocol. *Maternal Child Nursing, 19*(6), 321–324.

McKeel, A. J., & Sporakowski, M. J. (1993). How shelter counselors' views about responsibility for wife abuse relate to services they provide to battered wives. *Journal of Family Violence, 8,* 101–107.

Meskin, L. H. (1994). If not us, then who? *Journal of the American Dental Association, 125*(1), 10–12.

Messinger, R. W., & Eldridge, R. M. (1993). *Behind closed doors: The city's response to family violence.* New York: New York Task Force on Family Violence.

Miccio, K. (1995). Symposium on reconceptualizing violence against women by intimate partners: Critical issues: In the name of mothers and children: Deconstructing the myth of the passive battered mother and the "protected child" in child neglect proceedings. *Albany Law Review, 58,* 1087–1106.

Mills, L. (1996a). Empowering battered women transnationally: The case for postmodern interventions. *Social Work, 41*(3), 261–268.

Mills, L. (1996b). On the other side of silence: Affective lawyering for intimate abuse. *Cornell Law Review, 86,* 1225–1263.

Mills, L. (1997a). Benefitting from violence: A preliminary analysis of the presence of abuse in the lives of the new SSI disability recipients. *Sexuality and Disability, 15*(2), 99–108.

Mills, L. (1997b). Intuition and insight: A new job description for the battered woman's prosecutor and other more modest proposals. *UCLA Women's Law Journal, 7*(2), 183–199.

Mills, L. (1998a). Integrating domestic violence assessment into child protective services intervention: Policy and practice implications. In A. Roberts (Ed.), *Battered women and their families* (2nd ed.) (pp. 129–158). New York: Springer.

Mills, L. (1998b) (in press). Killing her softly: Intimate abuse and the violence of state intervention. *Georgetown Journal of Law, Sexuality, and Violence.*

Mills, L. (1998c). Mandatory arrest and prosecution policies for domestic violence: A critical literature review and the case for more research to test victim empowerment approaches. *Criminal Justice and Behavior, 25*(3), 306–318.

Mills, L., & Friend, C. (1997). *Assessment and case management of domestic violence in public child welfare* [Curriculum]. University of California, Los Angeles, School of Public Policy and Social Research, Department of Social Welfare. Project funded by the California Social Work Education Center (CalSWEC).

Mills, T. (1985). The assault on the self: Stages in coping with battering husbands. *Qualitative Sociology, 8*(2), 103–123.

Minow, M. (1997). *Between vengeance and forgiveness.* Unpublished manuscript.

Mitchell, D. (1992). Contemporary police practices in domestic violence cases: Arresting the abuser: Is it enough? *Journal of Criminal Law and Criminology, 83*(1), 241–249.

Mooney, D., & Rodriguez, M. (1996). California healthcare workers and mandatory reporting of intimate violence. *Hastings Women's Law Journal, 7,* 85–111.

Moore, K., Greenfield, W., Wilson, M., & Kok, A. (1997, July–August). Toward a taxonomy of batterers. *Families in Society: The Journal of Contemporary Human Services,* 352–360.

Morrison, E. J. (1996). Insurance discrimination against battered women: Proposed legislative protections. *Indiana Law Journal, 72,* 259–290.

Mullender, A. (1996). *Rethinking domestic violence: The social work and probation response.* London: Routledge.

Murphy, L., & Razza, N. (1998). Domestic violence against women with mental retardation. In A. Roberts (Ed.), *Battered women and their families* (2nd ed.) (pp. 271–290). New York: Springer Publishing.

National Council of Juvenile and Family Court Judges. (1994). *Model code on domestic and family violence.* Reno, NV: Author.

Neidig, P. H. (1984). Women's shelters, men's collectives and other issues in the field of spouse abuse. *Victimology, 9,* 483–489.

Neidig, P. H., Collins, B., & Friedman, D. H. (1984, August). *Attitudinal characteristics of males who have engaged in spousal abuse.* Paper presented at the Second National Conference for Family Violence Researchers, Durham, NH.

Neidig, P. H., & Friedman, D. H. (1984). *Spouse abuse: A treatment program for couples.* Champaign, IL: Research Press.

Nelson, K. (1994). Do services to preserve the family place children at risk? In E. Gambrill & T. Stein (Eds.), *Controversial issues in child welfare* (pp. 67–71). Boston, MA: Allyn and Bacon.

Newmark, L., Harell, A., & Salem, P. (1995). Domestic violence and empowerment in custody and visitation cases. *Family and Conciliation Courts Review, 33,* 30–62.

Nezu, A., Nezu, C., & Gill-Weiss, M. J. (1992). *Psychopathology in persons with mental retardation.* Champaign, IL: Research Press.

NiCarthy, G. (1987). *The ones who got away.* Seattle, WA: Seal.

Novello, A., Rosenberg, M., Saltzman, L., & Shosky, J. (1992). From the Surgeon General, U.S. Public Health Service. *JAMA, 267*(23), 3132.

Nurius, P., Hilfrink, M., & Rifino, R. (1996). The single greatest health threat to women: Their partners. In P. Raffoul & C. A. McNeece (Eds.), *Future issues for social work practice* (pp. 159–171). Boston, MA: Allyn and Bacon.

O'Keefe, M. (1995). Predictors of child abuse in maritally violent families. *Journal of Interpersonal Violence, 10*(1), 3–25.

Okun, L. (1986). *Woman abuse: Facts replacing myths.* Beverly Hills, CA: Sage Publications.

Orloff, L. E., Jang, D., & Klein, C. F. (1995). With no place to turn: Improving legal advocacy for battered immigrant women. *Family Law Quarterly, 29*(2), 313–329.

Pagelow, M. D. (1988). Marital rape. In V. B. Van Hasselt, R. L. Morrison, A. S. Bellack, & M. Herson (Eds.), *Handbook of family violence* (pp. 207–232). New York: Plenum.

Painter, S. L., & Dutton, D. G. (1985). Patterns of emotional bonding in battered women: Traumatic bonding. *International Journal of Women's Studies, 57,* 101–110.

Pate, A. M., & Hamilton, E. E. (1992). Formal and informal deterrents to domestic violence: The Dade County Spouse Assault Experiment. *American Sociological Review, 57*(5), 691–697.

Paternoster, R., Brame, R., Bachman, R., & Sherman, L. W. (1997). Do fair procedures matter? The effect of procedural justice on spouse assault. *Law & Society Review, 31*(1), 163–204.

Peled, E. (1993). Children who witness women battering: Concerns and dilemmas in the construction of a social problem. *Children and Youth Services Review, 15,* 43–52.

Peled, E. (1996). "Secondary" victims no more: Refocusing intervention with children. In J. L. Edleson & Z. C. Eisikovits (Eds.), *Future interventions with battered women and their families* (pp. 125–153). Thousand Oaks, CA: Sage Publications.

Pence, E., & Paymar, M. (1993). *Education groups for men who batter.* New York: Springer.

Pence, E., & Shepard, M. (1988). Integrating feminist theory and practice: The challenge of the battered women's movement. In K. A. Yllö & M. Bogard (Eds.), *Feminist perspectives on wife abuse* (pp. 282–298). Newbury Park, CA: Sage.

Pierce, G., & Deutsch, S. (1990). Do police actions and responses to domestic violence calls make a difference? A quasi experimental analysis. *Journal of Quantitative Criminology,* 17–42.

Pirog-Good, M., & Stets, J. (1986). Programs for abusers: Who drops out and what can be done. *Response, 9,* 17–19.

Pleck, J. (1981). *The myth of masculinity.* Cambridge, MA: MIT Press.

Post, R. D., Willet, A. B., Frank, R. D., House, R. M., Back, S. M., & Weisberg, M. P. (1980). A preliminary report on the prevalence of domestic violence among psychiatric inpatients. *American Journal of Psychiatry, 137,* 974–975.

Pozatek, E. (1994). The problem of certainty: Clinical social work in the postmodern era. *Social Work, 39,* 396–403.

Prochaska, J. O., Diclemente, C., & Norcross, C. (1992). In search of how people change: Application to addictive behaviors. *American Psychologist, 47*(9), 1102–1114.

Quinn, M., & Tomita, S. (1997). *Elder abuse and neglect: Causes, diagnosis and intervention strategies.* New York: Springer.

Raphael, J. (1996). Domestic violence and welfare receipt: Toward a new feminist theory of welfare dependency. *Harvard Women's Law Journal, 19,* 201–227.

Raphael, J., & Tolman, R. (1997, April). *Trapped by poverty, trapped by abuse: New evidence documenting the relationship between domestic violence and welfare.* Taylor Institute & The University of Michigan Research Development Center on Poverty, Risk and Mental Health.

Rebovich, D. J. (1996). Prosecution response to domestic violence: Results of a survey of large jurisdictions. In E. Buzawa & C. Buzawa (Eds.), *Do arrests and restraining orders work?* (pp. 176–191). Thousand Oaks, CA: Sage Publications.

Reg. v. Jackson, 1 Q.B. 671 (1891).

Reid, S. A., & Glasser, M. (1997). Primary care physicians' recognition of and attitudes toward domestic violence. *Academic Medicine, 72*(1), 51–53.

Reidy, R., & Von Korff, M. (1991). Is battered women's help seeking connected to the level of their abuse? *Public Health Reports, 106*(4), 360–364.

Rimonte, N. (1991). A question of culture: Cultural approval of violence against women in the Pacific-Asian community and the cultural defense. *Stanford Law Review, 43*, 1311–1326.

Rivera, J. (1994). Domestic violence against Latinas by Latino males: An analysis of race, national origin, and gender differentials. *Boston College Third World Law Journal, 14*, 231–257.

Roan, S. (1996, December 25). Law against domestic abuse may be backfiring. *Los Angeles Times*, p. E1.

Roberts, A. R. (1996a). Court responses to battered women. In A. R. Roberts (Ed.), *Helping battered women: New perspectives and remedies* (pp. 96–101). New York: Oxford University Press.

Roberts, A. R. (1996b). Epidemiology and definitions of acute crisis in American society. In A. R. Roberts (Ed.), *Crisis management and brief treatment: Theory, technique, and applications* (pp. 16–33). Chicago, IL: Nelson-Hall.

Roberts, A. R., & Burman, S. (1998). Crisis intervention and cognitive problem-solving therapy with battered women: A national survey and practice model. In A. Roberts (Ed.), *Battered women and their families* (2nd ed.) (pp. 3–28). New York: Springer.

Roche, S. E., & Sadoski, P. J. (1996). Social action for battered women. In A. R. Roberts (Ed.), *Helping battered women: New perspectives and remedies* (pp. 13–30). New York: Oxford University Press.

Rosenberg, M. L., O'Carroll, P. W., & Powell, K. E. (1992). Let's be clear: Violence is a public health problem. *Journal of the American Medical Association, 267*(22), 3071–3072.

Rosenfeld, B. (1992). Court-ordered treatment of spouse abuse. *Clinical Psychology Review, 12*, 205–226.

Russell, D. E. (1983). The prevalence and incidence of forcible rape and attempted rape of females. *Victimology: An International Journal, 7*, 81–93.

Russo, F. (1997, March 30). The faces of Hedda Nussbaum. *The New York Times Magazine*.

San Diego Department of Social Services. (1996). *Batterer's assessment form*. San Diego, CA: Author.

Sattel, J. (1976). The inexpressive male: Tragedy or sexual politics. *Social Problems, 28*, 469–477.

Saunders, D. G. (1992). A typology of men who batter women: Three types derived from cluster analysis. *American Journal of Orthopsychiatry, 62*(2), 264–275.

Saunders, D. G. (1996). Feminist-cognitive-behavioral and process-psychodynamic treatments for men who batter: Interaction of abuser traits and treatment models. *Violence and Victims, 11*(4), 393–414.

Scalia, J. (1994). Psychoanalytic insights and the prevention of pseudosuccess in the Cognitive-Behavioral treatment of batterers. *Journal of Interpersonal Violence, 9*(4), 548–555.

Schechter, S., & Edleson, J. L. (1994). *In the best interest of women and children: A call for collaboration between child welfare and domestic violence constituencies.* Unpublished manuscript.

Schneider, E. (1992). Particularity and generality: Challenges of feminist theory and practice in work on woman-abuse. *New York University Law Review, 67,* 520–568.

Schor, E. L. (1995). The influence of families on child health: Family behaviors and child outcomes. *The Pediatric Clinics of North America: Family-Focused Pediatrics: Issues, Challenges, and Clinical Methods, 42*(1), 89–102.

Schubmehl, W. (1991). Davanloo's intensive short-term dynamic psychotherapy in the treatment of battered wife syndrome. *International Journal of Short-Term Psychotherapy, 6,* 79–93.

Schulman, M. (1979). *A survey of spousal violence against women in Kentucky.* Washington, DC: U.S. Department of Justice, Law Enforcement.

Scott, C. J., & Matricciani, R. M. (1994). Joint commission on accreditation of healthcare organization, standards to improve care for victims of abuse. *Maryland Medical Journal, 43*(10), 891–898.

Sears, R., MacCoby, E., & Levin, H. (1957). *Patterns of child rearing.* White Plains, NY: Row, Peterson and Co.

Seybold, J., Fritz, J., & MacPhee, D. (1991). Relation of social support to the self-perceptions of mothers with delayed children. *Journal of Community Psychology, 19*(1), 29–36.

Sgroi, S. (1989). *Vulnerable populations.* Lexington, MA: Lexington Books.

Sherman, L. W. (1992). The influence of criminology on criminal law: Evaluating arrests for misdemeanor domestic violence. *Journal of Criminal Law and Criminology, 83*(1), 1–45.

Sherman, L. W., & Berk, R. A. (1984a). The Minneapolis domestic violence experiment. *Police Foundation Reports, 1,* 1–8.

Sherman, L. W., & Berk, R. A. (1984b). The specific deterrent effects of arrest for domestic assault. *American Sociological Review, 49,* 261–272.

Sherman, L. W., Schmidt, J., Rogan, D., Smith, D., Gartin, P., Cohn, E., Collins, D., & Bacich, A. (1992). The variable effects of arrest on criminal careers: The Milwaukee domestic violence experiment. *Journal of Criminal Law and Criminology, 83*(1), 137–169.

Shields, N. M., & Hanneke, C. R. (1983). *Violent husbands: Patterns of individual violence.* Unpublished report presented to NIMH.

Snyder, D. K., & Fruchtman, L. A. (1981). Differential patterns of wife abuse: A data-based typology. *Journal of Consulting and Clinical Psychology, 49*(6), 878–885.

Snyder, D. K., & Scheer, N. S. (1981). Predicting disposition following brief residence at a shelter for battered women. *American Journal of Community Psychology, 9,* 559–566.

Solloway, M., & Sonosky, C. (1996). *The role of maternal and child health in women's health* [Draft]. Washington, DC: The George Washington University Child and Adolescent Health Policy Center, The George Washington University Medical Center. Unpublished manuscript.

Sorenson, S. B., & Telles, C. A. (1991). Self-report of spousal violence in a Mexican-American and non-Hispanic White population. *Violence and Victims, 6*(1), 3–15.

Sorichetti v. City of New York, 65 N.Y. 2d 461 (1985).

Spagnoletti, R. Presentation at 1998 Georgetown University Law Center Conference on Violence and State Accountability. Washington, DC.

Stark, E., & Flitcraft, A. (1982). Medical therapy as repression: The case of the battered woman. *Health & Medicine, 1*(3), 29–32.

Stark, E., & Flitcraft, A. (1985). Spouse abuse. In *Surgeon General's Workshop on Violence and Public Health: Source book* (pp. SA1–SA43). Rockville, MD: U.S. Public Health Service.

Stark, E., & Flitcraft, A. (1988). Women and children at risk: A feminist perspective on child abuse. *International Journal of Health Services, 18,* 97–118.

Straus, M. A. (1991). Discipline and deviance: Physical punishment of children and violence and other crime in adulthood. *Social Problems, 38,* 133–154.

Straus, M. A., & Gelles, R. J. (1986). Societal change and family violence from 1975 to 1985 as revealed by two national surveys. *Journal of Marriage & the Family, 48,* 465–479.

Straus, M. A., Gelles, R. J., & Steinmetz, S. K. (1980). *Behind closed doors: Violence in the American family.* Garden City, NY: Anchor Press/Doubleday.

Straus, M. A., & Smith, C. (1990). Family patterns of primary prevention of family violence. In M. A. Straus & R. J. Gelles (Eds.), *Physical violence in American families* (pp. 507–526). New Brunswick, NJ: Transaction Books.

Subcommittee on Employer and Employee Relations. *Hearing on Equal Employment Opportunity Commission [EEOC] Administrative Reforms/Case Processing: Hearing before the Subcommittee on Employer-Employee Relations of the Committee on Economic and Educational Opportunities, House of Representatives,* 104th Cong., 1st Sess. 1. (1995).

Sugg, N. K., & Inui, T. (1992). Primary care physicians' response to domestic violence: Opening Pandora's box. *Journal of the American Medical Association, 267,* 3157–3160.

Sullivan, C. (1991). The provision of advocacy services to women leaving abusive partners: An exploratory study. *Journal of Interpersonal Violence, 6*(1), 41–54.

Taylor, R. (1997). *Preventing violence against women and children.* New York: Milbank Memorial Fund.

Thurman v. City of Torrington, 595 F. Supp. 1521 (1984).

Tilden, V. P., Schmidt, T. A., Limandri, B. J., Chiodo, G. T., Garland, M. J., & Loveless, P. A. (1994). Factors that influence clinicians' assessment and management of family violence. *American Journal of Public Health, 84*(4), 628–633.

Tolman, R., & Bennett, L. (1990). A review of quantitative research on men who batter. *Journal of Interpersonal Violence, 5,* 87–118.

Turner, S. F., & Shapiro, C. H. (1986, September–October). Battered women: Mourning the death of a relationship. *Social Work, 31,* 372–376.

Unified courts: A preliminary discussion. (1993). Minutes of conference, June 1, 1994, Palmer House, Chicago, IL.

United States Advisory Board on Child Abuse and Neglect. (1995). *A nation's shame: Fatal child abuse and neglect in the United States.* Washington, DC: U.S. Department of Health and Human Services.

United States Department of Health and Human Services.(1995, March 9). *Federal Register.* National Center on Child Abuse and Neglect and the Children's Bureau Discretionary Funds Program; Availability for Fiscal Year 1995 and Request for Applications; Notice. Washington, DC: Author.

United States Department of Justice. (1994a). *Violence between intimates.* Washington, DC: Government Printing Office.

United States Department of Justice. (1994b). *Violence against women, a national crime survey report.* Washington, DC: Government Printing Office.

United States Department of Justice, Bureau of Justice Statistics. (1997). *Violence-related injuries treated in hospital emergency departments* (Report No. NCJ-156921)[On-line]. Available: http://www.ojp.usdoj.gov/bjs/

United States Department of Justice [FBI]. (1992). *Crime in the United States, 1991.* Washington, DC: Government Printing Office.

United States General Accounting Office. (1991). *Elder abuse: Effectiveness of reporting laws and other factors.* (Publication HRD-91-74). Washington, DC: Author.

Valle Ferrer, D. (1998). Validating coping strategies and empowering Latino battered women in Puerto Rico. In A. Roberts (Ed.), *Battered women and their families* (2nd ed.) (pp. 483–511). New York: Springer Publishing.

Wagner, N. (1996, February 9). Utah Legislature domestic violence: 2 bills would seek to embolden battered women. *The Salt Lake Tribune,* p. A1.

Waitzkin, H. (1991). *The politics of medical encounters: How patients and doctors deal with social problems.* New Haven, CT: Yale University Press.

Walker, L. (1979). *The battered woman.* New York: Harper & Row.

Walker, L. (1984). *The battered woman syndrome.* New York: Springer.

Walker, L. (1989). *Terrifying love: Why battered women kill and how society responds.* New York: Harper & Row.

Warshaw, C. (1989). Limitations of the medical model in the care of battered women. *Gender & Society, 3*(4), 506–517.

Welch, D. (1994). Symposium: Vital issues in national health care reform: Comment: Mandatory arrest of domestic abusers: Panacea or perpetuation of the problem of abuse? *DePaul L. Review, 43,* 1133–1164.

Westra, B., & Martin, H. P. (1981). Children of battered women. *Maternal-Child Nursing Journal, 10,* 41–54.

Whalen, M. (1996). *Counseling to end violence against women: A subversive model.* Thousand Oaks, CA: Sage Publications.

White, E. C. (1986). Life is a song worth singing: Ending violence in the black family. In M. C. Burns (Ed.), *The speaking profits us: Violence in the lives of women of color* (pp. 11–13). Seattle, WA: Center for the Prevention of Sexual and Domestic Violence.

White, E. C. (1994). The psychology of abuse. In *Chain, chain, change: For black women in abusive relationships* (pp. 19–32). Seattle, WA: Seal Press.

Whitfield, C. L. (1987). *Healing the Inner Child.* Deerfield Beach, FL: Health Communications.

Wills, D. (1997). Domestic violence: The case for aggressive prosecution. *UCLA Women's Law Journal, 7*(2), 173–182.

Wisconsin Council on Developmental Disabilities. (1991). *Greater risk: Legal issues in sexual abuse of adults with developmental disabilities* (A training guide for caregivers). Madison, WI: Author.

Wolfe, D. A., Jaffe, P., Wilson, S. K., & Zak, L. (1985). Children of battered women: The relation of child behavior to family violence and maternal stress. *Journal of Consulting and Clinical Psychology, 53,* 657–665.

Wylie, M. S. (1996, March/April). It's a community affair. *Networker,* 58–65.

Yegidis, B. L., & Renzy, R. B. (1994). Battered women's experiences with a preferred arrest policy. *AFFILIA, 9*(1), 60–70.

Yllö, K. A. (1983). Sexual equality and violence against wives in American states. *Journal of Comparative Family Studies, 14*(1), 67–86.

Yllö, K. A., & Straus, M. A. (1990). Patriarchy and violence against wives: The impact of structural and normative factors. In M. A. Straus & R. J. Gelles (Eds.), *Physical violence in American families* (pp. 383–399). New Brunswick, NJ: Transaction.

Yoshihama, M. (1994, August). *Violence against Asian Pacific women perpetrated by male intimates.* Paper presented at the annual meeting of the American Psychological Association, Los Angeles, CA.

Yu, W. (1997, March 5). Doctors urged to be on lookout for victims of domestic violence. *The Times Union* (Albany, New York), p. B5.

Yung, V. (1997, April). Treatment strategies for the Asian-American community. Lecture given at UCLA, Los Angeles, CA.

Zambrano, M. (1985). *Mejor sola que mal acompanada: For the Latina in an abusive relationship.* Seattle, WA: Seal Press.

Zion, J. W., & Zion, E. B. (1993). Hozho' Sokee'—stay together nicely: Domestic violence under Navajo common law. *Arizona State Law Journal, 25,* 407–426.

Zorza, J. (1992). The criminal law of misdemeanor domestic violence, 1970–1990. *Journal of Criminal Law and Criminology, 46,* 46–72.

Zorza, J. (1995a). How abused women can use the law to help protect their children. In E. Peled, P. Jaffe, & J. L. Edleson (Eds.), *Ending the cycle of violence: Community response to children of battered women* (pp. 147–169). Thousand Oaks, CA: Sage Publications.

Zorza, J. (1995b, April 19). When divorce is best for children: Protecting children from abusive parents. Testimony before the U.S. Commission on Child and Family Welfare, Cleveland, OH.

Zorza, J. (1996, August/September). Most therapists need training in domestic violence. *Domestic Violence Report, 1*(6), 1–2.

Zorza, J., & Woods, L. (1994). *Analysis and policy implications of the new police domestic violence studies.* New York: National Center on Women and Family Law.

Indexes

Author Index

Subject Index

267

Springer Publishing Company

Battered Women and Their Families, 2nd Edition
Intervention Strategies and Treatment Programs
Albert R. Roberts, PhD, Editor

"...a landmark achievement. This is the first comprehensive book to examine domestic violence from a multi-cultural perspective. This brilliantly written and all-inclusive resource provides new clinical knowledge and practice wisdom to alleviate the emotional pain and trauma of battered women and their children."
—Jesse J. Harris, PhD, BCD, ACSW
Professor and Dean, School of Social Work, University of Maryland
Colonel, Retired

Contents:

1998   552pp   0-8261-4591-4   hardcover

536 Broadway, New York, NY 10012-3955 • (212) 431-4370 • Fax (212) 941-7842

SP *Springer Publishing Company*

Preventing Teenage Violence
An Empirical Paradigm for Schools and Family

John S. Wodarski, PhD
Lois A. Wodarski, PhD

"The Wodarskis deliver in this book—providing detailed assessment and intervention guides and tools as well as a wealth of literature support that can immediately be put to work. Both society and human services have yet to seriously invest in a prevention commitment. This book is an important contribution and an excellent place to begin."

—Paula S. Nurius, PhD
University of Washington School of Social Work

This volume is based on theoretical knowledge and research about violent children and discusses the factors that affect the development of violent behavior. After a discussion of empirically-based assessment and intervention methods, the authors present a specific intervention program (Teams–Games–Tournaments Method) as an effective approach that incorporates parent, peer, school, and community involvement.

Contents:
- Introduction
- The Intervention
- Assessment
- Teaching Teenagers to Control Anger: The Teams-Games-Tournaments Method
- Curriculum for Parents
- Violent Youth: A Critical Challenge for Parents, Schools and the Community by Lisa A. Rapp, CSW

Springer Series on Family Violence
1998   160pp   0-8261-1188-2   hardcover

536 Broadway, New York, NY 10012-3955 • (212) 431-4370 • Fax (212) 941-7842

Domestic Partner Abuse

L. Kevin Hamberger, PhD
Claire Renzetti, PhD, Editors

This volume breaks new ground in the understanding and treatment of couples abuse. The editors and contributors expand the models of abusive relationships to include the special concerns of gay couples, mutually violent partners, and abusive women, among others.

Based on a special issue of the journal Violence and Victims, this book shatters myths surrounding domestic violence and sheds new light on a complex social problem. For all counselors, therapists, and social workers concerned with domestic violence, as well as for students and educators in this field.

Partial Contents:

- Domestic Partner Abuse: Expanding Paradigms for Understanding and Intervention, *L. Kevin Hamberger*
- Gay and Bisexual Male Domestic Violence Victimization: Challenges to Feminist Theory and Responses to Violence, *Patrick Letellier*
- Are Bi-Directionally Violent Couples Mutually Victimized? A Gender-Sensitive Comparison, *Dina Vivian and Jennifer Langhinrichsen-Rohling*
- Counseling Heterosexual Women Arrested for Domestic Violence: Implications for Theory and Practice, *L. Kevin Hamberger and Theresa Potente*
- Lesbian Battering: The Relationship Between Personality and the Perpetration of Violence, *Vallerie E. Coleman*

1996   240pp   0-8261-9090-1   hard cover

536 Broadway, New York, NY 10012-3955 • (212) 431-4370 • Fax (212) 941-7842

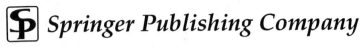

Springer Publishing Company

Empowering and Healing the Battered Woman
A Model for Assessment and Intervention
Mary Ann Dutton, PhD

The book spells out in practical, concrete terms what it really means to place the pathology outside the battered woman. The novelty in this approach lies in the implications for practice: battered women are not "sick"—they are in a "sick" situation.

——— A Model for ———
Assessment & Intervention

EMPOWERING
AND
HEALING
THE
BATTERED
WOMAN

𝕒

Mary Ann Dutton

Springer Publishing Company

"...practical and comprehensive, an excellent guide for clinicians and other interveners.... integrates psychological theory with detailed information on the real-life dimensions of abuse and threat in interpersonal relationships. Her discussion of abused women's posttraumatic responses and the strategies for assessment that form a part of each chapter are particularly valuable."
—Angela Browne, PhD

Partial Contents:

I. Conceptual Framework and Assessment: Women's Response to Battering: A Psychological Model • Understanding the Nature and Pattern of Abusive Behavior • Strategies to Escape, Avoid, and Survive Abuse • Psychological Effects of Abuse • Mediators of the Battered Woman's Response to Abuse

II. Intervention: Framework for Intervention with Victims and Survivors of Domestic Violence • Protective Interventions • Making Choices • Posttraumatic Therapy: Healing the Psychological Effects of Battering • Issues for the Professional Working with Abuse

1992   224pp   0-8261-7130-3   hardcover

536 Broadway, New York, NY 10012-3955 • (212) 431-4370 • Fax (212) 941-7842